Trevor Lummis spent t
in the Merchant Navy
manual worker he resi
mature student at New
is a graduate of the universities of Edinburgh,
London and Essex. He was senior research officer
at the University of Essex, where he specialized
in nineteenth- and twentieth-century social and
oral history. He is a past Honorary Treasurer of
the Oral History Society and held an Honorary
Fellowship in the Department of Sociology at
Essex. Trevor Lummis is married to a dealer in
modern British art and lives in north London and
the Languedoc.

Life and Death in Eden

Pitcairn Island and the *Bounty* Mutineers

TREVOR LUMMIS

PHŒNIX

A PHOENIX PAPERBACK

First published in Great Britain by Victor Gollancz in 1999
This paperback edition published in 2000 by Phoenix,
an imprint of Orion Books Ltd,
Orion House, 5 Upper St Martin's Lane,
London WC2H 9EA

Originally published in 1997 as *Pitcairn Island: Life and Death in Eden*
by Ashgate Publishing Ltd

A CIP catalogue record for this book
is available from the British Library.

ISBN: 0 75381 014 X

Printed and bound in Great Britain by
The Guernsey Press Co. Ltd., Guernsey, Channel Islands

For
Saskia Evans-Perks
with love

Contents

List of illustrations   *page*   9

Map   10

Prologue   11

I THE *BOUNTY*

1 Preparations   19

2 The Voyage   32

3 Tahiti   39

4 The Mutiny   55

II DEATH IN EDEN

5 Pitcairn   75

6 Revolt   90

7 Revenge   98

8 The Women   114

9 Rum   124

III REFLECTIONS

10 Evidence   133

11 Discovery   143

IV LIFE IN EDEN

12 A New Generation   159

13 Virtuous Lives   174

V BEYOND THE HORIZON

14 Return to Tahiti   189
15 The Adventurers   204
16 Abandoned and Resettled   219

Epilogue   231

Notes   242
Bibliography   249
Index   251

List of Illustrations

1. *The Mutineers Turning Bligh and Part of His Officers and Crew Adrift.* A hand-coloured aquatint after the painting by Robert Dodd, published October 1790.
By permission of the National Maritime Museum

2. *A Human Sacrifice in a Morae in Otaheite* by John Webber. Engraved by W. Woollett.
By permission of the National Maritime Museum

3. *A Young Woman of Otaheite, Dancing* by John Webber.
By permission of the National Maritime Museum

4. *Chart of Pitcairn Island* by Captain F. W. Beechey, RN, FRS.
By permission of the British Library

5. *Interior of Pitcairn* by Captain F. W. Beechey. Engraved by Edward Finden; published by Henry Colburn and Richard Bentley, London, 1830.
By permission of the British Library

6. *Interior of Pitcairn* by Lieutenant Conway Shipley, RN, published 1851.
By permission of the National Maritime Museum

7. *Portrait of John Adams.* Engraved from the original painting by Captain F. W. Beechey.
By permission of the author

8. *Friday Fletcher October Christian*, drawn and engraved by John Shillibeer.
By permission of the British Library

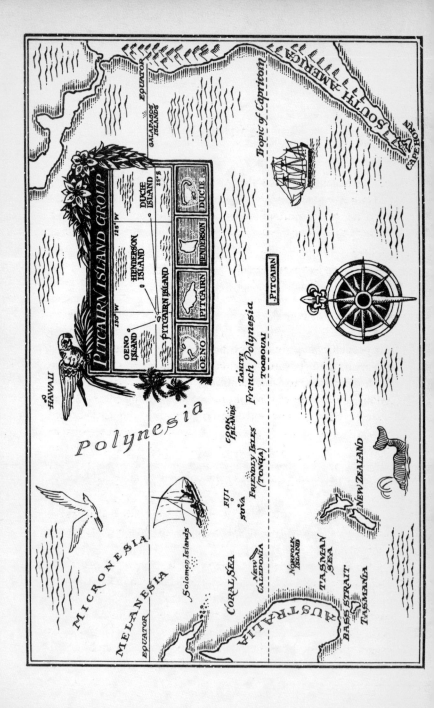

Prologue

In late September 1808 the American ship *Topaz* was sailing the empty expanses of the South Pacific Ocean. She had come from her home port of Boston, Massachusetts, down the east coast of the Americas and rounded Cape Horn. She was about halfway between South America and New Zealand and was just entering tropical latitudes when land was sighted. This was a surprise to her master, Captain Folger, for his charts showed no islands in the area. Nevertheless, land was a welcome sight, as he was cruising those waters hoping to find new sealing grounds and his ship was short of water: a strange island held the possibility of providing both those things. As the ship neared the island and its form became clearer through the telescope his hopes turned to disappointment. The island appeared fertile enough, but there was little hope of a safe landing-place. Wherever he looked there were precipitous cliffs and rock-bound shores pounded by heavy surf. As it was too dangerous to approach the land Folger was tempted not to waste time and sail on, but when night fell he saw lights on the coast. The fact that the island was settled meant that it had water, and there was a possibility that the inhabitants might be able to give him supplies; he was also naturally curious about who these unrecorded natives were. He hove to his ship until the next morning.

As the *Topaz* closed with the island at daylight, the surf was still too dangerous to risk landing in a ship's boat, but Folger spotted a canoe putting out from a small bay in spite of the danger. It contained two youths dressed in native clothing. When it arrived at the ship, Folger was stunned to be addressed in good English, but when he told them where he and his ship were from the youths had not heard of the United States of

America and inquired whether it was in Ireland. After some confused exchanges, Folger initiated the following conversation, later recalled by him in a letter to a friend.

> 'Who are you?' – 'We are Englishmen' – 'Where were you born?' – 'On that island which you see' – 'How are you Englishmen, if you were born on that island, which the English do not own, and never possessed?' – 'We are Englishmen because our father was an Englishman' – 'Who is your father?' With very interesting simplicity they answered 'Aleck'. – 'Who is Aleck?' – 'Don't you know Aleck?' – 'How should I know Aleck?' 'Well then, did you know Captain Bligh of the Bounty?' – At this question Folger told me the whole story immediately burst upon his mind, and produced a shock of mingled feelings, surprise, wonder, and pleasure, not to be described.[1]

Captain Folger had found the answer to a mystery which had fascinated the world since HMS *Bounty* had last been sighted leaving Matavai Bay, Tahiti, some twenty years earlier.

The story of the mutiny on the *Bounty* had reverberated around the world ever since it took place on 28 April 1789. It was a British *cause célèbre* from the time the news was received, and soon became a famous event throughout Europe, and in English-speaking countries and territories overseas. The *Bounty's* deposed commander Lieutenant William Bligh won fame by successfully conducting an epic small-boat voyage which took to safety himself and the eighteen of his crew whom the mutineers had cast adrift with him. The *Bounty* mutineers were assumed to have returned to Tahiti. No navy could allow mutineers to live unpunished, so once the news was received the Royal Navy sent a ship to find, capture and return them to England and to justice. A number of mutineers were recaptured on Tahiti, but the *Bounty*, under the command of the mutiny's leader, Fletcher Christian, had disappeared from the face of the known world. There might well have been a renewed effort to find the ship and to bring the missing mutineers to justice had not the French Revolution and the ensuing Napoleonic wars given the Admiralty far more pressing concerns. Not that the mutiny or Fletcher Christian were forgotten. The disappear-ance of the *Bounty* was spoken of by sailors throughout the world, and from time to time there were reports that Fletcher Christian had been seen in this or that foreign port, or on board a Spanish or French ship fighting against the English. But now rumour was at an end. Folger had found their hideaway. It was a tiny Eden only one mile by two, named Pitcairn Island.*

The *Bounty* was known to have disappeared from view with Fletcher Christian and eight other members of the crew, as well as six Polynesian men, twelve Tahitian women and one babe-in-arms. Their whereabouts had remained unknown for eighteen years when Captain Folger stepped into the canoe and was taken ashore to meet 'Aleck'. 'Aleck' was an able seaman from Wapping, London, whose real name was John Adams, but who – for reasons known only to himself – had signed on the *Bounty* as 'Alexander Smith'. Adams was the sole survivor of the fifteen men who had landed on Pitcairn in January 1790. It emerged that the settlement had a dark past: of the fifteen men only one had died from natural causes: twelve had been brutally murdered by their companions and one had committed suicide. Nine of the women were still alive, how-ever, and Folger saw a score or so of children playing in the village.

John Adams was the patriarch of this small community which, during his brief stay of five or six hours, impressed Folger as an ideal community. Everyone was well fed and healthy, and he, and later visitors, were unanimous in their compliments on the beauty of the women and the fine physique of the men. The islanders lived in harmony, followed a rigorous Christian practice based on the Bible, and appeared to be without the vices of the world at large. John Adams had taken it upon himself to instruct the children, who were assembled to demonstrate to Folger their skills in reading and writing, and in reciting the

---

* During Captain Carteret's Pacific voyage land was sighted on 2 July 1767 by 'a young gentleman' named Pitcairn. The island was named in his honour, and was originally known as 'Pitcairn's Island', but 'Pitcairn' is now common usage.

Creed and parts of the Bible. Folger left the island deeply impressed with the simple goodness of these few people. While he conversed with Adams the island's young men had replenished his water supply and, laden with gifts of fresh fruit, vegetables and meat, Folger took his place in the canoe to be returned to his ship and the crew who were anxiously awaiting him.

How had Pitcairn's murderous past given rise to such a harmonious society?' Establishing the narrative of events on the island is something of a historical puzzle. There are no contemporary documents recording what happened. The only written accounts are those of Captain Folger and those captains who called in later years, but these simply record what they were told by Adams, and he changed his version of events through subsequent retellings. He told Folger that all the men save himself had been killed in the course of one bloody day four years after they landed. During the following twenty years until his death he was to relate his story many times, and each telling revealed a rather more complex story of how his shipmates died on Pitcairn Island. Unfortunately, the women were never questioned in these early years and their version of events is lost to history. After their discovery, Jenny, one of the Tahitian women, left Pitcairn to return to her homeland, and was able to relate her story outside Adams's patriarchal influence, but most sources stem back to stories told by the sole white male survivor – John Adams – who, by his own account, played an innocent role in the blood-stained events. He also lived long enough to influence oral tradition. It would be unjust to doubt a man's word simply because he was fortunate enough to be alive, but one may legitimately wonder whether surviving such a series of murders called for a more active role than that which he ascribed to himself. He certainly changed his version of events many times. Nevertheless, John Adams emerges, if not as the hero of events, at least as their main witness, and he ended his days respected and admired for his prudent leadership: at the time of his death, he had made 'atonement for his past misconduct by bringing up no less than sixty-six young persons in the practice of pure and simple duties, with a success that has gained him a niche in the history of the human race'.[2]

The mutiny of the *Bounty* has been the subject of many books, but the events on the island, which require patient disentangling of the strands of the different accounts, have not been examined at length. Even as a simple narrative of events, it is a gripping drama in its own right. On such a small island no one could possibly be more than a mile away from anyone else and, during periods of conflict and killing, tensions must have been taut indeed. But the story has deeper resonances. A community of only twenty-eight individuals on two square miles of land provides a fascinating microcosm of the wider world, particularly in the clash of values and attitudes which led to the conflicts – between European sailors and the Pacific Islanders, between men and women, over religion and culture – and the environmental issues the islanders faced. No one could appeal to civil power or to common custom to enforce their assumptions about how society should be organized. Property rights, inheritance and the division of labour and social status all had to be negotiated; the strong had to be controlled and the weak protected, for without such basic principles society cannot survive for long. Internal conflicts brought the group close to total destruction; but miraculously, out of this explosive blend, society did survive and renew itself, and the new and strikingly egalitarian community of 'Pitcairn Islanders' emerged.

I

The *Bounty*

I · PREPARATIONS

Although the great Portuguese navigator, Magellan, had pion-
eered the route in 1519, by the mid-eighteenth century the
greater part of the Pacific Ocean remained largely uncharted
and its islands unexplored. Indeed, many scientists and geogra-
phers still believed that there must be a large undiscovered land
mass in the southern hemisphere to balance the land mass of
the northern hemisphere. Exploring and charting this huge
expanse was a formidable task. Square-rigged ships could not
sail very close to the wind and had to achieve their destinations
by following favourable winds no matter how roundabout the
route. Sections of the oceans which had proved sailable by one
ship in a given season were found to be bedevilled by contrary
winds, or by calms, by the next ship to attempt that crossing.
Knowledge was acquired slowly through hardship and determination. Eventually the circulation of the winds and their seasonal
variations became known and ocean currents were charted.
Landfalls where water, food and fuel could be obtained were
established, and bays and coves with tides suitable for careening
and repairing ships became known. Early voyagers planted fruit
trees and a variety of familiar food plants at these places for the
benefit of others who might follow them. The few European
ships which crossed the Pacific could sail week after week without sighting land, and the average voyage from the south of
England to Tahiti took about six months – provided that the
ship stopped only once on the way, usually at the Canary Islands
for water and fresh food. It then had no landfall except when
rounding Cape Horn.

The drive towards greater wealth through increased trade
and commerce was the main incentive for Europeans to send
ships to far destinations, but European curiosity ensured that

the simple urge to explore and the desire to pursue scientific inquiry were never entirely absent. From the fifteenth century onwards those voyaging to the Far East went from Europe via the Cape of Good Hope and the Indian Ocean to India or China; the Portuguese led the way, followed by the Dutch, English, French and other nationalities. Permanent European trading stations were established *en route*. When he was cast adrift, Captain Bligh headed for the Dutch settlements in Timor, Java and Sumatra (now Indonesia) – 3600 miles distant, but the nearest place where he could find security and ships returning to Europe. Australia had been discovered, but the coast was only partially charted, and the first European settlement was established only towards the end of the eighteenth century with the original penal colony at Botany Bay in 1788. Apart from that, and the scattered European presence in the area north of Australia through to the Philippines and China, the vast expanse of the Pacific stretching to the coasts of North and South America was little known. It was to be gradually explored and exploited by ships which ventured down the east coast of South America and entered the Pacific Ocean by rounding Cape Horn.

Nevertheless, the fact that the Pacific region was an immense ocean studded with comparatively small islands meant that, once European sea-powers turned their attention to it, it was rapidly explored. By contrast, Africa had been familiar for centuries, but very little of its interior was known to Europeans until the 1900s, and much of that not until quite late in the century. In Africa, land exploration and trade called for immense numbers of porters and guards, and goods for inland trade were often limited to what could be carried on the backs of humans and pack animals – both of which consumed a quantity of supplies daily. More crucially, explorers or traders were vulnerable to the power of the local inhabitants, and even large expeditions risked being attacked and plundered. It is no accident that one of the main trade goods out of Africa – slaves – could transport themselves to the coast. A European ship, on the other hand, was a floating fortress virtually immune to the hostility of the local populations. It could carry dry stores for two or more

years and was powerful enough to be able to land to trade for,
or otherwise obtain, fresh supplies from time to time when the
opportunity arose. Such ships floated away from Europe but
carried its technology with them. The Pacific economy had no
metal: ships carried not only cannon and muskets and all the
tradesmen's and domestic implements made of iron, but also
blacksmiths' forges on which metal could be worked. Natives
had to fell trees and work the timber slowly and patiently with
implements of stone and bone; the more technologically
advanced sailors felled trees, sawed them into planks and
repaired their ships with a full complement of hard-edged carpenter's tools, and they had knives, swords and bayonets as well
as all the metal fittings which were used to build a ship. Iron
was valued by the natives much as Europeans valued gold, and
it made the sailors wealthy beyond imagination. They could
purchase twenty coconuts for a single iron nail.[1]

Travellers by sea could explore and record in the spirit of
scientific progress with a thoroughness and detail which land
travellers could not. Ships could carry surveyors to measure,
map and chart; artists to record images of the many strange
plants, fish, birds and animals; botanists to collect, preserve and
store specimens on board and even bring living plants home.
A ship could serve as an institution for the gathering of knowledge. Even the ships' officers were encouraged to develop their
skills as draughtsmen so that they would be able to sketch an
accurate profile of coasts and landfalls and plans of natural har-
bours, not to mention foreign towns and their fortifications.
Drawing was part of the curriculum at the Portsmouth Naval
Academy from early in the eighteenth century. As Britain
developed to become the premier maritime power from the
mid-eighteenth century onwards, British sailors were active in
exploring and charting the empty Pacific wastes. Captain Cook
had been the greatest of these, and the two men who were
responsible for realizing HMS *Bounty*'s voyage – Sir Joseph
Banks and William Bligh – had both sailed with Cook in the
Pacific, and both had been to Tahiti.

More than any other place in the world, Tahiti (written as

Otaheite by the early visitors) captured the imagination and interest of Europe. Its inhabitants lived in a land so fertile and fruitful that work seemed scarcely necessary. They enjoyed a delightful climate, and were a well-formed, attractive and (usually) friendly people. They struck a chord in contemporary European thought and philosophy by seeming to embody all of the virtues and freedom of Rousseau's 'noble savage'; they were even compared to the Ancient Greeks with all the admiration which European culture had for that civilization. Joseph Banks claimed that:

> Tahitian women were the most elegant in the world. European ladies outvied them in complexion, but in all else the Tahitians were superior. Their clothes were natural and beautiful, such as were in Europe only upon statues and antique gems, or in the paintings of the great Italians who knew how to clothe their angels and goddesses in loose natural folds.[2]

A French expedition on the *La Boudeuse* under the command of Louis de Bougainville visited Tahiti in 1769 and called it New Cythera, after the Greek island where legend has it that Aphrodite, goddess of love, rose from the waves. For those less imbued with a classical education the image of Tahiti as relayed by European mariners came to epitomize the perfect tropical island of popular imagination, where food was to be had for the picking and people had little else to do but laze and make love. But Tahiti was something of an exception; most islanders throughout the Pacific proved to be fierce and warlike and quite prepared to attack the Europeans in spite of their superior armaments. The assumption that the newly discovered Hawaiian islanders would be as friendly or as easily intimidated by muskets as the Tahitians had cost Captain Cook his life.

William Bligh was an officer aboard Cook's ship on that fatal voyage. It was under Cook that Bligh had perfected his considerable skills as a navigator and surveyor, and it was because of those skills, and because he knew the natives and had a smattering of their language, that he was chosen to command

the *Bounty* – the commission that would make his name go
down through history. The *Bounty* was to sail on a unique
mission. The man who initiated the ill-fated expedition – Sir
Joseph Banks – had sailed with Cook on his first voyage to the
Pacific and to Tahiti during 1768–71. The ostensible purpose
of that voyage aboard the *Endeavour* had been scientific, and
the ship carried an astronomer to observe the transit of the planet
Venus across the sun; its other purpose, however, contained in
secret orders, was to explore the southern Pacific and discover
any new lands which may exist. On this and subsequent jour-
neys, Cook was to criss-cross the ocean so thoroughly that he
was able to rule out the possibility of any major land mass
between New Zealand and South America.

Joseph Banks was a wealthy amateur botanist who is said to
have contributed £10,000 to the cost of the first expedition;
among his personal entourage had been artists, botanists and a
draughtsman. That voyage made his reputation, and he went
on to become President of the Royal Society and a person with
immense influence over the scientific activities of the government. He wielded a great deal of patronage, both by virtue of
his personal wealth and through his office. He was not only
President of the Royal Society, a trustee of the British Museum,
a director of Kew Gardens and a privy councillor, but also a
friend and adviser on agricultural and botanical matters to the
'Farmer King', George III. It was through his intervention that
the project on which HMS *Bounty* was to be employed was
given royal support and the services of the Royal Navy. It was
he who recommended Bligh for command.

Britain was not the only European nation sending ships to
the Pacific, but within several years of George III's death it
was claimed that:

> The reign of George III was illustrated beyond every former
> era of English history, by mighty and successful efforts in the
> career of maritime discovery. Under the personal auspices of
> his Majesty, and with the means furnished by his government,
> voyages were made to quarters of the globe, and regions, the
> very existence of which had been unknown to former ages

... The pure interests of science, the diffusion among civilised nations of a knowledge of the globe which they inhabited, were the objects held mainly in view, and brilliantly fulfilled ... however ... nothing could be more laudable than to endeavour to draw from them the means of augmenting the subsistence and accommodations of mankind.

One source of subsistence was of particular interest:

The newly discovered islands of the great ocean presented many peculiar forms, both of animal and vegetable existence. Among the latter, the most remarkable and promising was a tree producing food for man, in such easy abundance, as seemed almost to exempt him from the original doom of earning his bread by the sweat of his brow.[3]

This marvellous plant was the breadfruit tree and the purpose of the voyage of the *Bounty* was to proceed to Tahiti, to collect a number of young breadfruit trees and to transport them to the West Indies. This was an example of commerce exploiting the earlier voyages of exploration and scientific inquiry, for the plan was that the breadfruit would provide a cheap and reliable source of food for the slaves who worked the plantations. The timing was apt, as the American War of Independence had resulted in the loss of British colonies on the mainland of North America and so the supply of grain and temperate foodstuffs to the West Indies was less certain than it had been. The breadfruit tree captured the imagination and envy of those who saw it growing, which it did with little or no attention or labour, and several visitors to Tahiti, including Captain Cook, made the observation that the Tahitians had escaped the biblical curse of having to 'eat bread by the sweat of their brow'. The breadfruit could be eaten just as it came from the tree. There was no need to plough and sow, reap and thresh, or grind – but simply pick and bake. If it could be successfully transplanted to the West Indies from halfway around the world, it could provide a cheap food for slaves and greatly increase the profitability of the plantations.

A committee of West Indian planters raised the question of

whether it was possible to transport young trees that distance and keep them alive through the rigours of a long voyage in a salt-laden atmosphere, but in the opinion of the influential Sir Joseph Banks it could be done. He used his extensive contacts to win support for the project and recommended that the botanist in charge should be David Nelson, who had been on Cook's third voyage and therefore knew the conditions and the natives. Banks also recommended how the ship should be adapted in order to preserve the plants.

William Bligh's previous experience and skills were such that he was bound to be among those considered for command of the voyage; but he also benefited from the fact that this was a period when appointments more frequently took account of an individual's influence than his abilities. Bligh's uncle by marriage, Duncan Campbell, was a West Indian planter active in the project. He was also a ship-owner, and had already employed his nephew as master on voyages to Jamaica. Bligh was a naval officer and had served full time in the Royal Navy, but had spent the previous five years as a lieutenant on half-pay – a type of reservist, who could be recalled at need, but was free to seek other employment while drawing his half-pay. In the summer of 1787 he was appointed to command the expedition charged with bringing about 1000 breadfruit trees from Tahiti to the West Indies. He was thirty-three years old, and although it was made through patronage, the appointment was an acknowledgement of his high skill as a navigator. He accepted the post with alacrity as his ambition was a career in the Royal Navy and full-time service was the only path to promotion.

After he had been appointed, however, Bligh expressed a growing resentment: he felt that the position warranted his promotion to captain, but the best he could extract from the Admiralty was a promise of promotion on the successful completion of the task. This was not simply a matter of status and climbing the promotional ladder, important though those concerns must have been; it was also a question of pay. As a lieutenant he was paid £70 a year (an able seaman received £14 8s. [£14.40]), and because the *Bounty* was a small vessel he was also to act as ship's purser. During his years on half-pay he had earned several times that amount as captain of one of his uncle's merchant ships plying to the West Indies. Thus he took the appointment at a considerable financial loss – although there was little doubt that the West Indian planters would have voted him a substantial purse had he arrived with the' trees. Even when the enterprise failed through mutiny, they awarded him 500 guineas.*

It was perhaps ungenerous of the navy not to promote Bligh before the voyage, but the ship was not of a size that required a captain as its master. The *Bounty* was an ex-merchant ship of 215 tons. She was only 91 feet long, 25 feet at her widest, and her hold was 10 feet deep. She had been specially purchased for the voyage and the whole after section of the ship where the captain would customarily have had his accommodation had been fitted with a false floor with holes to hold the pots of young trees. Suitable arrangements had also been made to supply them with water and light. As a result of this alteration space was at a premium. As captain of the ship Bligh was left with a cabin only 6 feet by 7 feet, so the overcrowding for the rest of the crew might be imagined:

> Everything but steering and sail handling went on below the flush main deck – cooking, eating, sleeping and the storage of supplies, both alive and dead. This microcosm of self-sufficient life was carried on in virtual darkness and impossible cramp. There were no portholes; fresh air and light came only through the three-foot hatches to the ladderways when conditions were suitable . . . so thirty nine of the forty five men had to live for months on end with an average space of 30 square feet. The other six were down companionways in even smaller cells on platform decks where headroom was only 5 feet.[4]

This lack of space was to be fatal to the enterprise, for it meant that Bligh had to sail without the usual complement of marines. Marines were placed on board ships partly to provide a trained

---

* Although not a captain *by rank*, Bligh is still referred to as the captain of his ship.

military force for protection when ashore in hostile circumstances, but also to serve as an armed guard to reinforce the authority of the captain against the crew should that be necessary. Also, had he been promoted to captain Bligh would have been given a lieutenant to serve under him, providing another commissioned officer to support his authority.

It could have been argued that the ship was too small for the expedition, but it had been purchased and adapted before Bligh was appointed. He joined it at Deptford to superintend the fitting-out, select his crew and take on supplies for eighteen months. Bligh's experience of the severe weather and sea conditions which circumnavigating the world entailed helped to ensure that the *Bounty* was as well prepared as possible for the rigours of the voyage ahead. He ordered that the masts should be shortened, and took less than half the prescribed amount of iron ballast. Given the battering they were to receive in attempting to round Cape Horn those decisions may well have saved the ship from foundering. He also rejected the 20-foot-long cutter that had been supplied, insisting on having one of 23 feet. An extra three feet may not seem much to the non-seaman, but it meant a much more substantial and seaworthy craft, and as it was to be the one in which he was cast adrift with eighteen men, Bligh's insistence was probably crucial to his, and their, survival.

As was customary, Bligh was responsible for choosing his own officers and crew. This was not of any great importance as far as the common sailors were concerned: at that time there was not the clear distinction between the Royal and Merchant navies that was to develop later, and crewmen in particular served indiscriminately in one or the other. But the officers owed their appointments to his patronage, which in the late eighteenth century was overt and accepted. The Royal Navy and merchant shipping had been suffering a slump since the end of the American War of Independence in 1783 and hundreds of officers and men were desperate to find a berth. By 1786 nearly seven men out of every eight had been discharged from the Royal Navy, and if that was a relief to many pressed men it spelt disaster for the thousands of officers who were placed on half-pay, and who, unless there was another war, had no realistic chance of serving at sea again, leaving their careers in ruins. Fortunate indeed was the officer who could secure royal service.

Bligh had been fortunate in becoming captain of a merchant ship through the patronage of his uncle; and it was also through family connections that Fletcher Christian, the man who was to lead the mutiny against him, first served under Bligh in 1785. Christian too had experienced long voyages, having been to Africa and India in the Royal Navy, and he had proved himself a capable officer. Like Bligh, he had been removed from active service and placed on half-pay. As a twenty-year-old with ambitions for a naval career he was so determined to be at sea and gain more experience that, exceptionally for a man from a good family and an officer, he had solicited Bligh for employment in the West Indian trade by volunteering to work as a seaman, asking only that he retain his status as a 'gentleman' by eating in the officers' mess. He so impressed Bligh with his abilities that on his second voyage he was promoted to second mate – and they became friends. It was because of this that he was chosen by Bligh to go on the *Bounty*. Christian's mutiny was to be a betrayal of patronage and friendship as well as of duty. The midshipmen, potential commissioned officers, were usually also recruited by the recommendation of influential families and friends. Edward Young, a midshipman who some blame more than Christian for the mutiny, was accepted because Bligh had obligations to his family – and so it went on. As for the crew, Bligh chose a number of men who had sailed with him or with Cook. In all a complement of forty-seven men was chosen for the voyage.

Conditions on board ship have traditionally been hard and restricted, and the late eighteenth-century sailor had much to endure. An able seaman's wage of £1 5s. [£1.25] a calendar month was hardly generous even by the standards of the day, but a seaman in the service of the Royal Navy could not count on that with any confidence – wages were supposed to be paid every eighteen months, but seldom were. It became customary always to keep back six months' pay in order to discourage desertion. Even in port, sailors often remained confined on board:

As late as 1811 Lord Cochrane quoted examples of one ship that had been eleven years out East, another fourteen, another fifteen, and none of the men had been paid at all. Penrose recalls how 'I was once paid off in a 74-gun ship in Plymouth and many of her men had never set foot on land for six or seven years, except in the dockyard at Jamaica'.[5]

During the war years merchant sailors returning home from long voyages ran the risk of being captured by a press-gang and forced aboard another ship before they had the opportunity to return home; they could even be taken off a homeward-bound ship in the English Channel and placed aboard a Royal Naval vessel, and forced into years more service without even touching foot on land, much less seeing their pay-offs or families. Given all they were subjected to, it says much for their basic character that they won and preserved a reputation for courage in war, good humour and ability at sea, and for genial high spirits and open-handedness when ashore. Few men earned a harder or more dangerous living.

Their dietary scale was, on the face of it, plentiful enough, although extremely monotonous:

basic ship's provisions per man were 1lb. salt pork or 2lb. of beef on alternate days. There was a daily ration of 1lb. biscuit and one gallon of beer, and a weekly issue of 2 pints of pease, 3 of oatmeal, 8oz. butter and 1lb. of cheese. On southern voyages a pint of wine or half a pint of brandy was substituted for the beer, which never remained fresh for long at sea. Rice was issued instead of oatmeal, olive oil for butter . . . The full measure of all articles was reduced by an eighth to compensate the purser for wastage or seepage.[6]

This would have been a substantial – if unhealthy diet – had the food been of good quality. But even given the limited technology for preserving food available to them, the contractors who supplied naval stores were frequently corrupt, and the men complained that when casks were opened at sea the meat was mainly bone and/or tainted, and the biscuit and dry stores were full of weevils and similar infestations. The ration could be – and usually was – reduced by the captain in order to conserve sufficient food for the length of the voyage: the scale above was more notional than actual. On exceptionally long voyages the basic dry stores were supplemented by some special foods in an effort to prevent scurvy (a potentially fatal disease caused by vitamin deficiency), and fresh food could be obtained when they touched land. Even on the best of ships, and in spite of the best of auguries when signing on, sailors remained subject to whatever cuts were deemed necessary by the captain. John Bechervaise was a quartermaster who in 1825 sailed on HMS *Blossom*, which, as part of its orders, was going to survey Pitcairn Island. Because the ship was subsequently bound for the cold northern latitudes Bechervaise records that everything was of the best: the stores were most liberal and of superior quality; the crew were to be issued with free warm clothing, and they were given six months' advance pay. They set off, apparently much better off than the seamen of the 1790s. But, despite having sailed with stores for a voyage of two or three years' duration, within four months rations which had already been shortened were halved. Food was issued:

> to each man at the rate of eight men on the allowance of four, little enough of any thing, but a necessary precaution for our safety. Each man's allowance of provisions for twenty-four hours was their eight ounces of soft bread baked on board daily, six ounces of salt beef or pork, alternate days, six ounces of flour for dinner one day, and a gill of pease the next; rum was not curtailed.[7]

Bechervaise wrote of the unremitting pain of continual hunger and how, in spite of having made port at Valparaiso in October, they still continued very short of food.

Given the length and nature of service, the uncertainty of pay and the atrocious food, it is not surprising that in the 1780s about a quarter of the men deserted their ships. Although the crew of the *Bounty* were not told officially what their destination was or the purpose of the voyage, it was obvious from the way the ship had been adapted that it was going to be a special voyage: perhaps that discouraged all but the bolder characters, for the *Bounty* had sixteen men desert during the weeks on board before she finally managed to clear the English coast.

Leaving England in a square-rigged sailing ship was no simple matter. The prevailing westerly winds could keep a ship wind-bound in harbour for weeks on end or force her back up the Channel once she had sailed. Bligh was ordered to proceed from the Thames to Spithead where he was to receive his final orders, and it took nearly three weeks of battling against gales before they managed to arrive on 4 November 1787. In spite of that slow passage, the final sailing orders from the Admiralty in London were still not ready for him. Time was now of the essence, for if the *Bounty* were to arrive in time to expect reasonable weather while rounding Cape Horn it needed to sail at once. They waited and waited for those orders during a period in which favourable east winds would have blown them out into the Atlantic, while Bligh cursed the incompetence of the Admiralty. By the time he received his orders on 24 November the winds had changed back to the west and the *Bounty* attempted to sail twice, only to be beaten back into harbour again. Bligh wrote to his uncle on 10 December:

> If there is any punishment that ought to be inflicted on a set of men for neglect, I am sure it ought on the Admiralty for my three weeks' detention at this place during a fine fair wind which carried all outward bound ships clear of the Channel but me, who wanted it most. This has made my task a very arduous one indeed for to get round Cape Horn at the time I shall be there. I know not how to promise myself any success and yet I must do it if the ship will stand it at all or I suppose my character will be at stake. Had Lord Howe sweetened this difficult task by giving me promotion I should have been satisfied . . . The hardship I make known I lay under is that they took me from a state of affluence

from your employ with an income of five hundred a year
to that of a lieutenant's pay four shillings a day . . .'

Bligh himself was already a bitter and disappointed man when
on Sunday 23 December, 1787, some two and a half months
after being ordered to sail from the Thames, his ship, on her
third attempt, finally managed to get away.

A fortnight later, on Sunday 6 January, 1788, the *Bounty*
anchored at Santa Cruz in the Canary Islands for water and
fresh food. Even here, the Admiralty's incompetence in delaying
them and the contrary winds which had prevented their prompt
departure were to their disadvantage, because in January fresh
vegetables and fruit were scarce and expensive. Having supplied
themselves as best they could, they left on 10 January under
orders to sail non-stop to Tahiti.

Although he was foul-mouthed and abusive, especially to his
officers, whom he berated and humiliated in public, Lieutenant
Bligh was not the callous, sadistic flogger of popular myth.
Flogging was a punishment viewed by his contemporaries as a
necessary adjunct to discipline and, provided it was not used to
excess, it was accepted by the crew. In fact, the first sailor
Christian approached to join the mutiny refused, and he was
one of the few men who had been flogged on Bligh's orders.
Bligh resorted to flogging very sparingly and was an exceptionally conscientious and progressive master who cared for the
health of his crew. When he was sailing master to Captain Cook
on his final voyage of discovery he had learned the value of
treating men humanely and ensuring the best possible diet and
dry quarters. The usual naval system of working was to divide
the crew into two watches, each of which worked four hours
'on' and then had four hours 'off' (although 'all hands' would
be called out in an emergency). The watches alternated
throughout the twenty-four hours, each man being on duty for
at least twelve, for as long as the ship was at sea. After they left
the Canary Islands Bligh split the men into three watches,
allowing them eight hours off for every four they worked, thus
reducing hours on duty by a third.

On Sunday 23 March, 1788 they sighted Tierra del Fuego and commenced their attempt to round the tip of South America and pass up into the Pacific. Whenever they made some progress, however, they were battered by one of the prevailing westerly storms which drove them back eastward again. The ferocious gales together with rain, sleet and snow tested the crew and the ship to their limits. Bligh recorded that the storm 'exceeded anything I had met with and a Sea higher than I had ever seen before'.[2] It was in these adverse conditions that his actions as a superb sailor and captain of his crew were at their best. As the decks of the battered ship began to leak, he moved the crew to the great cabin for their comfort. He left two men of the watch stoking fires below, to air the accommodation and dry the bedding and clothes of the crew. On 19 April he noted that their livestock was suffering even more than the men: 'To give the men a fresh meal tomorrow I ordered a hog to be killed, out of half a dozen I have remaining. We had a great abundance of Poultry, Sheep & Hogs but the Weather for this Month past has been so severe that we have scarce any left.'[3] They struggled to make progress for thirty days until finally Bligh decided to change direction:

> It was with much concern I saw it improper and even unjustified to persist any longer . . . a high sea running led me to determine to bear away for the Cape of Good Hope . . . I ordered the helm to be a Weather to the universal joy of all hands on 5 O'Clock [22 April], and as the Gale continued it was an additional satisfaction to think we had lost no time.[4]

They had survived a battering which might well have ended in the loss of the ship with all hands had not Bligh ordered much of the iron ballast to be taken out when they commissioned the ship. He writes a long justification for not persisting in following the Admiralty's preferred sailing plan, although he could not resist noting in his logbook that, had they left England a month earlier, they could undoubtedly have rounded the Cape without difficulty. Now, already four months at sea, he was obliged to circle the globe in an easterly direction, a much longer route

Before leaving Cape Horn the sailors supplemented their diet, showing no trace of the superstition which later became widely held by sailors that it was bad luck to harm an albatross:

> By Hooks and Line floating my People jigged (as they call it) two albatrosses. We have caught several of the Brown and of the White kind, between which there appears no difference but in their plumage, the same as may be observed among the Gulls in England. They measured six feet from tip to tip of their Wings. I have encouraged their eating these birds, and by cramming them with Ground corn like Turkeys they are as fat and not inferior to fine geese. We have done the same with the Pintada which are as fine and about the size of a Pidgeon.[5]

It was only ten years later that Samuel Taylor Coleridge's poem 'The Rime of the Ancient Mariner' was published, in which that graceful sea bird of the southern latitudes is first fed and welcomed on the ship as a bird of good omen, only to be shot by one of the crew. The bird is held to have brought fair winds, and killing it brings disaster to the ship. Perhaps the subsequent superstition about albatrosses is a case of nature imitating art, of a poet creating a belief rather than recording its existence.

The rest of the voyage passed without any great drama or incident. On 24 May they anchored in Simon's Bay (near Cape Town) where the ship and its rigging were repaired, the stores checked and replenished, and fresh water and supplies taken aboard. They sailed again after thirty-eight days' respite. On Thursday 21 August, after just over seven weeks at sea, they anchored in Adventure Bay, on the south of Van Diemen's Land (Tasmania). This was all but deserted, as the few inhabitants were extremely shy or fearful and Bligh managed only a fleeting contact, although he claimed to have recognized one man from when he was there with Cook in 1777. Here they set to work replenishing their water casks, cutting wood for fuel, and digging a saw-pit in which to cut tree trunks into planks. Bligh also planted some young apple and plantain trees he had carried from South Africa, and sowed cherry, plum, peach and apricot stones, along with Indian corn, pumpkins, potatoes, and other fruits and vegetables which might grow and prove of benefit to future voyagers – in the case of shipwreck they might even be the means of survival. After two weeks the *Bounty* continued its journey.

The ship sailed on eastwards, passing to the south of New Zealand, and after a run of fifty-two days dropped anchor in Matavai Bay, Tahiti, on Sunday 26 October, 1788, ten months after leaving Spithead. On this last leg from Van Diemen's Land Bligh lost one crew member, for which he blamed the incompetence of the ship's surgeon. The man had had a minor ailment, and although he recovered, the arm from which he had been bled became inflamed – leading to his death. The surgeon had been a bad choice: an alcoholic, he was seldom fit for duty, and was himself to die shortly. This spoiled Bligh's hope of returning with a complete crew. He had insisted on carrying sauerkraut, portable soup (vegetable soup boiled until it was solid) and essence of malt to prevent scurvy, which had hitherto taken such a toll of lives on long voyages. One could be cynical and ascribe his care to the fact that completing such a long and arduous voyage with a healthy crew would enhance his reputation. Equally, progressive sailors such as Cook and Bligh who undertook exceptionally long voyages at this period were aware that the safety of the whole enterprise could be compromised by sickness in the crew. It was also for the health of the men that Bligh had signed on board a nearly blind fiddle-player, and insisted that the men took their exercise in dance, as is shown by his entry in the log for Sunday 19 October, 1788:

> John Mills & Wm. Brown refusing to dance this evening, I ordered their Grog to be Stopt with a promise of further punishment on a Second Refusal. – I have always directed the Evenings from 5 to 8 Oclock to be spent in dancing, & that every man should be Obliged to dance as I consider it conducive to Health ... Mustered all hands & saw them clean and I think I never saw a more healthy set of Men and so decent looking in my life.[6]

To have refused a direct order while at sea as Mills and Brown did would have been followed by an instant and severe flogging with the cat-o'-nine-tails on virtually any one of His Majesty's ships. Even Captain Cook, with his wide reputation as a caring and humane officer who gained the loyalty and admiration of his seamen, resorted to the cat-o'-nine-tails more frequently than Bligh. In this case Bligh gave the offenders a second chance to avoid a flogging, a genuine piece of leniency that, with his concluding remark, made just a week before their arrival, suggests that he was looking after his crew well at this point in the voyage. Before their arrival, knowing from past experience what the reception would be from the women of Tahiti, Bligh had the surgeon inspect the crew and all were pronounced free of venereal infection. But despite his care for their physical well-being Bligh did not win the affection of his men. During this leg of their voyage across the Pacific he had been obliged to assemble the crew and to have a public reading of the Articles of War in order to enforce his authority as the ship's captain. It was normally considered a privilege to be able to dine with the captain, but after this incident the master and the surgeon refused to attend his table any longer. There is also some evidence that he had already fallen out with Christian. So, long before they had reached Tahiti, Bligh was an isolated and unpopular figure.

Tahiti was sighted on 25 October 1788. The following day the *Bounty* worked her way into Matavai Bay – where Captain Cook had stayed while he set up a shore station in 1768, so that the astronomer could record the transit of Venus. It had become the habitual anchorage for the few British ships to visit there. Long before they reached the point where Bligh wanted to anchor, the ship became unworkable as literally hundreds of natives of both sexes flocked aboard; it became impossible for Bligh even to see his men and so the *Bounty* was brought to a temporary anchorage. Native canoes brought very welcome gifts of fresh fruit, vegetables and meat – more sensationally, the women brought themselves. As night fell the native men were ordered ashore and the crew were left to enjoy the eager sexual attentions of the women who remained, who were more numerous than the sailors themselves. In one account after another from around this period (and for many subsequent decades) Tahiti is described as anything from the most fortunate and pleasant island in the world to an earthly, if not to say erotic, paradise. To the *Bounty*'s men, who had sailed 27,086 miles at an average speed of four-and-a-half miles an hour in their cramped quarters, enduring months of salt meat and ship's biscuit and all the hardship, danger and monotony of such an epic voyage, it was indeed a paradise: and a 'paradise' rather than a 'heaven', for it was populated with houris rather than with angels.

Eighteenth-century Europe was itself quite licentious, but the seaports of Europe, with their taverns and prostitutes which so quickly emptied a sailor's pockets, were in huge contrast to Tahiti, where sexual favours were unashamedly and freely bestowed by young women with full public approval. The friendship of the men and the open hospitality of the people were also striking, but it was the degree of sexual activity which, above all other aspects, impressed the sailors who were fortunate enough to be there before the missionaries subjected the Tahitians to other mores. It was within this culture that the *Bounty*'s men were welcomed with open arms during their stay of twenty-three weeks; as all the women who were to colonize Pitcairn Island with the mutineers came from it, it is worth a closer examination.

3 · TAHITI

Tahiti is shaped rather like an uneven hourglass, formed out of two circular pieces of land joined by a mile-wide isthmus. The larger end is about 18 miles in diameter and the smaller about 10, and both are mountainous, with land rising to well over 7000 feet. These central mountains were thickly wooded and provided an ample catchment area for small rivers and streams, which flowed across the coastal plain and into the sea every mile or two around the entire island. They watered fertile soil which, together with a favourable climate, provided crops with only a minimum input of labour. The lagoons and seas were full of fish and the Tahitians did not have to labour many hours a day in order to supply themselves with ample food and shelter; few, if any, worked beyond the morning. It was this plentiful supply of food which made Tahiti the most popular landfall in the western Pacific, used by virtually every one of the few European ships which travelled that area. Smaller islands and coral atolls simply did not produce enough surplus food from their resources to supply the needs of a shipload of strangers for more than a limited period. Indeed, inhabitants of some of the smaller islands could scarcely feed themselves.

Society on the island was organized along lines not dissimilar to those found in Europe. There were paramount chiefs who had religious as well as secular authority, and beneath them, under a rather loose authority, were the lesser chiefs. The main island had about three paramount chiefs who each, in turn, had three or four lesser chiefs under them. Under the chiefs were a number of farmers who owned and worked their land, and below them were landless workers of all kinds. There were more and less prosperous individuals within each of these sections. Although one could prosper within one's rank, it was not allowed to cross ranks – for example, intermarriage was not permitted and any child born to an alliance of two people of different ranks was killed at birth. Bligh compared the social hierarchy of the island to that of king, lord of a district, barons, esquires, citizens and servants. James Morrison, boatswain's mate on the *Bounty*, who was to spend some months on the island after the mutiny and who had the time and curiosity to learn much about the society in which he lived, stated that there were seventeen districts in all, each with its chief. Within those seventeen there were two groups (one of six chiefs who were always in alliance, and another of three), both of which usually recognized the same paramount chief. Other witnesses provide slight variations but it is clear that it was a complex society, which supported a structured political system.

The power of the paramount chiefs, however, was not accepted without question, and wars between districts and islands were quite common. The forces involved could be impressive – Captain Cook witnessed a war fleet of more than 300 canoes carrying some 8000 men to attack the nearby island of Moorea. Indeed, the first ship from Europe to visit Tahiti in the eighteenth century – the *Dolphin* under Captain Wallis in 1767 – had been opposed for several days by hundreds of canoes and a force of several thousand men until Queen Obarea made peace. The decision to go to war, or to support one, was made by each district chief – some would join and some would not. The enemy was warned in advance and a day arranged for the battle. Enemy prisoners would become human sacrifices, so it was quite acceptable for a commoner to run away from battle. Once a defeated army had fled, the victors took economic revenge by destroying (through 'barking') all the breadfruit and other food trees, thus condemning the enemy to five or six years of economic hardship until newly planted trees started bearing fruit again.

All this changed with the advent of the Europeans. Access to iron and, eventually, to muskets and powder gave any chief with whom the Europeans traded power over his rivals. It was by this means, as well as the backing of the Christian missionaries whose faith he professed, that Chief Pomare extended his power to become king over the whole of Tahiti in 1815. The attraction of European goods, particularly metal tools and, increasingly, arms and ammunition, meant that the chiefs tried to keep European ships anchored in their territory and trading under their auspices. This trade created economic pressures with political consequences: in order to supply the needs of the increasing number of ships, the paramount chiefs needed more and more land and people under their control, and so power was gradually centralized. The local chiefs, however, retained much power – they could requisition labour, food and material, as well as raise troops. One interesting element of their power was the ability to impose a taboo: the chief could order that certain plants were not to be harvested or animals to be killed, or that sections of the lagoon were not to be fished. While such taboos were most usually put in place for a brief period to ensure ample supplies for important forthcoming ritual feasts, they could be used to prevent over-fishing or the destruction of a plant species, giving the chiefs powers of conservation – essential to island living. They also gave the chiefs a strong hand in dealing with foreign ships, as they could cut off all supplies by placing a taboo against trading with the foreigners.[1]

Tahitians did not congregate in towns or villages but were dispersed, with each house on its own plot of land. Houses were oblong, and about 24 by 12 feet, although the size varied according to status – a paramount chief's house could be as large as 300 feet long and 40 feet wide. They had thatched roofs, no walls and very little furniture or furnishings. The climate was so favourable that life was lived mainly out of doors and all cooking took place outside the dwelling. At a time when large numbers of Europeans went hungry as a fact of day-to-day living and many were subject to periods of famine or near famine, Tahitians rarely suffered from shortages of food. The flat coastal area was like a huge, scattered and unplanned garden with breadfruit, coconut, banana, apple, sweet chestnut and almond trees. The soil was loose, easy and required little digging; spades were no more substantial than a sea shell on a stick, and

yams, sweet potatoes and taro were grown in abundance.* Sugar
cane provided sweetening. Every dwelling had its own small
garden plot and trees. Pigs, the main source of meat, were of
Chinese origin, and were quite small – weighing only up to
100 pounds – until crossed with European breeds. There were
also edible dogs which were fed a vegetarian diet and, according
to Captain Cook, tasted like lamb. They were of a breed which
was lost when it was crossed with dogs taken there by European
seamen. Fish were to be had for the taking and this, combined
with the availability of chicken, pork or dog, meant that fish
or meat were plentiful enough to be served with most meals.
The diet was sumptuous compared with that of a British farm
worker of the period, who could barely afford bread. To the
crew of the *Bounty*, who shared the local diet as soon as they
arrived, the abundance was princely. Once there, they were no
longer served the salt meat and dry stores of the ship, but were
fed on local produce – although they did continue to receive
their daily issue of grog.

Most cooking was done in earth ovens, as, lacking metal or
earthenware, the Tahitians had no fireproof cooking utensils.
Liquids were sometimes heated by dropping hot stones into
gourds, and blancmange-type puddings were thickened by the
same method. Tahitian cooking by fire-pits was highly com-
mended by Europeans for the way it preserved the flavour of
the food. A pit was dug and lined with stones and then a fire
burned in it until the stones were red hot. The fire was then
raked out and the stones covered with leaves (to provide steam
for cooking) before the food, again wrapped in leaves, was
placed in the oven. This was topped with stones, covered with
earth and left until the food cooked. All the cooking in these
pits was the work of the men, and once the food was cooked
men and women ate separately. Food was usually served on
leaves, but the more prosperous houses might have one or two
carved wooden platters, and, even more rarely, a wooden stool

---

* Taro is grown for its tubers and eaten rather like potato, although it
has a much higher food value. The tops, which can grow to six feet, can
also be used as a green vegetable.

to sit on. Most possessions and foodstuffs were stored in baskets made from reeds, leaves or vines, which were hung from the ceiling to protect them from the ever-present rats. The rats were small and served as useful scavengers, devouring the kitchen scraps as they were thrown away. The Tahitians tolerated them, even feeding them titbits while at their meals. Gourds and large sections of bamboo were used to store oils and liquids, while coconut shells served as drinking vessels. All implements were of wood, stone or shell: slivers of bamboo and sharpened shell made effective knives; stone was used for pestles and mortars. Fingers were used for eating and very few domestic implements were required.

Tahitian society was hedged with complex ritual and taboos, and, according to E. N. Ferdon: 'The Tahitians had several etiquette patterns related to food. One of these was a desire, or more probably a socially enforced custom, to share one's food with anyone who requested it, regardless of the smallness of the available amount.'[2] The Tahitians loved food and impressed visitors with their capacity to eat, but with this came an obligation to distribute food, so no one went hungry on the island. Indeed, Morrison, one of the *Bounty* crew who lived there for nineteen months, claimed that although people might trade their services – for example a fisherman might agree to supply a family with fish in return for garden produce – much food was simply given away. He explained that 'their Principal Method [of trade] is by Gifts and Presents to each other, and it is not Common to refuse the Greatest Stranger any thing he stands in need of whether Food raiment or any thing else.'[3] Travellers were always fed, and widows and children fed and cared for; under such a liberal system, poverty in the European sense did not exist.

The endemic thieving by Tahitians against which all Europeans had to guard themselves should be placed in the context of this widespread right to a share in the material possessions of others. There was also the lure of the great value of the iron tools and fitments on the ships:

A native of Otaheite goes on board a ship and finds himself in the midst of iron bolts, nails, knives, scattered about, and is tempted to carry off a few of them. If we could suppose a ship from El Dorado to arrive in the Thames, and then the custom-house officers, on boarding her, found themselves in the midst of bolts, hatchets, chissels, all of solid gold, scattered about the deck, one need scarcely say what would be likely to happen.[4]

It is almost impossible to exaggerate the value of iron in this society at this period. Apart from what they could trade or steal from the European ships, iron did not exist. All their huge canoes with intricately carved stems had to be cut from tree trunks felled, shaped and ornamented with tools of shell and bone. Iron tools simply revolutionized these tasks. Although the idle do not appear to have been obliged to labour, manual work was not demeaning. Chiefs and their wives and families would share in manual tasks with their servants without any loss of respect or status. The only disgrace was to be incompetent at such work. Although it was a very hierarchical society and chiefs had the power of life and death over their subjects and were treated with immense deference, the material differences were mainly symbolic (styles of clothing, colours reserved to particular ranks and so on), and there were no great differences in the material standard of living of the population. No one section of the population was overworked or exploited.

Although, in general, eighteenth-century Europeans held dark skins in low esteem, the Tahitians were seen as a physically attractive and well-formed race. The men were, on average, larger than European men, well fed and muscular, and the women were shapely. The majority of both sexes wore their straight black hair long. The men wore beards on their chins but shaved their cheeks and upper lips, and both sexes removed all other body hair. They were noted for their cleanliness, it being habitual for all to bathe twice a day – first on rising in the morning and again in the evening. Both men and women had pierced ears for wearing flowers as well as eardrops fashioned of shell, seeds and similar decorative elements. They loved scented flowers and wore them constantly. Knowing this, Bligh carried rose seeds from England as a gift. In terms of fashion and body ornament, however, the thing that the Tahitians were most noted for was tattooing (a word of Polynesian origin), an embellishment also much favoured by sailors.

Men did not appear naked in public but always wore a breechclout, a garment which covered the loins. Women usually wore at least a skirt, but would often appear naked in the ordinary course of the day. The clothing for both sexes was much the same: a wrap-around skirt and a poncho (an oblong piece of cloth with a hole for the head which rested on the wearer's shoulders). During brief periods when the climate was cool enough to warrant it, two or three ponchos were worn one on top of another and belted into the waist with a sash. Clothes denoted status: the upper classes wore a single rectangle of cloth draped around the shoulders, the lower classes a similar garment but tucked around the body under the arms, as it was necessary for lower ranks to bare their shoulders in the presence of their superiors.

Weaving was unknown in the Pacific and the cloth, *tapa*, was made from the barks of the paper mulberry, breadfruit and fig trees. The bark of young trees was stripped, soaked and softened in streams until the hard outer layer could be scraped off; the soft inner bark was laid in overlapping strips which were then beaten together to the appropriate thickness over a specially smooth baulk of timber. The normal width was 6 to 12 feet and the length could be continued indefinitely. Thicker material was made by pasting sheets together. This labour-intensive process was women's work and its production was endless, as the cloth was not washable and had to be replaced when soiled. It was usually worn white as it was produced, but some was dyed with a variety of colours and patterns: the use of red and yellow seems to have been limited to the chiefs, while those of lower status used black or brown. The clothing made from this cloth for religious and ceremonial use was as elaborate and complex as anything worn by the ladies of European Courts. *Tapa* was also used extensively for ceremonial gifts and ritual offerings. Such gifts were made by chiefs to the priests and to other chiefs.

Tahitian religion was complex and, given the problem of understanding the significance behind the ceremonies, accounts of Tahitian beliefs of this period are not altogether coherent. It is not easy to explain or understand the abstract beliefs of another culture, as Bligh was to acknowledge:

> He said their great God was called Oro; and that they had many others of less consequence. He asked me if I had a God? – if he had a son? and who was his wife? I told them he had a son, but no wife. Who was his father and mother? was the next question. I said he never had father or mother: at this they laughed exceedingly. You have a God then who never had a father or mother, and has a child without a wife! Many other questions were asked, which my little knowledge of the language did not enable me to answer.[5]

The limited command of each other's language and concepts inhibited understanding of such notions, but 'so numerous were the gods of Tahiti that the early missionaries came to the conclusion that there were almost as many of these immortal souls as there were people on the island'.[6] They had a supreme god Ta'aroa, who created the universe and all other gods and could not be given material form, and a whole hierarchy of lesser gods down to the particular gods of each home which were essentially the spirits of dead ancestors. In Christian terms perhaps the hierarchy could be compared to the different levels of veneration given to angels, disciples, saints and family tombs and graves. Tahitian gods could manifest themselves in natural phenomena, man-made images or in people, because 'the essential underlying principle of the Tahitians' view of life and the universe, and the interaction between gods and humans, was the dual concept of the sacred and profane'.[7] Religion, in the sense of the sacred and profane, permeated Tahitian life from birth:

> From the moment of birth a child was looked upon as a highly sacred being . . . the mother, having handled the sacred

child, could no longer touch her own food but had to be
fed by another person. Should that person . . . touch the
child, he or she immediately came under the same taboo.
Should the baby reach out and touch anything, it too became
sacred and was immediately appropriated to the child's use
. . . As is readily apparent, these restrictive taboos could not
last for any length of time without causing considerable disruption in the family circle. Somehow the sacred character
of the child had to be dispersed, or profaned, and this was
done through a series of rites known as *amo'a*.[8]

Not even the most royal European baby had the power to own
all it touched, as every child in Tahiti did. It took five of these
amo'a ceremonies, performed at intervals, before a child could
mix easily with its parents, kin and wider society. The child
was then tattooed on the arm to show that all the rites had
been performed.

That the great care and reverence given to children was
accompanied by the public and widespread practice of infanticide seems to contradict Ferdon's view that individuals were *born*
sacred. Christian missionaries were predisposed against much of
Tahitian culture and, as such, are something of a biased source,
but they questioned some of their converts on how many times
they had given birth and on how many of those babies they
had raised, and came to the conclusion 'that not less than two-
thirds of the children were murdered by their parents'.[9] Those
babies who were accepted as future members of society were
indeed sacred beings. A man whose wife gave birth to a child
conceived in adultery could demand its death but, in most
situations, it was the mother who had the right to choose
whether her baby would live or die. The killing had to take
place immediately, for once a baby had been permitted to live
it would have been murder to take its life. If the baby cried
out before it was smothered it won the right to live. As the
missionaries expressed it: 'Often, almost before the new-born
babe could breathe the vital air, gaze upon the light of heaven
or experience the sensations of its new existence, that existence
had been extinguished by its cruel mother's hands.'[10]

Acceptance into society, rather than biological origins, created the right to life and the right to a share in the duties and pleasures of that society, and a child's rights were extensive. Morrison wrote that as soon as a child was born it was superior to its parents: 'the Child is as soon as born the Head of the Family and the Honor and Dignity of the Father is transfered to the first born Child whether Male or Female, and before these rites [amo'a] are performed the Parents are not thought worthy to partake of its food.'[11] The higher one's rank in society the longer one remained sacred. This meant that some chiefs had to be carried everywhere, for if they touched the ground – or anything else – it would immediately become theirs. Life was much simplified when an heir was born, as the infant immediately became head of the family and the taboos on the old chief were transferred to the new. Danielsson gives an example of the power of both taboos and children among the Polynesians when he relates the account of a European visiting a chief only to find him and his wife and family camping in their garden because they had quarrelled with their eight-year-old son who, in revenge, had placed a taboo on the house (as was his right as chiefly head of the house) so only he could enter it. Among the lower ranks the sacred nature of their children was withdrawn (profaned) while they were still infants. In spite of their horror of infanticide, all European observers acknowledged that Tahitian children were exceptionally well cared for, raised with much affection, seldom rebuked, and led happy and care-free lives: 'They lay no restraint on their Children because they are the Head of the Family and therefore do as they please.'[12] Indeed, children had a great deal of power as they could place a curse on their parents and uncles and aunts – but not on their grandparents, and grandparents were the only ones who could curse the (grand)children.

Parentage had to be known as it was crucial to status and inheritance, but child-rearing was largely shared, as a child would feel at home and be cared for by any of its parents' kin, including its father's sworn blood-brothers; in any case, children could always be fed by whoever was nearby when food was ready. They had a childhood free from labour and spent their time in play. The Tahitians were almost as at home in the water as on land and learned to swim as soon as they could walk; surfing originated there, and European sailors – no mean boat-handlers themselves – admired the way in which Tahitians could pass through surf where Europeans could not. As children they had games and toys familiar to Europeans, such as kites, stilts, cat's cradles and ball games. Dancing was a popular activity throughout life and part of the social, religious and erotic texture of their lives. As they grew, and when *they* felt ready to do so, they learned their adult roles by assisting adults in their activities. Such was childhood in Tahiti at a time when British politicians, economists and industrialists insisted that it was absolutely necessary to keep ten-year-olds toiling twelve hours a day in field, factory and mine; and those fortunate enough to escape such work for the schoolroom were being disciplined with tawse and cane.

Girls reached puberty around the age of eleven or twelve and boys some two years later. It was at this time that both sexes were given the distinctive solid black tattoo over their buttocks which covered an area similar to a pair of modern swimming trunks. It was also at this age, or even earlier if they were so inclined, that they started the promiscuous sexual activity which so startled Europeans by its public nature – the Tahitians were vastly amused by the sailors' desire to retreat to a private location for the purpose. Single people were as promiscuous as they pleased, with teenagers often living in groups away from home in huts or shelters they built for themselves until such time as they chose to marry. During this period of their lives incest was the only taboo and limit to their sexual activity.[13]

Friendship between men was an important aspect of island culture and when men became *taio* to each other they became committed to lifelong friendship – blood-brothers in effect. Such brothers could have sexual relations with the wives of their 'brothers', as could a man's biological brothers, and any male guest approved by the husband. Thus a married woman had the choice of several sexual partners. Married men were under similarly loose restrictions in their choice of sexual liaisons. But once a couple had married sexual relationships with anyone beyond family and *tyos* were seen as adulterous and were forbidden. As it was something of a mark of status to have a European sailor as a *tyo*, the men of the *Bounty* were drawn into the privileges of this system, and 'for the women it was considered a prestigious triumph to conceive a half-European child, and they were as open in their appetites as their sentiments'.[14] Most marriages appear to have been long term, although there seem to have been no sanctions against separation, and marriages could be dissolved by mutual consent. When this happened the husband took any male children and the wife took the female. Possessions were divided, but the man had to maintain the woman and children until the woman paired with another partner.

Sexual activity was described as the Tahitian's main leisure activity, interest and subject of conversation. Bligh was horrified by some of the Polynesian sexual practices he witnessed – the public deflowering of a young girl by a youth, the uninhibited acceptance of sodomy, and what he called 'numerous sensual and beastly acts of gratification', including oral sex. Homosexuality was accepted as freely as heterosexuality, although, because many taboos and activities were gender based, it did carry a mild stigma in cases where the man concerned was treated as a woman. Bligh was shocked to discover that the queen shared her bed equally with her husband and his servant '. . . in the same hour and in the presence of the other',[15] surely a fine example of king and commoner sharing physical activities without prejudicing their respective status. Although erotic gratification was remarkably unrestricted and guiltless, it did take place within social rules and regulations. Much of the reputation for lasciviousness and sexual licence which so fascinated or outraged Europeans was caused by the *arioi*. These were members of a society which lived by special rules. They were the entertainers, performers of the lewdest dancing, who practised total sexual licence among themselves. Bligh described three men performing in one of these public entertainments which culminated in individual displays:

> the whole business now became the power and capability of distorting the Penis and Testicles . . . The Second [performer] brought his stones to the head of his Penis and with a small cloth bandage he wrapt them round and round up to wards the Belly stretching them at the same time very violently until they were near a foot in length which the bandage kept them erect at, the two stones and head of the Penis being like three small balls at the extremity. – The Third person was more horrible than the other two, for with both hands . . . it however afforded much laughter among the spectators.[16]

The *arioi* did no productive work, owned no property (the rest of society was obliged to keep them), and were not allowed any offspring: any children born to them were killed at birth. One explained to Captain Bligh that they lived like that because there were 'too many children', and it may well be that to keep the population in balance with the limited resources available to an island people, no matter how fertile the land, some form of population control was essential. As the majority of the *arioi* were recruited from the land-owning classes, however, it was more probably a method of preserving the social and economic position of the chiefly clans. If some of his offspring joined the *arioi*, the power of the chief and the succession through his child was assured and there were no, or fewer, sons and cousins to complicate inheritance.

The early visitors to Tahiti, when witnessing these public displays, did not, at first, grasp the real role of the *arioi* in society. They were actually a religious order given to worship through song and dance, and they were also expected to be prominent in any wars asserting the authority of their paramount chief – perhaps, in European terms, a combination of evangelical charismatics and Knights Templar. On the other hand, they also presented satirical plays, dances and theatrical performances which ridiculed and rebuked the powerful who transgressed the customary exercise of power or social custom. Theirs was a complex and powerful role in society. Novices had to spend a year proving their ability at singing and dancing and 'every member was bound to learn the society's sacred traditions and songs by heart' before being admitted to the order.[17] It had a hierarchy of some seven grades and, although it was recruited from all ranks of society, members of the chiefly classes had a privileged entry into the higher grades. There was total sexual liberty between members and, as pleasure and sexual gratification were considered positive goods, this liberty led to the invention and variation, publicly displayed, which featured so powerfully in European accounts of them. In fact they were the cultural and religious backbone of society: all their entertainments started with a religious subject and, however welcome as entertainment their dances and theatrical performances were, 'the divine mission of the *arioi* and their intimate relations with higher powers made them more welcome, for according to popular belief they could induce the gods to come down to earth and make them amiably disposed towards the inhabitants of the places they visited'.[18]

The Tahitians had structures and areas of land called morae, which were sacred and served the same purposes as a European church. They were open-air and the largest ones used for public ceremonials could be an oblong or square up to a hundred or so yards along each side, while private or family ones might be a piece of ground more appropriately measured in inches. The larger and more elaborate ones had a series of stepped stone rectangular platforms rather like a low Aztec pyramid. These had tables (altars) on which food was placed for the gods to eat. Nearby, and within the area of sacred ground that surrounded them, were the houses of the priests who served the gods. The largest, like cathedrals, were for events of national importance while lesser ones were equivalent to parish churches. Sometimes the ceremonies involved only the chiefly class, sometimes only men, but often men and women of all classes. Like the English eighteenth-century aristocracy the members of the chiefly class moved easily into secular or sacred office. All the higher offices of religion were the province of males, although at the lowest

level there were women priests. As with European religions,
special and very elaborate clothing, artefacts and symbols were
required to enact various rituals.

Human sacrifice was practised on some ritual occasions. Victims were always male and were usually killed by a blow with
a club at the back of the neck before the ceremony. Although
murder was a crime so rare that some European observers
claimed that it did not exist in Tahitian society, murderers were
executed, serving as the human sacrifice at a suitable occasion.
Thieving was a common crime with a scale of punishment
rising up to the death penalty for large-scale theft, but, as a thief
had actually to be caught in the act to suffer the penalty, this
was also rare. In fact, Tahitians appear to have had an aversion
to shedding blood. Sacrificial victims could not be killed by
knife or spear and were supposed to be unblemished. Executions
were by clubbing or drowning, and even food animals such as
pigs and dogs were strangled or suffocated, and edged weapons
were not widely used. The main sanction against criminal or
unsocial elements seems to have been an informal system of
marking them out as the next choice when a human sacrifice
was required. Even then they could escape that fate by fleeing
to sacred ground (where it was forbidden to kill anyone) and
staying there until the occasion had passed.

These sacrifices, however, were rare in comparison with the
frequent resort to the death penalty in Europe. Morrison was
on the island five months before there was a ceremony requiring
human sacrifice. This was the investiture of a new king, which
required the greatest number of deaths of any ceremony as each
chief had to offer a sacrificial victim. Finding so many seems
to have been a strain on the system given the length of time
since some of the victims had died: Morrison wrote, 'the human
sacrifices offered this day were 30, some of which had been
Killed near a Month. These were the First that had been offered
since our coming to the island. They never offer Men but such
as have committed some great Crime Nor then, but on particular Occasions.' On the whole the dead were respected and the
practice of keeping skulls above ground, which was viewed as

abhorrent and barbaric by Europeans, was viewed very differently by the Tahitians themselves. For them it was a mark of
especial esteem: 'Some who have great Veneration for the
deceased wrap up the Scull and Hang it up in their house in
token of their love and in this Manner is the Sculls of several
kept.'[19]

Religious taboos were undoubtedly powerful and did shape
and control individual and social behaviour, but the abstract
aspects of reverence seem to have been secondary to human
desire. When the British sent a ship to Tahiti to recapture the
mutineers, a shore detachment which had toiled up into the
mountainous interior in pursuit of mutineers found that:

> They were once also in danger of wanting victuals, till one
> of the natives ran to a temple, and brought out a roasted pig,
> ready dressed for the dinner of the god. On being taunted
> with the impiety of this act, he replied, with truth, that there
> was still more left than there was any chance of his divinity
> eating.[20]

Such was the island and the people with which the crew of
the *Bounty* lived for well over five months and, after the mutiny,
the society and culture of the women with whom they were
to found a new community on Pitcairn Island.

4 · THE MUTINY

After the *Bounty* arrived at Tahiti, the first task of the crew was to set up a shore station for the reception and potting of the breadfruit trees. Once the necessary protocols for peaceful trading had been completed between Bligh and the rulers and the desire for the plants broached and agreed to, the collecting began on 7 November 1788. According to one source, the required number of plants was collected within a fortnight,[1] and yet the *Bounty* remained at anchor for twenty-three weeks in all. Bligh has been criticized for this unaccountably long stay. During it, it is claimed, the crew became overly attached to the people and the place, which became a contributory cause of the mutiny. According to an earlier source, the collection took rather longer: 'In the course of six weeks, the English had collected 774 picked plants, having thrown out 302, which appeared to be assuming a less healthy appearance, and supplied their place with others.'[2] It must also have been sensible to wait a while in order to ensure that those plants which had been potted had survived the transplanting. In any event, although Bligh has been criticized for staying so long, that stay was, to a large extent, a consequence of the Admiralty's delaying their departure from England by two months. If they had been at Cape Horn at the right season to round it, thereby arriving at Tahiti in time to collect the plants during August, they could have left for home in September. But November to April was the hurricane and rainy season. Had Bligh left Tahiti during those months, during his voyage to the West Indies he would have been obliged to navigate through the very tricky waters of the Endeavour Straits north of Australia, during that region's season of adverse weather. His decision not to risk the whole enterprise by sailing during such an inauspicious period seems justifiable.

Others have criticized Bligh for making no constructive use of those weeks. As an officer with a sound reputation for the accuracy of his navigation and the quality of his charting, it has been argued that he should not have simply remained at anchor but should have made active use of his time there. If the *Bounty* had been under the command of Captain Cook, Hough writes, it 'would have been off every week or two, and at the end of five months they would have charted every bay, measured every hill, of all the Society Islands';[3] but that is an unfair comparison – Cook was on a voyage of exploration, Bligh was not. He was under orders to carry out a specific task of immense commercial import, and to have risked wrecking his ship in the sometimes hazardous business of charting strange waters, without specific orders so to do, would have been unforgivable. In his and the ship's absence the shore party might also have come into conflict with the natives and the primary purpose of the enterprise have been lost.

Bligh had comparatively few men and fewer officers to whom he could delegate varied activities. If he was culpable of laxness it was in permitting the crew to be indolent, and even letting the ship's equipment deteriorate through lack of proper inspection and care. Nearly six months swinging at anchor in such soft surroundings did nothing for the efficiency of the sailors or the seaworthiness of the ship: taking them out to sea and back even for a day every few weeks would have maintained the tautness of both. Although he was an excellent commander in difficult times, Bligh can be judged to have handled the time in Tahiti slackly. Certainly, while there he was anything but tyrannical; but given that the whole point of the voyage was to collect a thousand living plants, his most delicate task was to maintain good relations with the natives for a long period. Although he apparently never indulged in the free love that was so readily available, he did spend much time visiting and dining with the chiefs and having them aboard the ship on reciprocal visits.

For the crew the time at the island was a golden interlude, with little work, plentiful fresh food and compliant women. A number of the men 'went native' to the extent of having their buttocks, legs and feet completely tattooed in the Tahitian fashion, as well as with British motifs. After an initial period of promiscuity, one or two of the men settled down to a relationship with one woman. Fletcher Christian was the first to do this. Having been favoured by Bligh with the coveted post of commandant of the shore camp, he lived in plenty and some idleness ashore with Mauatua, a woman of exceptional beauty even by the high standards of the island.[4] She was the daughter of a chief for, as a hierarchical society, the Tahitians were conscious of status within the crew. The officers tended to have contacts with the chiefly class while the crew formed their relationships with women from the lower classes.

Moreover, any European male was prized as a friend as well as a lover: male Tahitians felt pleased to have sailors as their *tyos*. Three of the men determined to stay on the island forever. On 5 January 1789, Churchill, Musprat and Millward deserted, going ashore with the ship's cutter and several muskets. They then abandoned the cutter and took a canoe to a neighbouring island, hoping to elude any pursuit. In this they undoubtedly had the tacit agreement, if not active encouragement, of a chief, for two or three Europeans skilled in the use of muskets could be decisive in the wars between the islanders. Bligh's response was to pressure the local chiefs to find and return the fugitives. This was delayed for a while through claims of adverse weather but, inevitably, the superior influence of the ship and the power and wealth that it represented prevailed, and the deserters were returned. Desertion was punishable by death; the least sentence they could expect was a severe flogging. By the conventions of the day Bligh's sentence was not in the least severe: on 24 January Churchill was given twelve and the other two offenders twenty-four lashes each; they were then kept in irons and the punishment was repeated on 4 February.

The young midshipman, Hayward, had been asleep on duty the night the deserters stole the cutter, and he was kept in irons along with the others while waiting sentence for neglect of duty. The depth of friendship that a Tahitian could feel for a *tyo* is demonstrated by this account:

Hayward's male *tyo*, a man by the name of Wyetooa, had been aboard the *Bounty*, standing close behind Bligh with a club in his hand, on the morning when the three deserters had been flogged and Hayward had been publicly rebuked and ordered below in irons again. Bligh never knew how close to death he had been. If Hayward had been flogged, Wyetooa had planned to fell Bligh on the first lash, then leap overboard and gain the shore before anyone could reach him.

Instead, Wyetooa had bided his time, bitter at Hayward's humiliation and the loss of the company of his friend. Then on the black wet night of 5–6 February, he swam out and with a knife severed all but one strand of the *Bounty's* bower cable. There was a gale blowing, and the Tahitian reckoned that the remaining strand would soon snap and the *Bounty* be cast on to the shore.[5]

If Bligh had been attacked the native would have undoubtedly been put to death in turn. At the time no one knew who had cut the cable, and this was another incident at which Bligh quite rightly raged: he claimed that the watch had been careless in not being alert enough to prevent the event. For a while he suspected that the cable had been cut by the crew in a plot to wreck the ship and stay on the island permanently, a suspicion which grew to a conviction after the mutiny took place. It helped to persuade him that the mutiny had been long planned and was put in train as a result of the mutineers' failure secretly to cast the ship ashore.

There is no doubt that the native chiefs would have welcomed any deserter who cared to stay on the island. Because of their familiarity with muskets, ordinary crewmen were induced by offered grants of land and women to stay on the island but, apart from that one attempt by three of the crew, no one else was tempted, and Bligh was mistaken in thinking that the ensuing mutiny was fuelled by a desire to return to Tahiti. When the *Bounty* sailed for home all the crew sailed with her.

★

On 4 April 1789 the crew took leave of the Tahitians who had been their generous hosts, friends and lovers, and sailed for the West Indies to deliver their precious cargo of breadfruit trees on the way home. They headed west, towards the passage north of Australia and the Dutch East Indies, from where they planned to sail to the Cape of Good Hope and on to the West Indies. Accordingly, Bligh set course for the Friendly Islands, 1800 miles from Tahiti, where he intended to take aboard water and fresh food. They had a good passage, arriving on 23 April at Nomuka, where they met considerable hostility and watered with difficulty, setting sail again three days later. Less than two days after sailing, the mutiny erupted during the early hours of 28 April when Fletcher Christian and others burst into Bligh's cabin, arrested and bound him and took control of the *Bounty*.

The mutiny and its causes have been the subject of many books and films, and it is generally agreed that it erupted as a result of the personal conflict between William Bligh and Fletcher Christian. Had Bligh been a less abusive character and given Christian less reason for personal discontent no mutiny would have taken place, and in that sense their relationship was the catalyst. We know that Christian owed his position to Bligh's patronage, that he had served under Bligh on ordinary merchant ships, had been promoted by him and enjoyed his friendship. On the *Bounty*, Bligh continued his patronage of his friend and promoted Christian to acting lieutenant. The reason why the relationship went so sour is inexplicable. There has been speculation that the two men had a homosexual relationship, which Christian no longer wished to continue after having lived a vigorous heterosexual life for five months ashore, and that Bligh was particularly oppressive to him for that reason. But the evidence goes against that theory: such a relationship could hardly have been kept invisible on a small ship, where everyone lived cheek by jowl and where even Bligh's cabin was by a busy companionway. Bligh does seem to have been one of the few men, if not the only man, not to have had a sexual relationship with a Tahitian woman; but if that had been due to his homosexuality – rather than his morality as a married man, fear of venereal disease or any other reason – it seems unlikely that he would have parted himself from Christian for five months by giving him the favoured position of commander of the shore base. Given, too, that this explanation requires Bligh's pressuring of Christian to take part in such a relationship against his will, one would expect some rumour of this to have arisen at the time, given the bitterness and conflict the mutiny caused between powerful families in England: any hint that Bligh had been abusing his power to exploit a junior officer and younger man would have served as a partial justification of Christian's action.

Bligh had always been abusive and foul-mouthed to his officers, but on leaving Tahiti, he became particularly overbearing and unpleasant. His subsequent career suggests that his character as a supreme authority was somewhat defective. Perhaps at this time he also felt guilty for having neglected the ship and its crew for such a long period, for he worked them hard below and aloft exercising various manoeuvres. This might have been a necessary preparation for the difficult passage threading through the islands and reefs ahead, if rather abruptly enforced.

More seriously, the officers and crew who formed the shore party to collect water at Nomuka had a very dangerous experience in the face of native hostility, when lives were needlessly put at risk because Bligh would not permit the use of firearms. Under Christian, they carried out their task with considerable courage only to have Bligh accuse Christian, with no justification, of cowardice, an insult difficult for a naval officer to swallow. After some last-minute trading with the natives, who were becoming more and more hostile, they left Nomuka hurriedly, the decks still covered with piles of coconuts belonging to various members of the crew. The next morning Bligh claimed that some of his coconuts had been stolen and made a general accusation against the whole crew, but concentrated his venom on Christian and the officers. It was a petty, trivial and unprovable charge, perhaps existing only in his mind; but he reduced the rations and stopped the grog of the men. He was in such an ungovernable rage that he threatened his men with making their lives hard enough that 'I'll make half of you jump overboard before you get through the Endeavour Straits'.[6] As he had ordered them ashore to collect water in the face of hostile natives without the protection of firearms, such a threat could not be taken as an idle boast. That they had once been friends made it all the more difficult for Christian to bear this abuse, not least because Bligh made his position intolerable by often belittling him in front of the crew.

Christian's personal situation may explain why he was ultimately willing to lead a mutiny, but it does not explain why he found willing accomplices among the crew, for although they may have hated Bligh, mutiny meant that they would never see their homes and families again, and might either be captured by the Royal Navy or killed by natives. Mutiny was the final act of desperate men. Bligh believed that Tahiti was the attraction (although he was unlikely to blame his own actions) and he wrote:

> I can only conjecture that the mutineers had flattered themselves with the hopes of a more happy life among the Otaheiteans, than they could possibly enjoy in England; and this, joined to some female connections, most probably occasioned the whole transaction.

> The women at Otaheite are handsome, mild and cheerful in their manners and conversation, possessed of great sensibility, and have sufficient delicacy to make them admired and beloved. The chiefs were so much attached to our people, that they rather encouraged their stay among them than otherwise, and even made them promises of large possessions. Under these, and many other attendant circumstances, equally desirable, it is now perhaps not so much to be wondered at, though scarcely possible to have been foreseen, that a set of sailors, most of them void of connections, should be led away; especially when, in addition to such powerful inducements, they imagined it in their power to fix themselves in the midst of plenty, on one of the finest islands in the world, where they need not labour, and where

the allurements of dissipation are beyond any thing that can be conceived.[7]

Bligh's view is contradicted by the fact that Morrison (the boatswain's mate) wrote that when they sailed from Tahiti the crew's conversation was filled with expectations of arriving home and collecting their pay, and there was no mention of men wanting to return to Tahiti, and no thoughts of mutiny. John Adams was later to claim that there had been no real discontent among the *crew*. He said that the *officers* had much more cause for dissatisfaction, especially Mr Christian.

Whatever the reason for the ill feeling between Bligh and Christian, it was severe enough to put Christian into a state of mind bordering on madness at the prospect of being unjustly insulted, abused and publicly humiliated day after day, month after month without any redress or let-up. An oppressive commander could turn shipboard life into an unbearable torment.

After the incident with the coconuts, Christian decided to escape from the misery facing him on the long voyage home; he planned to slip overboard alone on an improvised raft in the hope of being able to reach one of the nearby islands. His state of mind and desperation can be measured by the fact that he tied a lead weight around his neck, ready to throw himself overboard and commit suicide should his escape plan be discovered and prevented. If Christian's desperate plan to escape became known he would have to go through with it, for in addition to whatever punishment might be decided on by Bligh or by a later court martial in England, at the very least his hopes of a naval career were ended. His plan did become known, for not only did he behave strangely in giving away various personal possessions to friends, but he also had to accumulate planks and spars for his raft and some supplies of food and water, both of which needed the help of others even if they did not know the precise reason for his activities. Edward Young and George Stewart, two of the midshipmen, learned of Christian's plan, derided it as impracticable and one, or both, suggested that he should lead a mutiny. It was true that to take to a raft could well mean death in one unpleasant shape or another – had he survived to reach land Christian would almost certainly have been killed by the natives. But for Christian to give up now, having gone this far, would have been humiliating and ended in disgrace. Mutiny offered him at least the possibility of life and dignity. He made his choice.

During the morning watch Christian broached the idea of mutiny to Matthew Quintal, one of the able seamen. He was a likely candidate for such an enterprise, for he had suffered a flogging at Bligh's orders and had formed a steady female attachment in Tahiti: at first Quintal refused. Once mutiny had been suggested to a crew member there was no going back, and Christian was in a desperate position, for he now had to abandon the ship in mid-ocean, face a hanging offence or push on to a successful mutiny. He approached another able seaman, Isaac Martin: Martin was enthusiastic. Christian then went to the others on watch. By daylight on 28 April 1789, the mutiny was underway. Of the mutineers who went on to settle at Pitcairn Island, Bligh named Adams, Mills and Quintal (who had changed his mind) as being with Fletcher Christian when the mutiny started and he was dragged from his bunk. Morrison, the boatswain's mate, goes further in blaming John Adams as an active mutineer in claiming that when he, Morrison, started planning with the master, John Fryer, how to retake the ship, it was Adams who betrayed them to the rest. Of the others who stayed loyal to Christian, Martin, McKoy and Williams were named among the main activists.

Adams and the others were ordered to secure the officers, while Christian and Charles Churchill, master-at-arms, seized Bligh in his bed, tied his hands behind him and took him on deck. Once he had been taken, the officers were allowed out of their cabins without guards, but the master, John Fryer, was the only one who tried to form a party to resist; he was quickly secured and confined below. The mutineers were then faced with the problem of keeping control. There were men on board who wanted no part in mutiny even if they were not enthusiastically loyal to Bligh. They wanted nothing more than to return to their homes. While such men were on board there was always the danger that they would retake the ship and imprison the mutineers. On the other hand, the mutineers felt the need to retain a sufficient number of men to work the ship and be numerous enough to confront hostile natives or any similar eventualities. They decided to set Bligh adrift in a small cutter with those loyal to him and with those men the mutineers did not want with them. After some argument, Christian conceded to Bligh's pleas to be permitted to take the 23-foot launch – a decision that probably made the difference between life and death for those set adrift. This must have been evident to the men, for once Bligh had been granted the launch Isaac Martin (who had also been flogged) changed his mind and wanted to join Bligh; he clearly had second thoughts about the mutiny and tried to re-establish his loyalty after having been one of the first to take part, for he was certain that Bligh would survive and bring retribution on them all. In Bligh's own account:

> Isaac Martin, one of the guard over me, I saw, had an inclination to assist me, and as he fed me with shaddock [a citrus fruit], my lips being quite parched, we explained our wishes to each other by our looks; but on his being observed, Martin was removed from me. He then attempted to leave the ship, for which purpose he got into the boat; but with many threats they obliged him to return.[8]

It was Quintal, a tough and headstrong man, who was not prepared to let Martin back out and levelled a musket at him until he complied. The armourer (Coleman) and two carpenter's mates (McIntosh and Norman) were also forcibly detained by the mutineers, as their skills might be needed, although the mutineers allowed the carpenter to go with Bligh.

The mutiny was not the result of some long-planned scheme to return to Tahiti as Bligh suspected. It erupted because Fletcher Christian had been driven by intolerable circumstances or, if one prefers, had not sufficient resolution to serve under a commander who demeaned him. Christian was popular with the men, who sympathized with him, and once he offered himself as a leader a proportion of the crew was willing to follow him. That willingness was more an expression of their preference for Christian over Bligh than the undoubted attractions of Tahiti. Fletcher Christian was as strong and able as any of them and could match them in the physical demands of all their tasks as sailors: he was respected by the men as a man. As an officer he was popular and he had gained the sympathy of the men as they witnessed Bligh's unreasonable treatment of him. On board ship, particularly aboard such a small ship as the *Bounty*, respect and authority become personalized, and wider obligations to articles, country and custom become attenuated by the lapse of time and of distance. Captain Bligh was unfortunate that the crowded conditions of the ship did not permit him to keep his distance and maintain his mystique as supreme authority from the usual dignity and isolation of a captain's quarters. The confined nature of the vessel meant that he was increasingly perceived and judged through his qualities as a man. Once Fletcher Christian challenged his authority there was no doubt that a number of the crew would actively support him, while few, if any, would risk their lives to support William Bligh.

At the time of the mutiny the *Bounty* had a complement of forty-four men (two having been lost since leaving England). Nineteen were set adrift in the launch under Bligh and twenty-five remained on the ship, some unwillingly, under Christian.

LAUNCH

William Bligh	captain
John Fryer	master
Thomas Ledward	surgeon (ex-surgeon's mate)
William Elphinstone	master's mate
Thomas Hayward	midshipman
John Hallett	midshipman
David Nelson	botanist
William Cole	boatswain
William Purcell	carpenter

Mr Samuel	clerk
John Norton	quartermaster
Peter Linkletter	quartermaster
George Simpson	quartermaster's mate
Lawrence Leboque	sailmaker
Thomas Hall	cook
John Smith	cook
Robert Tinkler	boy
Robert Lamb†	butcher
William Peckover	gunner

SHIP

★Fletcher Christian	master's mate
Peter Heywood	midshipman
George Stewart	midshipman
★Edward Young	midshipman
Charles Churchill†	master-at-arms
★John Mills	gunner's mate
James Morrison	boatswain's mate
Joseph Coleman	armourer
Charles Norman	carpenter's mate
Thomas McIntosh	carpenter's crew
★William Brown	gardener
★Alexander Smith [Adams]	able seaman
★William McKoy	able seaman
★Isaac Martin†	able seaman
★Matthew Quintal†	able seaman
★John Williams	able seaman
Thomas Burkitt	able seaman
Michael Byrne	able seaman
Thomas Ellison	able seaman
Henry Hillbrant	able seaman
John Millward†	able seaman
William Muspratt†	able seaman
Richard Skinner	able seaman
John Sumner	able seaman
Matthew Thompson†	able seaman

★ These nine men were to go to Pitcairn; the others stayed at Tahiti.
† These men had been flogged.

(John Adams signed on the ship as 'Alexander Smith' and did not resume his proper identity until after he was rediscovered on Pitcairn. For consistency's sake he is referred to as John Adams throughout, as that is how he is known to history. Adams's use of a false name does not necessarily imply a shady past: 'a fictitious, or "purser's" name, assumed on shipping, [was] a practice very usual with British seamen'.[9] One can only assume that by adopting a false name in the first place a man could more readily resume his proper identity on deserting a ship – as had sixteen of the original crew.)

After Captain Bligh and those with him had been cast adrift, Fletcher Christian refused to acknowledge that he was the mutineers' leader until he had been acclaimed as such by all the remaining men: to all he remained 'Mr' Christian – a Mr Christian who kept a loaded pistol always about him and enforced work and discipline. The work was now considerably heavier: because of their reduced numbers, the crew had to work the two-watch system rather than following the three-watch system Bligh had permitted them. Christian decided to settle at Toobouai, an island Captain Cook had discovered some 400 miles south of Tahiti, which confirms that a return to the attraction of Tahiti was not the purpose of the mutiny. They reached Toobouai a month later, but the natives were much more aggressive than the Tahitians and attempted to take the ship, losing eleven men and a woman and having many wounded in the conflict. In spite of the opposition and bloodshed, Christian insisted that it was a suitable place for a settlement and all that was needed to make a success of it was to return to Tahiti to collect some native men and women. On 6 June 1789 they returned to Matavai Bay only nine weeks after having left it amid so much genuine sorrow at the parting.

It was an embarrassing return. The breadfruit trees so carefully collected had been dumped overboard, and the captain and half the crew were missing. To explain away these awkward absences the mutineers invoked Captain Cook's name (the English had always maintained the fiction that Cook was still alive), saying that they had met Captain Cook who had taken the breadfruit trees, Bligh and half the crew to help him found a new settlement, and sent the *Bounty* back for other supplies and assistance in this project. Captain Cook was venerated by the Tahitians of Matavai Bay. He had left them his portrait (an oil painting by John Webber), which was an object of worship and was paraded as part of some of their most solemn religious rituals; as a mark of honour the portrait had been kept aboard the *Bounty* while she was there and had been one of the last things to be taken ashore when she sailed – it being the custom for each ship to record its name and the date of its visit on the back of the portrait. The Tahitians responded to Cook's name and to their English friends with their usual trust and generosity, and on 16 June the mutineers were able to sail from Tahiti with the decks crammed full of livestock, including 460 hogs, fifty goats, plus fowl, cats and dogs. They persuaded nine men, eight boys, and ten women (one with a baby) to accompany them. If they had been told the truth, they might never have gone. Morrison later wrote that in addition to these there were 'some stowaways', without specifying a number. They arrived back in Toobouai a week later.

The venture was never a success. The island of Toobouai was divided into three chiefdoms, which were in more or less perpetual conflict. The arrival of such a powerful new group with their invincible armaments threw the whole political and economic balance of the island into disarray. Christian started badly: he negotiated with one chief for a grant of land on which to settle, but then decided there was a more suitable site elsewhere and transferred his location and favoured relationship to another chief, creating an enemy. The chief in the new area did not want them to settle, but the mutineers demanded land and food and let their livestock loose to multiply in the 'wild' – the hogs causing immense damage and loss to the native crops. They also demanded women, whom the natives refused to grant them. In keeping with the easy sexual relations of that part of the Pacific the native men had no objections to the European men having intercourse with their women as long as it was a

casual relationship taking place in the native villages They
would not agree to the loss of their women, which permanent
residence as European wives would have entailed. Shortage of
women was a constant source of friction among the mutineers,
and was later to have disastrous effects. On Toobouai, the fact
that some men could not obtain a 'wife' led to resentments and
indiscipline, which undermined Christian's authority. The risk
of men being killed while searching for women posed a danger
to the whole enterprise. Adams was held captive overnight on
one occasion, and when Quintal and Sumner subsequently spent
a night ashore without permission Christian held his pistol to
Quintal's head and threatened to blow out his brains if he
refused to obey orders in future. He then had the two of them
put in irons. Ill feeling between the natives and the sailors
became endemic, and the Europeans were often beaten and
stripped of their clothing by the natives if they were found
walking alone. Throughout the time that these troubles were
simmering, work to establish an impregnable settlement ashore
continued. Patriotically named Fort George, with a Union Jack
flying proudly from its flagstaff, it was square, 50 yards on each
side, protected by 12-foot tall walls and a ditch 20 feet wide.
Cannon were mounted on the walls and one huge gate gave
access. It was difficult to venture far alone without being in
constant danger, so normal agricultural, hunting and fishing
pursuits necessary to their survival were undertaken only with
great difficulty.

This tense situation was bought to a head by the Tahitian
men who had sailed with the Europeans. In a foretaste of what
was to happen later on, they proposed joining the Toobouains
in a surprise attack to kill all the mutineers. One of the Tahitian
women, Jenny, related the story in later years:

> One of the Otaheitians, who belonged to the Bounty, pro-
> posed to the Tabouai people, that in case the Englishmen
> should settle on the island, they should unite and take the
> ship, murder the crew, and share the property. This coming
> to the ears of Christian's wife, she informed him of the plot,
> but did not tell him that an Otaheitian was the contriver of

it. The secret having transpired, led to a battle between the
mutineers and the Tabouai people, in which the latter were
defeated with considerable loss. One of the mutineers was
mortally wounded with a spear.[10]

Christian had taken the offensive on learning that the
Toobouains were planning to wipe them out, and sixty-six
natives were killed in the battle. Jenny was wrong, or misre-
ported, in saying that one of the mutineers died: one was badly
wounded but recovered. For the first time, although not for
the last, the Tahitian women proved their loyalty to their European men. They were not, however, prepared to denounce the
treachery of their fellow islanders at this early stage.

In spite of this slaughter, or perhaps because he was convinced
the successful outcome could be repeated as necessary, Christian
never deviated from his original intention to stay on the island,
but a 'mutiny' forced his hand. The crisis came when he ordered
that the *Bounty* be dismasted and the timber and cordage used
in building the fort. This would have been the first irrevocable
step towards permanent settlement, leaving the mutineers no
choice but to stay forever. A majority of the men objected, and
during the discussion, when Christian would not issue more
alcohol, they ignored the authority they had accorded him and
broke into the liquor store to help themselves. Eventually sixteen men voted to return to Tahiti. Faced with such widespread
discontent, Christian did not contest the decision, he simply
stated that he personally would never remain at Tahiti to be
captured and returned in disgrace to England, to the shame of
his family. He, rather romantically, requested that once returned
to Tahiti they give him the ship, set the sails to let the ship go
where it would before the wind, to founder or ground, with
only him aboard to meet his death. At this, eight of the men
swore their loyalty to him and expressed their determination
to stay with him no matter what their fate; they would crew
the ship with him and seek an unknown haven.

Such a split was not unexpected. The active mutineers had
kept some of the crew aboard the *Bounty* against their will
because they felt the need for their special skills. Bligh himself

had encouraged some of the men loyal to him to stay with the mutineers so as not to overload the open boat; those men felt certain that they had nothing to fear from being apprehended by the Royal Navy, and, indeed, it would be their one chance of seeing their homes and families again. Others, perhaps wisely, had not the stomach to settle on an island where the natives showed every sign of maintaining hostilities, the outcome of which was unpredictable. The welcome they had received at Tahiti, the goodwill towards them which had been expressed by the chiefs, the prospect of peace, security and comfort proved more and more attractive whatever the longer term risks of capture and trial.

It was agreed that those who chose to remain with Christian could take the *Bounty* provided they divided the arms, ammunition and stores with those who wanted to settle at Tahiti. With the policy agreed they left Toobouai for Tahiti once again on 18 September 1789, after two-and-a-half months of wasted effort. They took with them, as part of Christian's party, two Toobouain natives, a chief named Oha and his nephew Titahiti, who had been so active on the Europeans' side that they feared they would be killed by their tribe if they remained.

During the four-day voyage back to Tahiti, the two parties were busily dividing the arms, ammunition, tools, alcohol, stores and other equipment. Once in Matavai Bay these were hurriedly ferried ashore in the ship's boats and canoes with the men who had chosen to stay. The mutineers planned to keep Joseph Coleman, the armourer, with them because they felt that his skills were invaluable, but he managed to escape and swim ashore. At last, all the sailors remaining on the ship with Fletcher Christian were there of their own choice. Christian had said that they would stay for two or three days, but during the night he slipped the anchor and stole out to sea without a word to the mutineers on the beach. As the *Bounty* slowly disappeared from view in late September 1789 she and all who sailed in her were to disappear from the known world for almost twenty years.

II

Death in Eden

The *Bounty* sailed with thirty-five people on board, but not all were willing passengers. A number of women had been tricked into sailing: they were invited on board to eat and drink, and as the ship moved out of the bay they were told that it was only moving to another part of the island. One woman was mistrustful enough to jump overboard and swim away, but the others were forcibly detained. When it became abundantly clear that they were being abducted, the women kept protesting and, as they passed close to the Island of Moorea (visible from Tahiti), a canoe came out and six of the oldest women and most determined protesters were sent off on it. From there they could be returned home. Nine mutineers, six Polynesian men, twelve women and a baby were all that remained on board.

They faced a daunting future. The ship was undermanned and such a small crew could not sustain the heavy labour of working against contrary winds for long, so they were more at the mercy of the prevailing winds than ever. In spite of their firearms they were a small party and could not have defended themselves indefinitely against a hostile population: an uninhabited island would be an ideal refuge. If it were part of an archipelago, however, their existence would hardly remain secret for long, as the Polynesians were great voyagers and stories about the location of a white colony would soon spread. They touched briefly at Rarotonga in the Cook group and, as usual, bartered for fresh food, but the island was thickly populated and they quickly moved on. They continued through the islands, searching without success, and eventually found themselves in the Friendly Islands still with no prospect of finding a suitable haven. While at Tongatapu, taking on water and supplies,

Christian read in one of Bligh's books a description of Pitcairn Island.

Pitcairn lies in isolation in the South Pacific Ocean, on the outer edge of island clusters southeast of Tahiti, roughly halfway between South America and Australia, and close to the line of the Tropic of Capricorn. First recorded in 1767, it had been sighted subsequently only once or twice by European sailors. It was described as having steep and precipitous cliffs with one tiny and dangerous landing-place subjected to a continuous heavy swell and no safe anchorage: a place most sailing ships would avoid like the plague. It seemed ideal for the mutineers, and they decided to try to reach it. They were then at the Fiji islands some 3000 miles to the west of Pitcairn, and in order to get there they needed to sail south down into the colder latitudes where they could pick up the westerly winds and then, having travelled far enough to the east, swing back to the north at the appropriate longitude. This was a hard voyage, which discouraged all and exposed the Polynesians to temperatures lower than they had ever experienced. Given the large margin of error possible with the clocks and navigational instruments of the time, Pitcairn Island was not easy to locate. It was two long and miserable months before, on 15 January 1790, the distinctive outline of the island appeared on the horizon. It was now nearly four months since they had left Matavai Bay and joy at the prospect of living a normal life ashore again must have been particularly strong in the women and Polynesian men who had no previous experience of long, dreary weeks of shipboard life.

Pitcairn was a rough oblong about one mile wide and two miles long, with very mountainous terrain rising to over 1000 feet. It was precipitous and rocky, and most parts were heavily wooded with thick undergrowth. Soon after their arrival the mutineers and their party were fortunate enough to enjoy a rare period of calm seas. Although the island proved to have a climate as agreeable as they could assume from its latitude, the open ocean surrounding it could send huge waves rolling up day after day, which crashed as surf on the rocky coast and

could make the one small bay unusable to ships' boats for days
or even weeks on end.

One of the women, Jenny, later related the mood on board
after the long ocean wanderings:

> Two months elapsed before land was again seen, during
> which all on board were much discouraged: they therefore
> thought of returning to Otaheiti. Pitcairn's Island was at
> length discovered in the evening. It was then blowing hard,
> so no landing could be effected till the third day, when the
> boat was lowered down and the following persons went on
> shore Christian, Brown, Williams, M'Koy, and three of the
> Otaheitian natives.
>
> The ship now stood out to sea, and returned to the island
> the second day, by which time the boat returned. The crew
> reported that there were no natives on the island; that it
> abounded with cocoa-nuts and sea-fowl, and that they had
> found traces of its having been once inhabited. Charcoal,
> stone axes, stone foundations of houses, with a few carved
> boards were discovered.[1]

The initial inspection confirmed that the island had sufficient
water, and a variety of trees suitable for both building and food.
In this, Brown's expertise as a botanist was invaluable and there
was little doubt that the livestock, plants and seeds they had
brought with them would also flourish here. There was a small
plateau of fertile land which they could cultivate and where
they could construct a village. At first they were a little uncertain
whether the island was still inhabited, with its population in
hiding, but confidence grew that the traces of occupation were
from a considerably earlier period of habitation, as proved to
be the case. Later they found a group of four stone images,
similar to, but much smaller than, the famous stone heads of
Easter Island, along with rock carvings and innumerable graves.
This was all most heartening, especially to the Polynesians, as
it not only proved that others had managed to live there over
a long period, but also that they were somewhere where their
culture had flourished and their gods had been worshipped. To
the mutineers it offered a haven far from the world frequented

by European ships, any one of which would have reported their whereabouts and brought retribution upon them. In any case everyone was sick to death of roaming the ocean month after month. They decided to settle.

It's doubtful whether they could have made a better choice. Pitcairn was on the far edge of the populated archipelagos where the restless, ocean-travelling Polynesians might come across them, and it was misplaced on European charts. To be able to chart longitude correctly required chronometers that remained accurate over the long months of a voyage. Due to inadequate equipment when it was discovered, Pitcairn Island appeared on the charts 200 miles from its actual situation, so ships hoping to sight it would be searching the wrong area. The only practical landing-place, now known as Bounty Bay, was exposed and dangerous, and it was not a place where many ships' captains would be keen to put a party ashore – for fear that any deterioration in the weather would make it impossible for them to get back on board. If strong winds prevailed, as they often did, a square-rigged sailing ship could be driven away from the island, leaving the shore party abandoned for an indefinite period. If a shore party should land, the mountainous interior offered many concealed places where it might be possible for the mutineers to hide until the intruders were obliged to leave. There were many caves and narrow defiles where a few determined men could make a stand against considerable numbers. From Bounty Bay there was a steep muscle-sapping ascent to the plateau some 100 yards higher, facing northeast, where their settlement would be built, and from where they would catch an early sight of any approaching sail. It would be difficult to imagine a location more suited to their needs of concealment and security.

Jenny's account continues:

> Christian got the vessel under a rocky point and came to anchor. The mutineers began to discharge the ship, by means of the boat and a raft made out of the hatches. The property from the ship was landed principally on the raft, by means of a rope fastened to the rocks.[2]

Having seen during the previous few days how difficult landing
on Pitcairn could be, everyone worked flat out to get all the
stores on dry land while the weather held. First ashore was the
poor livestock, perhaps even more relieved than the humans to
be released after long weeks of confinement. The pigs, goats,
chickens and cats were carefully tended; but the depth of the
mutineers' fear of discovery is evident in their decision to
slaughter all the dogs. It was feared that the noise of their barking
could carry out to sea and betray the presence of their masters
to any ship passing close to the island. As well as the obvious
arms and ammunition, plants, seeds, dry stores and clothing,
the *Bounty* was also stripped of sails and cordage; her yards and
masts were dismantled, and planks and beams salvaged. Every
scrap of metal had become as precious to them as it was to the
Tahitians; the forge and metal tools were now the most valuable
part of their heritage. Finally there was little more than the
floating hulk to be considered. The choice was a stark one.
Any passing ship that might otherwise ignore the island would
be duty bound to investigate when it spotted the hull of a
European vessel; it would be obliged to discover the name of
the apparent wreck and the fate of any survivors. But if they
destroyed the ship then the decision to settle would be irrevocable: they would have to expect to live on Pitcairn for the rest
of their days. The natives were not consulted and the nine men
were divided in their opinion.

Jenny gave two accounts of what happened:

> When all they wanted was brought on shore, they began to
> consider what they should do with the vessel. Christian
> wished to save her for a while. The others insisted on
> destroying her, and one of them went off and set fire to her
> in the fore part. Shortly after two others went on board and
> set fire to her in different places. During the night all were
> in tears at seeing her in flames. Some regretted exceedingly
> they had not confined Capt. Bligh and returned to their
> native country, instead of acting as they had done.[3]

In this account she avoids naming the men who fired the ship.

This reticence occurs quite frequently in accounts of what happened on Pitcairn and is often obviously deliberate concealment. There were no outside witnesses to the crimes which were committed during the years of isolation on the island, and the surviving participants had their own reasons for giving different versions at different times. In constructing a narrative of events therefore, it sometimes becomes necessary to test one source against another. On another occasion Jenny actually named the man who first fired the *Bounty*: 'Fletcher Christian wanted to preserve the ship, but Matt [Quintal] said, "No, we shall be discovered": so they burnt her.'[4] Jenny's first account states that two other men helped in the firing. This is not supported by any other source but, if true, it does imply a deeper division between the mutineers than would an arbitrary act by one individual. Quintal was undoubtedly a tough and formidable individual, but it is questionable whether he would have acted against the will of all his shipmates.

The suggestion that the mutineers were already disunited at this early stage of their enforced life together is supported by a later account which claims that when Christian first landed to inspect the island, John Mills suggested to those left on the ship that they take the opportunity to desert him and sail back to Tahiti. The authority of Fletcher Christian either as an ex-officer or as the elected leader of the mutineers was already being defied, and loyalty to him was waning. It seems that in burning the ship against Christian's wishes Quintal may have had the tacit support of some of the men, but that he was not willing to wait for an agreement to emerge, and acted according to his own inclination. Adams is the name most frequently associated with loyalty to Christian and in wanting to preserve the ship; while McKoy is linked with Quintal. Remember that at Toobouai Christian had threatened Quintal with a pistol and put him in irons for disobeying orders. At that time there had been twenty-five mutineers and Quintal had submitted, but now that he was one among only nine white men he was no longer willing to accept orders. From now on personal determination and physical strength, not the rule of law, were to predominate. If nothing else, Quintal's wilfulness deprived everyone of the opportunity of salvaging much English timber suitable for building, planks which could only be cut from living trees with much labour. Burning the hulk destroyed more than the remnants of recognized authority.

No one attempted to punish Quintal in any way. How could they? Every hand was valuable and they could not start quarrelling among themselves. The women wept, but neither tears nor the ocean could extinguish the fire, and the *Bounty* burned to the waterline, hissing at the salt water as it dropped beneath the surface, boiling off a cloud of steam and leaving a pall of smoke to disperse across the now cold waters. The ship which had been their sole refuge for so long had gone, and the mutineers and their companions were now transformed into 'islanders'.

When Captain Bligh was cast adrift in the *Bounty*'s launch, one of his first tasks was to write a list of the mutineers and append a brief description of each of them. These provide a vivid picture of the European contingent of this new community.[5] According to the list, Fletcher Christian, master's mate promoted to acting lieutenant by Bligh, was 26 years old in 1790, when they arrived at Pitcairn. Born in Cumberland, he was described as handsome, 5 feet 9 inches tall and strongly built with a very dark brown complexion and dark brown hair. During his stay in Tahiti he had, like many of the sailors, become heavily tattooed in the native fashion over his backside and had a star on his left breast; he was 'a little bow legged', and suffered from excessive sweating, notably on his hands.

Edward Young, midshipman, was 28 years old, and came from St Kitts in the West Indies; he was 5 feet 8 inches tall, 'strongly made', with a dark complexion and dark brown hair. He had lost several front teeth, and many of those remaining were rotten. On his right arm was a tattoo of a heart with a 'dart through it and "E:Y" and date 1788 or 89'. Bligh continued, 'Young was a Person recommended to me by Sir George Young Captain in the Navy. He appeared to me to be an able and Stout Seaman and therefore I took him, he however always proved a Worthless Wretch.' Others described him as being part negro.

The oldest man by far, at 40, was John Mills, the gunner's mate. Born in Aberdeen, he was 5 feet 10 inches tall with a fair complexion and light brown hair. He was physically raw-boned, and had a 'Scar in his Right Armpit Occassioned by an Abcess'. William McKoy, able seaman, was also Scottish, from Ross-shire. He was 27 years old, and 5 feet 6 inches tall with a fair complexion and light brown hair; he was thickset and tattooed on his body, and he also had a 'Scar where he had been Stabbed in the Belly and a Small Scar under his Chin'. His friend Matthew Quintal, an able seaman from Padstow, was aged 23, and at 5 feet 5 inches, he was short and powerful. He had a fair complexion and light brown hair, and was 'very much tatowed [sic] on the backside and several other places'.

Isaac Martin, able seaman, was a lanky American from Phila-delphia, who was 5 feet 11 inches tall and also 'raw boned' (one of Bligh's most common expressions); he was aged 32, with a sallow complexion and short brown hair, and was tattooed with a star on his left breast. John Williams, a French-speaking able seaman from Guernsey, aged 27, was 5 feet 5 inches tall and slenderly built, with a dark complexion and black hair; he was also tattooed. William Brown, born in Leicestershire, who was employed at Kew Gardens previous to the voyage, had sailed as the botanist's assistant. He was 29 years old, 5 feet 8 inches tall and thin with a fair complexion, dark brown hair and tattoos. He had a 'Remarkable Scar on One of his Cheeks which con-tracts the Eyelid & runs down to his throat occasioned by the King's Evil'.★

Finally, John Adams (Bligh knew him as 'Smith'), able sea-man, was a Londoner from Wapping, aged 26. He was 5 feet 5 inches tall, and strongly built, with a brown complexion 'much pitted with small pox', and brown hair; he was also

★ 'The King's Evil' was scrofula – a form of tuberculosis, which it was believed could be cured if the sufferer was touched by the King.

'very much tatowed [sic] on his Body, Legs, Arms and Feet,
and has a Scar on his Right Foot where he has been cut with
a Wood Axe'.

The frequency with which Bligh uses tattoos to identify individuals shows how widespread it had become among these
sailors. He describes one as having a tattoo of a garter inscribed
Honi soit qui mal y pense, and another as having his name tattooed
on his right arm dated 25 October 1788. The wide variety of
tattooing with European motifs – pierced hearts, initials, stars
and names – reflects their own culture, wherever it was done.
But the tattooing on the buttocks, feet and legs mentioned in
several of the descriptions had been done according to Tahitian
custom – an indication of the degree to which various individuals had 'gone native'. Given Christian's social background
these tattoos might have been something of an embarrassment
had he returned to English society.

There were six native men among the settlers. The two who
had left Toobouai when the mutineers abandoned their attempt
to establish a settlement there (because they had become too
closely identified with the white men and feared for their lives
should they remain) were Oha, a chief, and his nephew Titahiti.
Menalee, Timoa and Nehow came from Tahiti and Menalee
was of the chiefly caste. Tararo was also from Tahiti but 'of
exalted blood because he came from Raiatea' – a different island
– and so of a different status from the others.[6] The ages of these
men is not known, and indeed the widespread reference to
them as *men* by historians is erroneous. Jenny specifically refers
to Nehow as a *boy*, which implies that he was very young,
possibly pre-pubescent. Titahiti too, as nephew to Oha, was of
a different generation and probably quite young. The ease with
which these natives accepted the domination of the white men
in the early days on the island may, in part, be explicable if one
assumes that some of them were little more than boys when
they joined the venture.*

* The spelling of names varies from source to source. For example, Oha
is also written as Ohoo, Oopee, and Oho.

Contemporary descriptions of the twelve women from Tahiti are also lacking. Of those twelve, only the six who had had steady relationships with mutineers during the *Bounty*'s long sojourn at the island came willingly. Mauatua, a chief's daughter, had been Christian's partner during his stay. He called her Isabella, but the other Europeans nicknamed her 'Mainmast', as a tribute to her tall, straight figure. Mary had been the wife of McKoy, and she had a baby in arms when they left Tahiti – the identity of the father is not known, but the baby was called Sarah; Quintal's wife was another Sarah. Young's wife was called Susannah and she is the only woman for whom we are given an age: she was fifteen in 1790. When she was nearly seventy years old a visitor described her as 'short and stout, of a very cheerful disposition [with] dark and curling hair, flowing profusely over her shoulders, and as yet but little frosted by the winter of her life'.[7] Jenny had been partnered with Adams – indeed, she had his initials and the date ('A.S. 1789') tattooed on her arm – but after leaving Tahiti and during the voyage to Pitcairn, she became Martin's woman. Vahineatua partnered Mills. Those who were tricked into sailing with the mutineers and effectively kidnapped were Mareva, Pashotu, Paurai, Prudence, Teatuahitea and Toofaiti. The predominance of Tahitian names in this group is perhaps an indication of their greater separation from white culture. Some were given European names but these seem to have stuck less firmly.

THE SETTLERS

Mutineers:	Fletcher Christian
	Edward Young
	John Mills
	William Brown
	John Adams [Smith]
	William McKoy
	Isaac Martin
	Matthew Quintal
	John Williams

Polynesian men:
   from Toobouai Island   Oha
                                Titahiti

   from Tahiti Island   Menalee
                                  Timoa
                                  Nehow

   from Raiatea Island   Tararo

Tahitian women: Mauatua (Isabella)
                                  Mary
                                  Sarah
                                  Susannah
                                  Jenny
                                  Vahineatua
                                  Mareva
                                  Pashotu
                                  Paurai
                                  Prudence
                                  Teatuahitea
                                  Toofaiti
                                  Sarah (Mary's baby)

The production and reproduction of the necessities of life – food, warmth and shelter – required immediate attention from this motley group of people: their whole future now depended on co-operating to create a replenishable supply of food for an indefinite future. The island may well have been a virtual Garden of Eden in terms of nature's bounty but, like Robinson Crusoe or the Swiss Family Robinson, the settlers were not newborn and their society could not be created afresh from innate human nature – they took their histories and cultures with them. If they were to create a new society it could not be freely planned or instinctively executed but would, of necessity, emerge from an amalgam of pre-existing values and inherited relationships. The nature of the settlement, the distribution of land, the allocation of property rights, the choice of sexual partners and the establishment of 'family' units for the reproduction of the population was initially carried out largely according to European cultural values and by, and to the advantage of, the white males.

The first year was a busy one, filled with hard work for all. Land had to be cleared and planted, animals raised and houses built. They lived in tents made from sails while the settlement was established. In felling the trees and clearing the brush, care was taken to leave a screen between them and the sea, and trees were left singly and in clumps dotted at random around the village, giving pleasant shade. All the cultivatable land on the island was divided among the nine white men. They also divided the rock pools between them as these were essential sources of salt, and convenient places from which to fish. The Polynesians apparently accepted this without protest. Perhaps it did not appear significant to them: they knew the necessity of the work undertaken and shared in it as they shared in the food that was produced. Coming from a society where all accepted the obligation to feed and care for others, they may well have been comparatively indifferent to the issue of ownership.

Food was not to be a problem. The settlers still had their share of the stores from the *Bounty* as well as the existing natural produce – coconuts, fish, sea birds and their eggs – which would supply them for several months until their gardens and livestock began to produce. A number of goats and pigs were turned loose to colonize the uncultivated areas and provide a supply of 'wild' meat, but each white man kept his own livestock and cultivated his own land for his personal provision. They planted banana, plantain, melon, yam, taro, sweet potatoes, appai, tee and cloth-plant.

Eventually they built the substantial houses later described by a visitor.

All these cottages are strongly built of wood in an oblong form, and thatched with the leaves of the palm-tree bent round the stem of the same branch, and laced horizontally to rafters, so placed as to give a proper pitch to the roof. The greater part have an upper storey, which is appropriated to sleeping, and contain four beds built in the angles of the room, each sufficiently large for three or four persons to lie

on. They are made of wood of the cloth-tree, and are raised
eighteen inches above the floor; a mattress of palm-leaves is
laid upon the planks, and above it three sheets of the cloth-
plant, which forms an excellent substitute for linen. The
lower room generally contains one or more beds, but is
always used as their eating-room, and has a broad table in
one part, with several stools placed round it. The floor is
elevated about a foot from the ground, and, as well as the
sides of the house, is made of stout plank, and not of bamboo,
or stone, as stated by Captain Folger; indeed they have not
a piece of bamboo on the island; nor have they any mats.
The floor is a fixture, but the side-boards are let into a groove
in the supporters, and can be removed at pleasure, according
to the state of the weather, and the whole side may, if
required, be laid open. The lower room communicates with
the upper by a stout ladder in the centre, and lead up through
a trap-door into the bedroom.[8]

The main village was supplemented by other dwellings. The
far side of the island proved more suitable for the cultivation
of yams and was higher and cooler, so summer houses were
built there, both so that they could enjoy the coolness and as
temporary shelters while they tilled these crops. Even within
such a small island there was a degree of privacy and movement,
with people in different places at different times. Christian found
a cave on the northern tip of the island, approachable only by
a narrow and dangerous path, which he kept stocked with
provisions and arms, and from where he was determined to
conduct a last fight should any ship be sent in pursuit of them.
Near it he built a small hut which he used as a watchhouse.
During various fits of melancholy, to which he became increasingly prone, he would spend much time alone in his eyrie.

It is clear from his behaviour that Christian would rather die
than be returned to England for public trial and the shame and
humiliation that would entail. Even earlier, when the mutineers
finally returned to Tahiti, he had stated that he would sail alone
if necessary rather than be captured. It is understandable that
he might have regretted his actions in leading the mutiny: he
had thrown away his position in English society and a promising

career as a naval officer. The mutiny had not entailed such a sacrifice for the seamen. They may have suffered the same degree of homesickness, but they had exchanged the hard, dangerous and low-paid life of a sailor to become well-fed peasant farmers with wives and families. Their losses were partly balanced by their present gains. When Christian withdrew into himself, Young was left isolated. As a midshipman he was an officer in the making and had been Christian's friend. While Christian's authority declined, and the sailors went their own ways, Young drew closer to the Polynesians, becoming a particular favourite of the women.

Each of the mutineers had a woman who was exclusively his own. How these relationships were formed and to what degree the women concerned had a say in the matter is not known. Like the property distribution, it was an arrangement which favoured the white men, but it is not certain whether it was enforced by them, or whether it was also the choice of the women. In Tahitian culture, the lighter skin was, the greater it was prized. The chiefs were a much lighter brown than the lower classes, so white men had an immediate desirability and high status, and it was more prestigious for a woman to be associated with one than with a native man. However it arose, the arrangement left only three women between the six native men. Tararo had a woman of his own, and two of the men, Oha and Titahiti (uncle and nephew), shared a woman called Prudence. The remaining three men, Menalee, Timoa and Nehow, shared the third woman, Mareva. Once again, the Polynesian men seemed to consent to this situation without protest, and it may well have been accepted because it was the way the women wanted to arrange their liaisons. The comparatively free and open sexual relationships of Tahitian culture also meant that men were used to sharing wives with their brothers and special friends, and the women were used to having such relations outside their marriages, so the notion of sharing sexual and domestic services was not one which presented a difficulty for them.

This initially amicable arrangement did not last long,

however. Shortly after landing on the island, Pashotu, Williams's wife, died of a throat disease. He then resented being the only white man without a woman and claimed that he should be given a wife taken from the Polynesian men. The European men refused to support his claim, pointing out that this would be too great a deprivation for the native men and would lead to trouble. Williams became insistent and even threatened to leave the island in one of the small boats which had been part of the *Bounty*, unless the others helped him take one of the women. Even so, he could not persuade any of the mutineers to help him and he was not strong-willed or powerful enough to challenge the natives on his own. In spite of his threats, he did nothing to disturb the original arrangement, although his bitterness against his old shipmates and his isolation as the only womanless man might well be imagined. As a precaution against his making good his threat to leave the island, the mutineers destroyed all the small boats.

This situation lasted for about a year until another woman died – this time in a tragic accident. In the spring of 1791, John Adams's wife Paurai fell to her death from a precipice while collecting birds' eggs from the cliffs. Adams also refused to tolerate being without a woman, and he was made of sterner stuff than Williams: in this new society physical presence must have counted for a good deal, and many observers commented on Adams's physique and strength. Only about 5 feet 5 inches tall, he was described as having the shoulders and body of a man a foot taller, and he was undoubtedly not someone many of his companions could overawe or restrain. Loyal friendships were as important as physical strength and character, and when Adams resolved to have a woman he won the backing of the other white men in a way the slighter and less forceful Williams had not. According to Jenny, the Europeans took the three women from the natives and cast lots for them, with the result that Adams took Prudence from Titahiti and Oha; while Williams, his wishes at last granted, took Toofaiti from Tararo.

This was the first disruption: it led to the first killings.

The Europeans had made it obvious that they did not consider the Polynesians – men or boys – to be their equals in any way. This had been implicit in the partition of the land, and was now confirmed by their taking two out of three women from the Polynesians. They were not even prepared to live by the original inequitable arrangements, and accept the contingencies of life, but were ready to make good any of their own losses by taking more from those already disadvantaged. It was a particular blow to Tararo, whose chiefly status had granted him a wife of his own. Three of the Tahitian men were unaffected by the change, but the two natives who had become friendly with the mutineers when they attempted to settle at Toobouai had been left womanless. In autumn 1791, the deprived men decided that they would not tolerate the loss of their woman. They planned to kill the whites.

The earliest oral account of the events that follow was not given until some fifteen years later, and a full report was not written until fifteen years after that; the truth of what happened is therefore not easy to establish. It is hard to deduce who exactly was involved, and whether the intention was to kill all of the Europeans or simply those who had taken the women. Most of the evidence was provided by John Adams, the only man who lived long enough to tell his tale to outsiders, and he changed his story at virtually every telling. Jenny gave her own version of events, and other stories became current after Adams died. Like the detailed arguments over evidence and the veracity of witnesses in a court of law, choosing one account over another calls for close examination of the stories that were given by the various witnesses, and the different versions given by the same witness at different times, as well as any imputations of motivation and self-interest in the narrators. To avoid interrupting the narrative of these events, and those to follow, the most convincing account will be presented, with only a partial examination of conflicting evidence. Any remaining contradictions will be considered more generally at the end.

Shortly after Toofaiti had been taken from Tararo and given to Williams, she was doing her chores and, as was customary with the women, singing softly to herself a rhythmic, repetitious chant to set the pace for her work with words of her own devising. She was overheard by two of the other women, one of whom, Isabella, was the wife of Christian, and they immediately ran to him with the news of Toofaiti's song: she had been chanting over and over again, 'Why does the black man sharpen an axe? To kill white man. Why does the black man sharpen an axe? To kill white man.'[1]

Although one would assume that the men most at risk were Williams and Adams, Christian's sense of leadership and authority are evident in the fact that he took immediate action without informing the other whites or waiting for them to help him. He seized a musket and made his way towards the hut which Oha and Titahiti shared with Tararo. According to one version he did not place a ball in the musket, intending only to scare them into submission. He met Oha on his way and challenged him and, meeting defiance, eventually fired his musket in his direction. Oha, assuming that it had been fully loaded, derided Christian's poor marksmanship and fled into the forest. The other two natives, realizing that their plot to kill the whites had been discovered, also fled. Another account claims that the three natives fled into the forest once they saw Christian heading towards them with a gun and before a shot was fired. In either case it demonstrates that the whites assumed a considerable superiority over the natives, taking for granted that one of them would be enough to quash any incipient revolt.

On an island only two miles by one, no one, neither assassin nor victim, could be more than a mile away from the main settlement located in the centre. The disappearance of three

Polynesians who were planning to kill at least some of the European men must have generated enormous tension. The white men could not be sure whether the three Tahitian men still in the settlement – Nehow, Timoa and Menalee – were part of the plot, nor which of the women were loyal to them – apart from the two who had reported the plan. Toofaiti's role was ambiguous. She knew of the plot and could have disclosed it directly had she so wished. As she did not warn the white men, her song can be more plausibly interpreted as one of anticipation and gloating rather than a means of spreading the knowledge to those she knew would warn the European men.

The Europeans suspected that other Tahitian men were involved and placed them in irons while they discussed their future. It was a difficult decision, as such a small society could not cope with dissidents; if someone threatened the life of another they did not have the resources to place them in perpetual imprisonment, not could they work or sleep constantly on their guard. Ultimately, anyone threatening another's life had to be killed or trusted to be at liberty again. Although the Tahitians denied being part of the plot, they remained in irons. During this period Toofaiti disappeared from the village and was assumed to have left Williams and fled into the hills to join Tararo – thus confirming her loyalty to her original man. Others claim that Tararo surprised her while she was out collecting food and forced her to go with him.

Eventually the Europeans agreed that they would not kill the captive Tahitians, provided they bought their freedom by hunting down and killing the three who had fled. The Tahitians agreed to prove their loyalty to the whites (and perhaps to the majority of the women) on those terms. Tararo was to be the first target. Menalee was chosen to make the initial search while the other two remained secured, as the white men could not risk letting all six natives band together. Letting Menalee go was a risk, but after being at liberty he returned to report that Oha was alone in hiding on the south of the island, while Titahiti was with Tararo and his wife, Toofaiti, on the west of the island. Menalee was sent to win Tararo's confidence by posing as a friend and a supporter of his action. Tararo instructed him to return with food, and to help kill the white men.

In the knowledge that the fugitives would welcome food, a rather naïve plan to poison Tararo was concocted. Menalee took three puddings with him, one of which was poisoned, and was charged with the task of ensuring that Tararo ate it. Tararo remained suspicious of him however, and quite rightly, for he could not understand why the white men permitted Menalee to come and go so easily unless they were sure of his loyalty. He threw away the food offered to him and shared the food given to his wife. Menalee then claimed that his own wife, Mareva, had also fled from the white men and was now in the mountains with him and that they should all join together. As they made their way single file along the narrow path, Menalee pulled out his pistol, thrust it into Tararo's back and pulled the trigger. The pistol misfired and Tararo, his mistrust of Menalee confirmed, ran for his life. But he was caught by Menalee and the two engaged in a hand-to-hand struggle. Tararo called to his companion for help, but Titahiti was frightened by events and took no part in the fight. When Toofaiti caught up with the men the two antagonists were struggling on the ground and Tararo then called to his wife for help. Her intervention was decisive: she joined the fray on the side of his enemy. She hammered Tararo's head with a stone, and killed him, her husband.

She and Menalee returned to the village where she resumed her place as Williams's new wife, while Titahiti was placed in irons and kept in close captivity. Menalee was now ordered by the Europeans to go out and find the remaining Polynesian fugitive. Having proved his loyalty by securing the death of the most dangerous rebel, he was trusted to take Timoa to aid him. By this time Oha had been living alone and in hiding for some two weeks, an experience which had done much to demoralize him. He had often been seen close to the village, almost as if he wanted to be found and to rejoin the group; indeed, there was little choice open to him. He had nowhere to flee, no other human group to join, and he could not hide indefinitely

– he would be obliged to face the others at some not too distant time. When he had been found and was within earshot, he heard what he wanted to hear: assurances from Menalee and Timoa that they meant him no harm and that they came in friendship. He allowed them to approach him. They signified their sincerity by sharing the Polynesian ritual of combing his hair for him as a symbol of joint sorrow and grief

> [Oha] suspecting treachery, would have fled, but the two men, through their fair speeches and the food they had brought him, quickly disarmed him of his suspicions. To further assure him they produced a comb, and prevailed on him to let them comb his hair.

However, this was a treacherous ploy, for:

> Having thus decoyed him into their power, the rest was easy enough, and a few seconds sufficed to dispatch the poor fellow.[2]

As with so many details, the story of Oha's murder is reported differently in different accounts: some say that he was shot, others that having moved behind him while combing his hair Menalee cut his throat – a difference of as minor importance to the victim as it is to us. The writer of the above account, a Pitcairn Islander, claims that the murdered native was Titahiti rather than Oha, but other well-authenticated sources account for Titahiti's death much later; the error obviously crept in as the story passed down the generations.

The Tahitians had hunted down and killed the two who were most responsible for the plan to kill the white men, but they had been forced into it to save their own lives. The killings were the result of collective action, but John Adams must bear much of the responsibility: it was he who refused to live without a woman, triggering the sequence of events that led not only to those deaths but also, arguably, started the train of events that was to lead to so many more. John Williams had lived without a woman for over a year, admittedly with a great deal of bitterness and resentment, but he had been unable to persuade his fellows to support him in taking even one woman from the

natives. John Adams refused to accept his misfortune and caused
the white men to act unjustly to the Polynesians who had
previously been their friends and allies.

From his account of events, it seems that John Adams was
well aware of this culpability. For years after the event he always
told the story as if only Williams had lost his wife, and as if
Williams was the only man to take a wife from the natives.
This appears to be largely confirmed by Jenny's version, except
for slight differences in details, which one might expect from
two participants recalling events years later:

> One of the women who lived with Williams died of a disease
> in her neck about a year after their arrival ... Williams,
> whose wife had died, now proposed to take one of the
> Otaheitian men's wives, there being only two among them;
> and lots were drawn which it should be. The chance fell on
> the wife of an Otaheitian, called Tararo. Williams accordingly
> took her from her husband, who was in consequence much
> afflicted, and betook himself to the hills. After three days he
> returned and got his wife away, and took her to the moun-
> tains with him. The native men now proposed to kill the
> English, who were, however, upon their guard: three of
> the principals in the plot thought proper to take refuge in
> the mountains. One of the natives who remained with the
> English, was sent by Christian to the mountains, for the
> purpose of shooting the principal conspirator, whose name
> was Oopee [Oha], promising to reward him handsomely if
> he succeeded, but, if he did not, he was to lose his own life.
> This man took a pistol with him as directed: he found Oopee
> among the craggy precipices and killed him. Tararo, who
> had taken his wife from Williams, and was still in the moun-
> tains, was shot by order of the Europeans: his wife was now
> returned to Williams. After this the mutineers lived in a
> peaceful manner for some years.[3]

This gives a different timescale to events, in that it claims Tararo
fled alone to the mountains *before* there was a plot to kill the
whites: a plot which had Oha [Opee] as the leader and the first
to be killed, rather than Tararo. Whatever the true sequence,

the result was much the same. Jenny makes no mention of the role of the women in warning the mutineers, nor does she mention the attitude or actions of Williams's new wife, who, according to other accounts, actually killed her native husband. In this she may have been glossing over the women's role to protect Toofaiti from any legal action which might be taken against her. Jenny implies that Toofaiti was abducted by Tararo which would explain why she helped to kill him – if that was the truth. In general Jenny has been credited as a reliable witness, but it is obvious that she was always very guarded in what she said. She names the dead but carefully avoids naming anyone responsible for the killings.

These may have been unintentional omissions from a brief account; but there is one worrying inconsistency, which implies deliberate intent to mislead as well as an understandable reluctance to name the guilty. Earlier in her account she states that there were originally twelve women (as does *everyone*: it is one undisputed fact), but in the above she said that when Williams's wife died he decided to take one of the *two* women living with the native men. If only one woman of the twelve had died, nine women would have been left for the nine white men and two for the natives, so Williams's action would have been unnecessary. If, on the other hand, after Williams took his wife the natives had only one woman left to them, and the whites had nine, then one other woman is left unaccounted for. In order for the arithmetic to add up it makes more sense for us to believe the alternative story that Adams also lost a wife, and joined with Williams in taking another. This also makes more sense of the native men's behaviour. Tararo had a wife of his own – therefore the others originally had two between them, one for the three Tahitians, and one for the two men from Toobouai. The three most involved (Jenny also spoke of three 'principals' in the plot), or perhaps the only three involved, were Tararo, Oha and Titahiti. The three rebels lived in one hut, and if one postulates that they lost both their women, their actions are understandable. The three Tahitian men, who were, from the beginning, living with only one woman, were not affected by the change and had no greater reason to rise against the whites than they had ever had.

The subsequent history of the islanders fully accounts for the lives and deaths of *ten* women so it is beyond reasonable doubt that two women died in this early period and that *two* women were taken from the unhappy native men. One suspects that Jenny knowingly concealed Adams's role in events to shelter his reputation; after all, he had been the island's and her patriarch and 'chief' for close on twenty years before she left the island in 1817 and related her version of events. When writing down Adams's account, Captain Beechey (who recorded the fullest account while surveying the island in 1825) never noticed that the arithmetic did not add up. Adams and the women were then still intent on maintaining that he was not in any way responsible for the crimes which had taken place since the mutiny. But Arthur Quintal (son of Matthew), who was thirty-two years old when Adams died and well informed on the history of the island by Adams and the surviving women, asserted that in his old age Adams acknowledged that he as well as Williams lost his wife.

The rebellion was over, but the revenge of the Europeans had been severe. Whatever the truth of the details, within two years of landing on Pitcairn the first murders had been committed. They were not to be the last.

In the two years following the killings, the small population of Pitcairn grew. A couple of babies had already been born before the killings in 1791; in 1792 another three were born, and two more were born in 1793. The small population was becoming more viable with the birth of a new generation and the consolidation of their livestock and food supplies. The needs of personal survival were met. However, the four remaining Polynesian men had been brought to the point of virtual slavery. They were set to work labouring at the behest of the whites, as the servants of McKoy and Mills (who worked together), Quintal, Martin and Brown. The *tyos* of Tahiti, proud of their white friends and valued by them, had been reduced to inferiors in this new society. The degree to which the oppression exercised by the whites was racist is a moot point. Clearly their different place of origin was the main dividing line between the men, and yet the Tahitian women appear to have shared in the exercise of white male power. Timoa, for example, stole some yams, but was informed on by a woman and severely beaten, as was Menalee for stealing a pig from McKoy: unsurprising offences given that they had no land of their own. McKoy and Quintal had a reputation for being particularly oppressive. They beat the natives for the most trivial reasons, even literally rubbing salt into their wounds to increase the severity of the punishment.

In September 1793, violence once again broke out on the island, ostensibly in a 'slave' rebellion through which the Polynesians again attempted to redress their wrongs. The reality of what happened was probably more complex, as we shall see below; but whoever was involved, the way the plot was planned and accomplished seems to show that the European men assumed they had broken the spirits of the natives and had nothing to fear from them. Indeed, they were so confident of their mastery that they allowed them access to firearms. The European reaction to the revolt, once it started, shows an almost unbelievably high degree of individualism in the whites, almost amounting to indifference towards each other. This indicates that the rebellion might have had more complicated origins than some accounts claim. They also showed a degree of over-confidence in the loyalty of their women and their readiness to inform the European men of any planned threat from the natives.

The Polynesians' actions were well-enough conceived. The village routine was firmly established by now, and it was not difficult to choose a morning when the Europeans were dis-persed about the settlement, each working his own lands, some in the village, others on the yam patches on the higher ground. On this particular day, many of the women were away on the cliffs collecting sea birds' eggs. As usual, accounts of what happened vary slightly in detail. According to Adams, Nehow and Timoa had stolen muskets and fled to the forest, and were in hiding for some days, awaiting the right moment to join Menalee and Titahiti in their attack. If that is true then the response of some of the white men to the Polyesians' attempt to murder them all was even more extraordinary than it appears in the following narrative. It demonstrates that only three years after settling on the island, the Europeans lacked the unity to undertake concerted action and seek out the two armed fugi-tives, as they had done previously. In Jenny's account, however, after they decided to kill the whites, all four native men con-tinued to go about the village in their normal manner, but they 'went about from day to day with their muskets, on a pretence of shooting wild-fowl' so that the whites would get used to seeing them armed and not be suspicious. They then simply waited for a suitable opportunity to strike.

Nehow and Timoa were armed, together and concealed in the village when the plot was put into action. Titahiti went to his master, Isaac Martin, and asked to borrow a musket in order to shoot a wild pig he had seen. Few actions could demonstrate the overweening confidence of the whites more than the fact that Martin let him have the gun without hesitation. With equal lack of hesitation Titahiti, having so easily armed himself, hurried off and linked up with the other two. John Williams was putting up a fence around the garden by his house when the three descended on him and shot him. Martin heard the shot and exclaimed 'Well done! we shall have a glorious feast today', assuming that a pig had been the target, and continued working unperturbed.[1] Mills and McKoy, who worked their land jointly, were tilling it with their slave Menalee when they also heard the shot. To allay any suspicion they may have had that all was not well, Titahiti ran over to them and asked Mills if he would allow Menalee to help carry the pig he had just shot. Mills agreed. Now consolidated into a single force, the four Polynesians left McKoy and Mills at work and carried on with their mission. Christian Fletcher was the next victim:

> The natives next proceeded to shoot Christian: they found him clearing some ground for a garden, and while in the act of carrying away some roots, they went behind him and shot him between the shoulders – he fell. They then disfigured him with an axe about the head, and left him dead on the ground.[2]

McKoy and Mills were working in their garden close enough to hear Fletcher Christian's dying groans. McKoy became suspicious and turning to Mills said that it was 'the sound of someone dying', but Mills reassured him 'It is only Mainmast (Christian's wife) calling her children to dinner.'[3] They turned back to their work. Two of the nine white men were now dead.

Although McKoy and Mills were unarmed, the four Polynesians did not feel confident enough to attack them directly. This was not necessarily due to cowardice or excessive caution, given that they appear not to have been very competent in the use of firearms: time and again the flintlock muskets failed to fire at crucial moments. They concocted a ruse to separate the two white men – Timoa and Nehow concealed themselves inside McKoy's house and Menalee hid himself outside. Titahiti then ran again to where the two white men were working and told McKoy that he had just seen Timoa and Nehow stealing things in his house. Titahiti stayed in the field with Mills while McKoy hurried off to safeguard his possessions. Although there were two natives, known to be armed, McKoy did not hesitate to drop his tools and face them alone and unarmed, in order to deter or apprehend them. As he rushed into the house they both fired at him from their hiding places in the room, but both missed. As McKoy backed out of the house, Menalee jumped on him from behind. McKoy was a powerful and desperate man and managed to throw Menalee off his back into a pigsty before the others had time to reload their muskets. His suspicions about the earlier shots and groans all too graphically confirmed he ran to warn Mills of the danger. He told him of the attempt on his life and that it must be part of a plot, because their slave Menalee was not away helping to carry a pig but was also involved in the attempt to kill him. Given that he had been sent into the trap by Titahiti who had stayed with Mills, it seems almost inconceivable that Mills should not have immediately fled with McKoy to link up with the others and arm themselves. Yet John Mills refused to take alarm or to assist McKoy, saying that he was a good friend of one of the natives and was sure that they would not harm him. William McKoy, stunned by his friend's indifference, did not stay to argue the point but ran on to warn Christian.

Given the previous plot against the whites and the fact that McKoy had been the target of a well-planned attempt on his life, it is impossible to believe that Mills reacted as he did unless he had some reason to feel confident that his own safety was not at risk. But his confidence was misplaced. When he and Titihati were rejoined by the other natives, John Mills was shot. Although dreadfully wounded, he managed to reach his house before the natives closed in and beat out his brains.

Isaac Martin and William Brown, each working on his own land and apparently totally unaware that any untoward events were in train, were the next to be slaughtered. As Jenny related it:

> They now went to Martin's house and shot him: he did not
> fall immediately, but ran to Brown's house, which was not
> far off. He was there shot a second time, when he fell; they
> beat him on the head with a hammer until he was quite
> dead. Brown at the same time was knocked on the head
> with stones, and left for dead. As the murderers were going
> away, he rose up and ran. One of them pursued and overtook
> him. He begged hard for mercy, or that they would not kill
> him until he had seen his wife. They promised they would
> spare his life; however, one with a musket got behind him
> and shot him dead.[4]

It seems that individual native men did consider some of the
white men as friends but they were not agreed on whom they
wished to save. Five Europeans were now dead.

Having escaped from the attempt on his life and urged an
unheeded warning on his friend Mills, McKoy fled to Christian's place only to find him already dead in his garden. Running
on to the next plot he encountered Matthew Quintal. Quintal
had been alarmed by the unusual number of shots and had
already armed himself and sent his wife to warn the others of
his fears. Once McKoy had told him about Christian's death
and McKoy's own near death, the two made no further attempt
to find out who had survived or to plan resistance, but fled to
the mountains.

The first person Quintal's wife, Sarah, met was John Adams
in his plantation; she asked him, 'Why are you working at such
a time?'[5] He did not understand the import of her question,
but seeing her obvious agitation followed her back towards the
settlement. It is unclear whether he could not fully understand
her message because of language difficulties (which is unlikely),
or because she was too distressed to be lucid, or because she
was being deliberately ambiguous and was simply enticing him
back to his death as part of the conspiracy. However, like
Quintal, Adams (in his own version) was more alert to danger
than many of the others and it was enough for him to catch a

glimpse of the four Polynesians, together and armed, for him also to take to his heels and hide in the woods.

Williams, Christian, Mills, Martin and Brown were dead and had they not bungled their attack on McKoy the Polynesians may well have made a clean sweep of all the Europeans – if that was their intention. As it was, numbers were now balanced at four each. They no longer had the advantage of surprise, as by now they could assume that McKoy had alerted the others. Nevertheless, they did have the advantage of unity. Quintal and McKoy were together somewhere in the mountains, and Adams had gone to earth nearby in the woods. What of Edward Young? He remained safe and secure in his own house and it has been claimed that he was hidden and protected by the women, with whom he was a particular favourite. Young was the only European whose life was neither taken nor threatened.

Adams proved to be a bold and hungry man, for some three or four hours after he went into hiding:

> thinking all was quiet, [he] stole to his yam-plot for a supply of provisions; his movements however did not escape the vigilance of the blacks, who attacked and shot him through the body, the ball entering at his right shoulder, and passing out through his throat. He fell upon his side, and was instantly assailed by one of them with the butt end of the gun; but he parried the blows at the expense of a broken finger, Tetaheite [Titahiti] then placed the gun to his side, but it fortunately missed fire twice. Adams, recovering a little from the shock of the wound, sprang on his legs, and ran off with as much speed as he was able, and fortunately outstripped his pursuers, who seeing him likely to escape, offered him protection if he would stop. Adams, much exhausted by his wound, readily accepted their terms, and was conducted to Christian's house, where he was kindly treated.[6]

It was a remarkable offer and, even more remarkably, Adams trusted them. Perhaps he had little choice: he was severely wounded and was unlikely to live long unless the bleeding was stopped and he received proper nursing. Even so, to place himself in the hands of those who were intent on ending his life moments before was a desperate decision – especially when Tararo and Oha had been killed after professions of friendship and good faith. But the Polynesians were not employing a ruse to finish him off – they took him back to the village and placed him in the care of the women. There the other two native men wanted to kill him, but Jenny records the active role of the women: 'He [Adams] was saved by the women, who were at this time assembled. The murderers after wounding him, permitted him to take farewell of his wife. The women threw themselves on his body, and at their entreaties his life was spared.'[7] While all the killings were happening, Edward Young had installed himself in Christian's house where the injured Adams was taken.

The situation at the end of the day confirms that these events, long reported as a rebellion by the natives against the whites, were actually far more complex. By the end of that day the wounded Adams and the unthreatened Young were living in the settlement with the four Polynesian men who had just killed five of their old shipmates, while Quintal and McKoy were fugitives in the forest and mountains. This seems to imply that the split between the men was not a simple racial one. Perhaps more accurately, there was a division between the Europeans, and the natives were on one side of that division.

It was not a situation that could last indefinitely. The island was too small and contained too few people for it or them to be divided. Given the great cruelty with which Quintal and McKoy had treated the native men, one might have assumed that the natives' first task would be to hunt the two seamen to their death, but this was not the case. Tahitians were always more interested in sex than in war, and one thing the deaths had done, from the point of view of the male survivors, was ensure that there was no longer a shortage of women. As the highest status white man and a favourite of the women, Edward Young took the greatest advantage of the new situation by moving into Fletcher Christian's house and taking both Christian's widow and the widow of John Williams as his wives. His original wife, Susannah, was temporarily ignored by him, but

Timoa and Menalee competed for her favours. Although there was now a surplus of women, male competition for sexual favours remained intense, which suggests that the women were not passive objects, there to be taken if not already claimed by a man. This competition soon led to more bloodshed.

Timoa appears to have been the most successful in wooing Susannah, and one evening as he was playing the flute and she was singing, the disappointed Menalee appeared with a loaded musket, shot and wounded Timoa, reloaded and shot him again, this time fatally. When Titahiti protested at the killing, Menalee prepared to murder him too, but by now the women had been drawn to the scene and they united against him and drove him out of the village. Thus, a week after the killing of the Europeans one Polynesian was dead and another had fled to the forest. Seven men were left: Quintal, McKoy and Menalee on the loose, and Adams, Young, Nehow and Titahiti in the settlement with the women and children.

Menalee was the most combative and dangerous of the native men but his situation was now perilous. Driven from the group in the village, he was on his own in the forest, which also sheltered Quintal and McKoy, whom he had previously attempted to kill. He managed to approach them, however, and expressed his desire to join forces with them. They suspected that Menalee had been sent to serve them the way he had served Tararo and Oha, but if he was sincere he would be a much needed reinforcement. If they allowed him either to rejoin the others or to roam on his own they could hardly feel more secure than they would with him under their surveillance. Eventually they accepted him on condition that he hand over his musket as a sign of good faith. Quintal and McKoy then indulged in attacks on the village, taking up positions on the ridge and shooting down into the settlement. This shows that there was now an entrenched split between the remaining whites as well as between the native men.

The two groups remained at war with each other for three weeks. Initially, the two sides were evenly balanced – Adams was recovering from his wound, which left Young, Nehow and Titahiti in the settlement opposing Quintal, McKoy and Menalee in the mountains. This must have been an almost unbearable period: on the tiny island, murder could have come from behind any bush or tree. There would have been suspicion and mistrust within as well as between the small groups of men, with no one sure that his 'friends' would not turn on him. Events show that any such suspicion was well placed. According to Jenny:

> One or two of the women now went in quest of M'Koy and Matthew Quintil. They met with them, and strongly advised them to kill Manarii, which was accordingly done that night. The two remaining Otaheitian men next went in search of M'Koy and Quintil to kill them; they found them among the mountains, shot at them, and supposed that one was wounded; this however, was not the case.[8]

Apparently, Nehow and Titahiti believed that they'd wounded either Quintal or McKoy because they found traces of blood along the track where the two men fled. But McKoy had simply gashed his foot on a piece of wood in his hurry to escape.

The women seem to have been able to move freely between the two camps. This is confirmed by another version, current on Pitcairn in later years, which, however, places the initiative in killing Menalee with the white men:

> Adams and Young wrote them [McKoy and Quintal] a letter, and sent it by Quintal's wife, to persuade them to kill their new friend, Manale; which they succeeded in doing.[9]

Despite this collaboration, Quintal and McKoy had still mistrusted their two old shipmates who were living peaceably with the natives who had attempted to kill them. This mistrust was confirmed when, having killed their would-be ally Menalee, they were again hunted down and ambushed by the two native men.

But after the failure to kill Quintal and McKoy the plot changed: now Titahiti and Nehow were marked as victims. Jenny's account continues:

The Otaheitians proceeded to the house where the women, with Smith [Adams] and Young were, and boasted that they had wounded M'Koy. One of the women proposed to her two countrymen to go into the mountains to see if this was the case, and bring them correct information. To this proposal they gladly acceded; but the real object of the woman was to advise M'Koy and Quintil to come privately at a certain time that night, and assist the women to kill the two remaining natives. The Englishmen promised to do this, but did not keep their word. Next day the women agreed with Smith [Adams] and Young to kill the two Otaheitians. About noon, while one of the Otaheitian men was sitting outside of the house, and the other was lying on his back on the floor, one of the women took a hatchet and cleft the skull of the latter; at the same instant calling out to Young to fire, which he did, and shot the other native dead.[10]

Adams was still recovering from his wound, which left the execution of the plan to kill Nehow and Titahiti to Young. Young planned and carried out their deaths with the active help of his original wife, Susannah, and with the consent and involvement of all the women. In order not to alert the victims, the deaths were planned to take place almost simultaneously, and to achieve that the first had to be accomplished silently. It was Susannah, Young's cast-aside wife, who entered the room with an axe. Nehow was sitting with Young while Young loaded and primed his musket. When Nehow asked why and was given the customary reason that it was for shooting pigs, he is said to have advised putting a good charge in it. Young killed him with the single shot – a tragic end for Nehow who was only a 'boy' when he set off on a great adventure with his white friends. Titahiti, too, was probably very young when he ventured away from his homeland and was recorded by Jenny as having been 'dreadfully afraid of being killed; but Young took a solemn oath that he would not kill him': Young arranged matters so as not to be forsworn.[11]

The women had taken a very active role in the conflict by placing themselves on the side of the Europeans and agreeing to the deaths of the remaining Polynesians. Jenny stated that the women did this out of revenge for the deaths of their husbands, but if that is so, it was not a decision taken in the immediate aftermath, when shock and grief were most intense. As the native men were not killed until about a month after the massacre of the women's five husbands, there was evidently an element of reflection and calculation in that decision. It was only after the failure to kill Quintal and McKoy that the women came to the conclusion that peace could return only if the two remaining Polynesians were murdered. Edward Young then sent Susannah and Martin's widow to inquire if it were true that one of them was wounded and to tell them that they had decided to kill the two natives and so allow the white men to come together again. Jenny was well-informed on these events because, although she never acknowledged it, she was the woman who accompanied Susannah – she was Martin's widow.

Adams made a rapid recovery and, according to the story he told Beechey, after about a month he was fit enough to go out of the village and have a meeting with Quintal and McKoy to negotiate an end to hostilities, to put to rest the suspicions and the division between them, and to break the stalemate that had ensued. Thus, according to his own testimony, Adams had the role of making peace between the white men. He also claimed to have carried the news that both the remaining natives were dead.

> But so many instances of treachery had occurred, that they would not believe the report, though delivered by Adams himself, until the hands and the heads of the deceased were produced, which being done, they returned to the village. This eventful day was the 3rd October, 1793.[12]

The slaughter was over, peace had returned.

The sequence of events narrated above is as accurate as can be established from the various sources: an account of the events written by Edward Young, seen and partially copied by Captain Beechey and supplemented by the accounts of Adams and Jenny. But it cannot be the whole truth, for it is clear that there was more to it than a desperate uprising of the four abused Polynesian men. A question mark also lies over the conduct of the women and the degree to which they knew what was planned. In her first (very brief) account of the massacre Jenny stated that it took place 'when the women were gone to the mountain for birds' and she mentions no role for the women save that 'Ned Young's life was saved by his wife'.[13] In a later and more detailed account, she does not repeat that the women were absent in as many words but, having described the murders up to the attack on John Adams, continues, 'He was saved by the women who were at this time assembled,' which implies that the women were dispersed around the island when the killing started and that it was their intervention which halted it. This version of how Adams's life was saved is quite convincing, although his own account of events cannot be entirely discounted. Jenny's only specific indication of the whereabouts of individual women is her statement that Young's wife was there because she saved his life. But Quintal's wife was sent to warn Adams, so she was also in the village as the murders took place. As we have seen, the 'warning' she gave was so ambiguous that Adams followed her back to the settlement, which, if true, suggests the possibility of entrapment.

It may well be that many of the women were absent from the houses, collecting eggs in the mountains as Jenny states; but it is unlikely that they all went together and took all the young infants and babies with them on what was very dangerous work, at which one of them had already fallen to her death. It is more reasonable to suppose that they shared and alternated the labour of egg collecting and child minding. It is said that Isabella, Fletcher Christian's wife, gave birth to a daughter on the very day he was killed, so presumably she would have had at least one of the other women with her. In any event, there was an inexplicable lack of women or children around the settlement willing to raise the alarm as the Polynesian men went from house to house and garden to garden killing the whites. The one certain fact is that this time the women gave the white men no prior warning that their lives were in danger, as they had done twice in the past, which raises the suspicion that on this occasion at least some of the women were aware of the plot, but kept silent.

Edward Young's life was not endangered and it has become widely accepted that he planned the deaths of all the other white men in league with the blacks. His motive was to take Christian's wife, which he promptly did and Christian's house as well. Yet it is also widely suggested that he did not want Adams killed and that the attack on him was due to the over-excited natives exceeding their orders – his escape made them realize their error and then take him into care.

That Young should have planned to kill *all* of his fellow mutineers (except perhaps Adams) simply because he coveted the wife of one of them strains credulity. Nevertheless, we have seen ample evidence that the conflict was not along simple racial lines. If Young and Adams had no connection with the slaughter of their old shipmates, why didn't they flee the village once they had the chance and regroup with Quintal and McKoy? If the natives had planned to kill all the white men why were Young and Adams so confident that they would not be slaughtered while they were off guard or asleep? The natives even went into the woods in attempts to kill Quintal and McKoy – if they still wanted to kill whites why then did they not kill Young and Adams who were alongside them in the village? The weight of rational interpretation favours the opinion that both Young and Adams were in alliance with the natives against the other whites.

If we accept that Young planned the deaths of his erstwhile shipmates with the Polynesians but wanted at least one left alive for company, then the evidence suggests that at least one more name should be added to those marked to survive. There was one man who, on the evidence, would appear to have had prior knowledge of the event in a way in which Adams may have not: John Mills showed an extraordinary confidence in his own security. He smoothed down McKoy's suspicions after hearing Christian's dying cries and groans by assuring him it was Christian's wife calling his children. He left McKoy to go alone to his house when it was reported that the two natives who were known to have guns were robbing it. Most incredibly, he refused to take any notice of McKoy's warning that the three natives had tried to murder him. It seems unbelievable that at that point, if not before, Mills would not have feared that the natives were out for revenge and that it would be as well to take some precautions until the situation became clear. We have seen that the whites operated a system of private ownership and cultivation of the land, and Mills and McKoy were the only two who shared their land and labour, which suggests that they were closer to each other than were most of the mutineers. That Mills should have allowed his friend to be shot at and flee for his life without intervening is bizarre, and was surely the behaviour of someone who *knew* what was happening and had some prior reason to believe his own life was not under threat.

If any white men were involved with the Polynesians in a plot to kill *some* of the whites then Mills's actions suggest that he was part of it. His immediate death is also proof that if any white men other than Young were involved, the Polynesians were playing a deeper game. If Young was the ringleader it would be reasonable to assume that he would want at least one white companion, and Mills, a much older man than the others, might have seemed the least threatening choice. Whatever possible knowledge some whites may have had of the coming attack, and whatever the degree of collusion, the natives' motive was clearly to rid themselves of their oppressors, and once the massacre started they attempted to kill all except Young.

Adams never told any outsiders of Young's treachery, and during his lifetime he always maintained to those who questioned him that it was a native plot. That Young committed the unthinkable and planned the treacherous slaughter of the other white men did not become generally accepted until the 1840s, when it was told to one visitor by Arthur Quintal, son of Matthew, who was given the story by Adams himself. Adams had also said that one of the natives told him Young had given orders that Adams's life should be spared but that in the heat of the moment they 'forgot'. On the reasoning given above it seems likely that Mills was also included among those to be saved. That the natives should want to kill Quintal and McKoy for their sustained cruelty is not surprising; Martin had taken Titahiti as a slave, so his death is also explicable; the attack on Adams (which so narrowly failed) is understandable given that Adams had stolen Titahiti and Oha's wife when Williams took Tararo's. But there was no real reason to kill Christian, Mills and Brown. If it is true that Young planned the attack on his fellows, there can be little doubt that he would, of necessity, have included Christian. If he could command the four native men to kill on his orders then he would have been the *de facto* chief of the island. He would have also had to convince the natives that the white men would not be numerous enough after the killings to exact their revenge. Yet he could hardly have viewed being a sole European with four native men as a position of security: he needed one or two companions as a counterweight.

The final question is whether Adams himself was aware of the plot from the beginning, or even planned it with Young. In spite of the fact that he was shot, this appears to be a strong possibility. Adams survived all the killings, and although it would be unfair to condemn a man simply because he was fortunate enough not to be murdered, the question arises whether it would not have required rather more than good luck and passivity to have been the last survivor. According to his own account, Adams went back into the village with one of the women who had been sent to warn him of danger and, according to Jenny's account, he was shot in his own house. In both accounts he was the last man to be attacked. He must, then, have ignored an exceptional amount of musket fire and unusual activity as the women ran back to the village to halt the slaughter. Jenny's statement that the women saved him suggests that he was in the village when shot and that, like Mills, he had no expectation of being attacked. That the native men might have been willing to go beyond a plan made by Young and any others would not be surprising, and is understandable given that Adams had stolen a wife from them in

1791. Judged solely by their actions on the day, and by subsequent events, it seems more than possible that Adams and Mills were involved in the plot with Young from the beginning. The whole truth will never be known.

The community – if that is the appropriate word – was united again, about a month after the Polynesians had started their rebellion. Four years after twenty-seven people had landed on Pitcairn, all six of the native men, two of the women and five of the mutineers were dead. The adult population had been brutally reduced to four white men and ten Polynesian women.

8 · THE WOMEN

The women of Pitcairn had not been simple pawns in events. They had consistently committed themselves to the European men in preference to the Polynesian. They had twice warned the Europeans of plots against them, and two Polynesian men had been killed by the women's own hands. They had also colluded in the death of the others. Their affections and loyalties – or their fears – bound them to the Europeans. But that commitment was not abject or unreflective; they intervened as and when they judged their own best interests were to be served. They behaved with an eye to their own advantage and survival. When they first willingly sailed with the mutineers to settle with them at Toobouai, Isabella protected Christian's life, and those of his companions, by revealing the plot to capture the ship; but neither she nor the other women were prepared to denounce the plotters. It was Isabella again, with Brown's wife Teatuahitea, who betrayed the first plot to kill the whites at Pitcairn, but that incident indicated divisions among the women, for the singer of the song had not informed the whites of the plan to murder them. There is no reason to doubt that Isabella would again have saved her Christian and the white men had she known of the second plot. If she was actually giving birth to a daughter on the day that Fletcher Christian was killed and if the women attending her were aware of the planned murders they did not share the knowledge with Isabella. The fact that the white men had no warning of the planned massacre, and the absence of women when it started, are signs that by this time, like the men, the women were not all of one mind.

After the death of the Polynesian men, the remaining four Europeans self-consciously attempted to bury the hostility between them in a renewed effort to sustain themselves. During the months that followed they set about the tasks of tending their crops, fishing, trapping wild-fowl and 'constructing pits for the purpose of entrapping hogs, which had become very numerous and wild, as well as injurious to the yam-crops'. But 'the only discontent appears to have been among the women, who lived promiscuously with the men, frequently changing their abode'.[1] The slaughter of two-thirds of the men had surely unsettled the women, and perhaps their grief for the dead turned to resentment of the living. If the white men had originally had the power to select a woman each at the expense of the Poly-nesian men the power of choice had now shifted decisively to the women. Among Polynesians, whose sexual mores were so different from those of Europeans, this restlessness might not necessarily be a sign of moral breakdown after a series of trau-matic events; perhaps the women were simply reasserting a more collective lifestyle.

By this point events on the island had left Polynesian culture dominant in terms of numbers. They had also prompted some of the women to live separately from the men, and had generated a great longing among them to leave Pitcairn and return to their homeland. These separate currents were to fuse together, and create conflict between the women and the remaining men, which led once again to the plotting of violence.

One result of murder is that there are bodies to be disposed of, and the manner in which people dispose of their dead is an important ritual in any culture. There seems to be no firm evidence on who buried the bodies after each bout of killings, nor whether any religious services were observed. According to one author the slain were not even buried:

> the bodies of those who had been murdered remained where they were killed. Some had their heads removed by the women . . . Although there is a definite Polynesian tendency to forget someone once he is dead, it is, nevertheless, an appalling thought that the late husbands of these Tahitian women, the fathers of their young children, lay rotting in the sultry summer of 1793/4.[2]

The slain were not only husbands, and by implication their corpses the responsibility of the women; they were also fellow countrymen, co-religionists and old shipmates of the men, and it might be thought more natural that the men should have buried them. After all, in European culture it was men who dug graves, bore coffins and conducted funeral services. If the bodies remained unburied it was not the fault of the Tahitian women. The women had charge of children and domestic life during this period, and were the predominant bearers of culture, a culture in which the dead were not buried but exposed above ground until the flesh had rotted from the bones. If the dead were not buried, the disrespect came from their old shipmates not the women. Nevertheless, the assertion of their native values in the face of the men came directly from a clash over how to treat the dead. The evidence was provided by Young himself, who, after the massacre started keeping a journal. It is now lost, but it was seen and partly copied by Beechey, who wrote:

> Young says, March 12, 1794, 'Going over to borrow a rake, to rake the dust off my ground, I saw Jenny having a skull in her hand: I asked her whose it was? and was told it was Jack Williams's. I desired it might be buried: the women who were with Jenny gave me for answer that it should not. I said it should; and demanded it accordingly. I was asked the reason why I, in particular, should insist on such a thing, when the rest of the white men did not? I said, if they gave it to them to keep the skulls above ground, I did not. Accordingly when I saw M'Coy, Smith [Adams], and Mat. Quintal, I acquainted them with it, and said, I thought that if the girls did not agree to give up the heads of the five white men in a peaceable manner, they ought to be taken by force and buried'.[3]

Given that Edward Young objected to only the *skulls* of some of the slain being kept above ground, it would seem more likely that the corpses had been buried. If he had been content to leave the rotting corpses above ground he would be unlikely to object to unburied skulls. We know from Morrison's observations during his stay in Tahiti that the Tahitians respected the dead, for as he wrote: 'Some who have great Veneration for the deceased wrap up the Skull and Hang it up in their house in token of their love and in this Manner is the Skull of several kept.' Clearly the women were expressing their attachment to the dead by keeping the skulls and according them due honour and respect in keeping with their own cultural and religious beliefs. Their action may not have been one of simple piety – there might have been a more pragmatic reason. Land owner-ship was held by marriage and descent, and proof of title to land was associated with 'the occasional practice of carefully conserving parts of bodies, such as the head, bits of hair. [This was] somehow linked to land and, in some cases, represented title inheritance from the deceased party'.[4] Given the way in which the Polynesian men had been excluded from any share in the land, it would seem that these women were intent on guarding their and their children's right to hold and inherit the land of their white husbands, of which the skull of the previous owner served as title deeds. It would be unreasonable to expect Young to be aware of such economic importance attaching to the skulls, but it is extraordinary that he should have insisted on them being buried according to European custom, as the mutineers had not practised any religious ceremonies or prayers during their time on the island. To antagonize the women over treating their dead in a familiar way was a mistake. It opened and entrenched a division between the sexes that had not previously existed. The women persisted in their refusal to accept Young's orders to bury the skulls. This was quite an assertion: not only were they disobeying the orders of a European male who had been accorded high status back in their own island, but they were also denying the authority of a 'chief' among them, once again in sharp contradiction to the great authority accorded to chiefs in their own culture. It is as if the cultural traditions which afforded males status and superiority had been undermined by the conflicts, while the cultural traditions of the women were emerging as supreme values. If the community was to survive those values were far more necessary than those so far displayed by the males.

Being disobeyed by the women – whose general favourite he had been – was a threat to his status which Young was not prepared to ignore. He tried to convince the other men that the skulls should be taken from the women, by force if necessary, and buried according to European custom. The others were indifferent to the issue and were anxious not to antagonize the women unnecessarily; the women were now a much more powerful group and had to be accepted as such. Whatever the balance of pressures and power, the skulls, for the time being, remained above ground. Jenny seems to exemplify the ambivalence apparent in the actions of the women. She appears to have had a genuine attachment to the European men: she had been Adams's woman during the time that the *Bounty* had stayed in Tahiti; then during the voyage to Pitcairn she became Martin's wife and remained so until his death, although Adams and Martin are reputed to have swapped wives (or their wives to have exchanged men) occasionally. But she was also the leader of the movement among the women to return home and, clearly, one of the upholders of Polynesian culture and values. She was not alone: Young's journal recorded that it was the women 'with Jenny' who refused his orders to bury the skulls.

It may be significant that Jenny and some of the other women remained childless. Polynesian women were reputed to have the ability to induce abortion through external massage, and childlessness may well have been a conscious rejection of the fruits of enforced cohabitation, or a determination to remain unencumbered by children and so remain free to seize any opportunity to return to their own island and people. The latter explanation is more likely: none of the Polynesian men fathered a child, so if it was a conscious policy not to give birth, it was not aimed at the white men alone. The ability of Tahitian women to induce abortions seems to conflict with the widespread practice of infanticide. As we have seen, missionaries to Tahiti claimed that most families raised only two or three children but that women gave birth eight or ten times, and thus killed some two-thirds of their babies. The raising of two or three children by each couple would be the right number to keep an island population static and in balance with the resources available to maintain it. Either the method of abortion was frequently ineffective or going to full-term was considered less injurious to the health of the women.

For whatever reason and by whatever means, some of the women did not have children, which left them free to seize any opportunity to leave the island. Rosalind Young, a Pitcairner, published a story which came to her through the oral tradition of the islanders:

> So constant was the dread experienced by some of the women, that they contrived, in secret, to construct a rude raft, with the intention of returning to Tahiti, or be lost in the attempt. They had their raft launched, and ventured a little way beyond the breakers; but their hearts failed them, and the entreaties of some of the women left behind, who had found out their intention, prevailing, they returned to the shore again.[5]

Jenny was among the group of women most anxious to leave Pitcairn and, after the killings had taken place, the most active in her determination to leave. After the failed experience with an unwieldy raft, she urged the women to force the men into building a boat so that they could leave the island.

For the men such a departure was out of the question. Arguably they could survive without the women – after all they were used to doing so in long months and years at sea – but as they aged they could not have survived without children. The Jewish formulation 'Honour thy children that thy days will be long in the land of thy fathers' has great practical force in a subsistence society. Without a younger generation capable of performing all the necessary agricultural and domestic labour, and willing to care for them, the men could look forward to old age with very little comfort. Moreover, if the women succeeded in regaining contact with the wider world, their location would not be secret for long. Their necks were at stake. However slim the chances were that the women would manage to reach land or encounter a passing ship, the mutineers dared not take the risk.

The pressure from the women on the men was so strong and unrelenting, however, that a month after Young's quarrel with the women over the burial of the skulls, the men agreed to start building a boat. Jenny was so anxious to forward this work that she tore down her house in order to furnish planks and nails, although she was unsuccessful in her attempts to persuade the other women to follow suit. The men toiled at their task for four months and then tested the boat; but it proved unseaworthy:

> On the 13th August following, the vessel was finished, and on the 15th she was launched: but, as Young says, 'according to our expectations she upset,' and it was fortunate for them that she did so; for had they launched out upon the ocean, where could they have gone? or what could a few ignorant women have done by themselves, drifting upon the waves, but ultimately have fallen a sacrifice to their folly?[6]

It is most unlikely that four experienced sailors of that period could not have built a seaworthy boat – however dangerous or foolhardy it may have been for inexperienced sailors to attempt a return to Tahiti in a small craft. The other mutineers who had been left behind at Tahiti built a boat in similar circumstances which was no makeshift job but one known as a fine sailer, used long afterwards as a Pacific ocean trader – although they did have a skilled carpenter among them. Young's acknowledgement that they expected the craft to upset, however, implies that the men had planned to placate the women by outwardly acceding to their wishes, while deliberately constructing something totally unstable. We can also deduce that the boat was part of a bargain made with the women about the remains of the dead; for Young wrote that the day after the unsuccessful launch a grave was dug, and the skulls were interred according to European notions of decency. The women had kept their part of the agreement even if the men had not.

After this transparent piece of trickery the women:

continued much dissatisfied with their condition; probably
not without some reason, as they were kept in great subordi-
nation, and were frequently beaten by M'Coy and Quintal,
who appear to have been of very quarrelsome dispositions;
Quintal in particular, who proposed 'not to laugh, joke, or
give any thing to any of the girls.[7]

As the men became more surly, the women took a stronger
line in their relations with them. A number of women withdrew from the men and lived on their own for periods of
time. Quintal became very unpopular and increasingly brutal
towards the women. He frequently ill-treated his wife as well
as handing out beatings to other women who incurred his dis-
pleasure.

On 3 October 1794 the men held a dinner to celebrate the
first anniversary of the killing of the Polynesian men and to
acknowledge their success in burying their differences and living
in peace. Their celebration was a little premature, however,
for on 11 November they discovered that the women were
conspiring to kill them while they slept. The men seized all the
women and, when questioned, the women admitted that it was
true – they had planned to murder them. Once the men had
learned the truth there was little they could do to safeguard
their lives short of a general slaughter of all the women. That
was unthinkable, yet how could any of the men sleep peacefully
knowing that such a plan had been made by the women whose
beds they sometimes shared? And by women who had already
proved their capacity to swing an axe into a sleeping man's
skull? It was a problem which could not be solved by force or
by reason. Only the renunciation of violence by all parties could
bring peace and security. The men were less confident, or
over-confident, than they had been when the Polynesian men
rose against them; this time they agreed upon a plan. Young's
journal stated: 'We did not forget their conduct; and it was
agreed among us, that the first female who misbehaved should
be put to death; and this punishment was to be repeated on
each offence until we could discover the real intentions of the
women.'[8] This time, at last, they appreciated that collective

action was necessary to their survival. They had yet to learn that violence was not the means.

Young did not record how the men learned of the plot, but it is difficult to see how it might have been discovered unless one of the women had acted as an informant. There is an outside possibility that a child could have repeated something heard from the women and alerted the men, but as they lived with the women and only three of them were older than three years, this is unlikely. But it is clear that some of the women were always reluctant to concur in permitting the deaths of all the men. During this period the conflict between the sexes reached its peak. The men remained very nervous and after the plot had been discovered they concealed two muskets in the woods for the use of any of the four who might survive a sudden attack. Two weeks later an attack came:

> On the 30th November, the women again collected and attacked them; but no lives were lost, and they returned on being once more pardoned, but were again threatened with death the next time they misbehaved. Threats thus repeatedly made, and as often unexecuted, as might be expected, soon lost their effect, and the women formed a party whenever their displeasure was excited, and hid themselves in the unfrequented parts of the island, carefully providing themselves with fire-arms. In this manner the men were kept in continual suspense, dreading the result of each disturbance, as the numerical superiority of the women was much greater than their own.[9]

Quite clearly at this stage there was a gender war, albeit one deepened along racial lines and influenced by the brief but eventful history they had shared. What is unclear is how long this situation of outright hostility and suspicion endured. The women did eventually return to the men on the promise that none of them would be harmed – although with a renewed threat from the men to kill any one of them who attempted to harm them. The women themselves were divided – some of them had little to do with the men and often lived away from them, sometimes arming themselves and keeping the men in a state of fear, while others cohabited with the men. Certainly from the peak of hostility at the end of 1794, relations slowly improved and a sense of trust was gradually established. In the end the women either lived willingly with the men or separately if they chose, but everyone lived in harmony.

The women of Pitcairn gradually abandoned their hopes of leaving, and between 1795 and 1797 six more children were born: two each fathered by Young, Quintal and Adams. According to Young's journal, in April 1798 McKoy set in train a series of events which destroyed this peaceful interlude. At some time in his career before he became a sailor, McKoy had been employed in a Scottish whisky distillery, and he had been attempting to produce alcoholic liquor on the island for some time, using sugar-cane with various vegetable bases and a primitive still. In 1798, according to Young's journal, he succeeded in distilling his first bottle of spirits from the roots of the tee-plant. This started a period of drunkenness by McKoy, Quintal and Adams. Young claimed that he kept himself apart from the group during that time and did not indulge in the alcohol, but some of the women joined the three men and lived in a near-perpetual state of inebriation and licentiousness.

The behaviour of Quintal and McKoy soon degenerated, and Quintal returned to his old violence against women, even biting off Sarah's ear in a rage when she failed to catch enough fish to satisfy him. McKoy became increasingly disturbed, disappearing into the forest for days at a time. Finally he met a tragic end: he 'came to his death through drinking spirits, which brought on derangement, and caused him to leap into the sea, after having tied his own hands and feet.'[1] Other accounts say McKoy committed suicide by tying a stone to himself. The result, whatever the precise detail, was that towards the end of 1798 five-year-old Dinah Adams ran back to the village one morning to report that McKoy could be seen lying at the bottom of one of the rock pools. Young had given up his journal before McKoy's death, which was not therefore recorded precisely to date, so the evidence comes from what Adams told Beechey and others. The event shocked Adams: he claims that he gave up drinking after McKoy's self-destruction. Quintal, in contrast, continued to drink heavily after McKoy's death, and his behaviour became increasingly uncontrollable. With only three men left, Adams became something of a pivotal character in the balance between the rational behaviour of Young and the excesses of Quintal. He saw less and less of his erstwhile drinking companion and drew closer to Young.

After a year of this uneasy situation, Quintal's wife, the unfortunate Sarah, was killed in a fall from the cliffs while collecting bird's eggs, as Paurai had been eight years before. It was an accident, but she might have been taking undue risks simply for fear of being beaten if she returned empty-handed. Sarah seems to have been the one woman who was unreasonably attached to her man: she had formed a stable relationship with Quintal while the *Bounty* was collecting breadfruit at Tahiti, and remained loyal to him for the rest of her life. When Quintal also took Jenny, Martin's widow, as an additional wife after the massacre, Jenny refused to tolerate his behaviour and left him after a very short time. As there were women living separately from the men, sometimes in armed independence, sometimes only loosely affiliated to them, it is a mystery why Sarah stayed. If the women were capable of controlling fertility, it is even more surprising that she had four children by Quintal – more children from the same father than any other woman. Whatever the nature of their relationship or the cause of her death, Quintal was now left without a wife.

In spite of the fact that there were now nine women and only three men, Quintal demanded Young's wife Susannah. Young and Susannah had been together for the ten years on the island, and their relationship had probably been formed back at Tahiti. Quintal's demand that another man should give up his wife was irrational, especially given the horrific results of similar demands in the past. Perhaps no unattached woman was prepared to live with Quintal because of his violence and drunkenness, but that objection should have applied to Susannah as well. His behaviour again threatened the peace between the islanders. According to the account Adams gave to Beechey, Quintal attempted to take the wives of both Young and Adams by force:

> Of course, neither of them felt inclined to accede to this unreasonable indulgence; and he sought an opportunity of putting them both to death. He was fortunately foiled in his first attempt, but swore he would repeat it. Adams and Young having no doubt he would follow up his resolution, and fearing he might be more successful in the next attempt, came to the conclusion that their own lives were not safe while he was in existence, and that they were justified in putting him to death.[2]

Young was the man most under threat, as it was his wife Quintal wanted above all. By this time he was quite ill (with asthma or pulmonary tuberculosis), and no match for the burly Quintal. He needed the protection afforded to him by Adams. They soon found their opportunity:

> one day when he was in John Adams' house, [Quintal] was set upon and overpowered by the two other men. By means of a hatchet the dreadful work of death was soon completed. The daughter of John Mills (who lived to the age of ninety-three), then a young girl of eight or nine years of age, was an eyewitness of the awful deed, and used to relate how terrified were all of the little band of women and children who beheld the blood-bespattered walls.[3]

It would be only fair to Quintal to record that the justification for his murder comes from Adams, his executioner. It is not entirely clear that Quintal's attentions to Susannah were unwelcome to her. She was pregnant at the time of his death and after his murder she gave birth to Edward *Quintal*: one can be sure she was certain who the father was, especially as this paternity was proclaimed after Quintal's murder. She may have been raped by Quintal, but if that were the case it is strange that Adams did not say so, as it would have demonstrated how criminally Quintal was abusing the women, and would have been an added justification for his death. By that time, Susannah had lived for ten years with Young and had remained childless. If she wanted to have children, her liaison with Quintal could have been natural and voluntary. Perhaps Young was jealous of Quintal and his success with Susannah.

Jenny's memories of McKoy's and Quintal's deaths, although arriving at substantially the same result, are a little different. She gave two accounts: 'Old Matt, in a drunken fit, declaring that he would kill Fletcher Christian's children, and all the English that remained, was put to death in his turn. Old McKoy, mad with drink, plunged into the sea and drowned himself' and 'In a drunken affray, Matthew Quintal was killed by his *three* [author's italics] countrymen. M'Koy came to his death through drinking spirits, which brought on derangement, and caused him to leap into the sea, after having tied his own hands and feet.'[4] In the first extract, which is the earliest account of her memories, Jenny confirms the threat that Quintal posed, but relates his death as if it were *before* that of McKoy. In her later version she specifically confirms this impression by stating that three men killed Quintal, and adds a little detail on McKoy's suicide. This is a puzzling discrepancy, and there is no obvious reason for deliberate deception on either side. In this instance Adams's account, in which McKoy died first, may be the more trustworthy. One suspects that if McKoy had been alive when Quintal was killed, Adams would have laid the major part of the murder on him rather than acknowledging it happened by his own hand with the prior planning and assistance of Young. We must remember that according to Adams the sole reprehensible action he committed was to kill Quintal, and as that was in defence of his and his companion's lives it was a necessary and justifiable act.

This does not entirely rule out Jenny's version, for if McKoy was still alive at the time of the murder he might have been excluded from the plan as a hopeless drunk or as a friend of Quintal. Given that all agree McKoy was found drowned in a rock pool with his hands and feet bound and, according to some accounts, a weight tied to his body, perhaps it was not suicide. It's not unreasonable to speculate that he was murdered by Young and Adams, but there is no evidence for this.

It is also worth reflecting on how much confidence can be placed in the above version of the production of alcohol. Once again, it came mainly from the word of John Adams and from a journal kept by Edward Young, the only contemporary written source. The veracity of both must be tested.

The dramatic contrast between its dissolute, drunken and blood-stained past and the honest, amiable and religious society that was eventually discovered was one of the things that made this tiny community a subject of interest. It was either seen as an example of how the nature of man reveals its innate goodness once removed from the corrupting influence of civilization, or as an example of the benefits of total abstinence from alcohol and conversion to Christian religious belief and practice. The period in which the Royal Navy effectively took the Pitcairners under its wing was a period of religious revival in Britain. Over-indulgence in alcohol was held responsible for a great deal of British poverty and immorality, and in the eyes of moral reformers, a major black spot, if not the major black spot, in the island's history was the production of alcohol. This was held responsible for the degeneration in behaviour, particularly that of McKoy and Quintal after the massacre. Virtually all historians accept Beechey's account, based on the authority of Young's journal (verbally confirmed by Adams), which blames McKoy for producing the first bottle of spirits on the '20th of April' 1798. However, Jenny disagrees with that account, both on the time that alcohol was distilled and by whom. She should not be ignored.

According to Jenny, alcohol was available on the island at the time of the original massacre, perhaps only shortly before it happened. Here is her description of the death of Susannah's unfortunate suitor, which happened only a few days after the massacre of the five white men: 'Inflamed with drinking the *raw new spirit they distilled* [author's italics], and fired with jealousy, Manarii killed Teimua by firing three shots through his body.'[5] She was there, and if alcohol was available within days of the

1. The mutineers turning Bligh and his accompanying officers and crew adrift.

2. A human sacrifice in a Tahitian morae (sacred place).

3. A Tahitian woman of the period, like those who became the mutineers' companions, wearing a dress made out of the native *tapa* cloth.

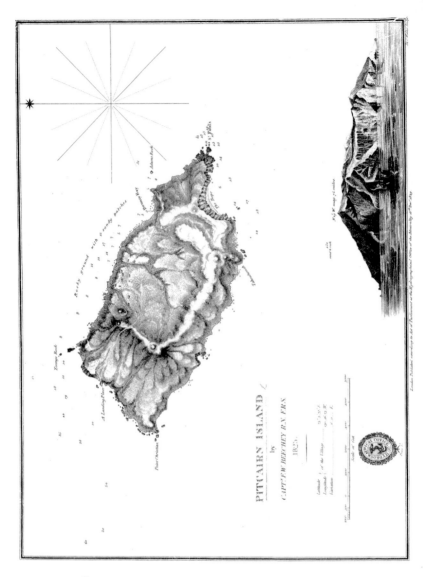

4. A chart of Pitcairn Island by Captain F. W. Beechey. The scale shows that the island is two miles long and one mile wide. The houses of the settlement are to the left of Bounty Bay.

5. An engraving of a painting by Captain F. W. Beechey of the interior of Pitcairn Island, showing John Adams with children and women roasting a pig.

6. A view of the interior of Pitcairn by Lieutenant Conway Shipley, who visited Pitcairn on HMS *Calypso* in 1848. The house was Fletcher Christian's.

R. Beechey Esq. del. J. Vinter lith.   *Day & Son, lith. to The Queen.*

John Adams

Obiit 1829. Ætat 65.

Engraved by permission of Capt. Beechey R.N. and J. Bentley Esq.

7. A fine portrait of the last survivor of the Pitcairn mutineers,
engraved from the original painting by Captain F. W. Beechey.
The illustrations by Beechey and Shipley demonstrate the
artistic ability which naval officers of the period were
encouraged to develop.

Friday Fletcher October Christian

8. Friday Fletcher October Christian, wearing the clothes
which caused much amusement to visiting seamen.

massacre, over three years before Young's journal claims that it was produced, then it might have been the fuel which fired the courage of the natives into rebellion – and it might also account for their exceptional incompetence with the firearms. Jenny is as unambiguous about who started it: 'Neddy Young taught them to distil spirits from the tea root.'[6]

Who was recording the truth, Jenny or Young and Adams? Support for Jenny's version came, as usual, long after Adams was dead. Arthur Quintal told a visitor in 1850 that: 'Young was half West Indian, born in St Kitts, whilst there he learned how to make spirits. By his knowledge of making them there he *soon* [author's italics] made them here, out of the ti-root, by the aid of a large copper boiler which came out of the *Bounty*.'[7] This version carries most conviction. Sailors received a daily ration of half a pint of spirits – usually rum or brandy – and to be deprived after years of such an alcoholic intake was not something to be easily faced. The alcohol aboard the *Bounty* is unlikely to have supplied them for more than a year. It is reasonable to suppose that the problem of producing their own spirits was one of their very early concerns. Alcohol on Pitcairn would have had to be made with tropical produce reduced to a kind of molasses, and this was much more likely to have been a skill possessed by Young, with his West Indian origins, than McKoy with his experience in a Scottish grain distillery. Shifting the responsibility to McKoy was not difficult, given his reputation for drunkenness. It has the appearance of a calculated lie designed to shift the moral odium for the production of alcohol, and its subsequent effects, from Young to McKoy.

The disintegration of Quintal's personality was probably due to excessive drinking, and McKoy's suicide almost certainly so. In spite of this, Adams continued to drink heavily, demoralized, no doubt, by being the only man left. He later claimed to have stopped after having some religious visions. During subsequent years, as visiting ships became more regular, Adams always claimed that the stills had been destroyed and that Pitcairn was alcohol-free, which earned him the approbation of well-wishers in England. But, as usual where John Adams was concerned, this was considerably less than the whole truth, and alcohol continued to play its part in the island story for a number of years.

William McKoy and Matthew Quintal met their ends between 1798 and 1799. Of the fifteen men who had landed on Pitcairn a decade earlier, thirteen had met violent deaths; but the final year of the century saw an end to the bloodshed. By this time there were twenty children, nine boys and eleven girls. Despite the brutal behaviour of their parents, they were to grow up happily, and form a remarkably peaceful society.

III

Reflections

The conflicting accounts of what happened on Pitcairn oblige one to reflect on the evidence and evaluate which is most likely to be valid. This is normal historical practice, although it is frequently performed behind the scenes, historians only presenting the reader with their final opinion. Here the evidence is from such limited sources that the process can be shared. What is more puzzling and disquieting than the contradictions is the *lack* of evidence concerning events on the island from the time the mutineers first landed until they were discovered. Why are there these 'silences' in the record? There can be no doubt that someone kept a minimal daily log from the moment of the mutiny onwards. This is proved by the fact that the islanders knew exactly how many days had passed since the mutiny. For eighteen years someone had been disciplined enough to note each passing day, at the very least. It's most likely that Fletcher Christian kept that record while he lived, and most likely that it was more than a mere calendar. As an experienced watch-keeping officer, Christian would have formed the habit of keeping a logbook and recording significant events. It seems inconceivable that, while writing down the day and date every day, one would not note a birth, death or murder. That no such record ever came to light could not have been for lack of ink or paper, as there were still ample supplies of the *Bounty*'s stationery being used in the school when Folger first landed. If Fletcher Christian had kept a journal it was lost or destroyed after his death. If it was destroyed, the reason could only be that it contained observations the survivors did not want to be seen.

The only contemporary written document seen by outsiders was Edward Young's journal which Captain Beechey saw and partially copied, but then that too was lost. As the only contemporary written evidence, albeit at second hand, Young's journal has been granted much authority as a true account of events. But was it? Young did not start his journal until after the massacre of his shipmates, which virtually confirms that the daily record until then had not been kept by him. Christian as the other, and senior, officer is the only person likely to have done so. As Edward Young planned the deaths of his shipmates, including that of his co-officer Christian, his version of events was written to mislead, not inform. The journal which Young started after the massacre included some quite lengthy descriptions, as the sections copied by Beechey demonstrate: on the affair of the skulls and its consequences, for example. Young's observation that McKoy produced his first bottle of spirits on the '20th of April' 1798 shows a surprising degree of precision from a journalist who did not find the date or circumstance of McKoy's death worthy of even a mention, and did not record either Quintal's death or the reason for it – odd omissions from someone who found many other trivial details worthy of his attention. For example, Young noted that on the '4th of May, two canoes were begun' (the first craft they had permitted themselves); and he made the precise observation that on the '27th of December following, they were greatly alarmed by the appearance of a ship close in with the island. Fortunately for them there was a tremendous surf upon the rocks, the weather bore a very threatening aspect, and the ship stood to the S.E., and at noon was out of sight.' Life on the island could be uneventful and Beechey notes 'So little occurred in the year 1796, that one page records the whole of events.' The next year Young took the trouble to record their efforts to salt meat, their attempts to produce syrup from the tea-plant, and that McKoy sustained a number of injuries in falling from a coconut tree. This is what one might expect from a journal of island affairs, but then Beechey records without question or comment that 'The journal finishes nearly at the period of M'Coy's death, which is not related in it: but we learned from Adams [etc.].'[1] The problem of Adams as the sole source returns once more.

For all that we should appreciate the amount of information Beechey wrote so laboriously with quill and ink (and the record would be sparse without him), his passivity is frustrating. He never questioned Adams on why Young's journal failed to record such important events as the death of their last two shipmates, or why there was no journal for the earlier period, or how, without a daily record, a calendar was kept.

History is, of course, written by survivors, so where existing fragments conflict one is obliged to consider the circumstances in which they were produced and the self-interest of the person producing them. For example, Jenny's versions of events are, in general, preferable to Adams's early versions of events – and Adams's later versions to his early ones.

Jenny never changed her mind about wanting to leave the island and as soon as possible she begged passage on a ship in 1817 and eventually found her way back to Tahiti. She was, therefore, not under Adams's influence when she was questioned about the mutineers' fate. She was not present throughout the years when Adams managed to conceal the truth and change his story in spite of the presence of a number of women who could have given the visitors a different version. Either they were under Adams's influence and supported his story because he was their accepted patriarch and the leader who alone among them understood and could deal with the visiting Europeans or, as appears often to have been the case, the naval officers concerned never questioned the women, whether because of their limited English or because they felt that Tahitian women could add nothing worthwhile to the information given by a European man. At all events, the islanders presented a collective front to the world and John Adams was their mouthpiece. Jenny's memory was not necessarily clearer than that of Adams, but she had no reason to distort events – although she frequently avoided naming names so as not to incriminate others.

Adams had strong reasons for inventing stories: he was a mutineer and needed to put the best face he could on that fact. He was also the sole survivor of the fifteen men who had landed on the island, and their deaths had to be explained if murder

was not to be added to his offences. His first version, told in
1808, was simple:

> Smith said, and upon the point Captain Folger was very
> explicit in his inquiry at the time as well as in his account
> of it to me, that they [the mutineers] lived under Christian's
> government for several years after they landed; that during the
> whole period they enjoyed tolerable harmony; that Christian
> became sick and died a *natural death*, and that it was after this
> that the Otaheitian men joined in a conspiracy and killed
> the English husbands of the Otaheitian women, and were by
> the widows killed in turn on the following night.[2]

This version of events presented Adams as a blameless, if somewhat fortunate witness to the violence. First the native men
killed all the European men save him in one fell swoop, the
native women then killed all the native men the very same
evening, and lucky John Adams was left the sole man with the
women and children. The very improbability of the account
shows that Adams had not prepared a tale to explain the deaths
of his shipmates. During the following twenty years until his
death he was to relate his story many times, and each telling
revealed a rather more complex version of how his shipmates
died on Pitcairn Island.

Folger was an American and, having no obligation to the
British naval authorities, was no threat to Adams. Adams's first
test came when Captain Sir Thomas Staines and Captain Pipon
arrived off the island in two frigates on 17 September 1814. He
was very cautious and prepared to go into hiding, but the two
captains went ashore in the islanders' canoes, and Pipon wrote
'we reached the shore with only a good wetting; and soon after
old John Adams, when he learned that we had landed without
arms, and were not come to seize his person, met us on the
road, and conducted us to his house'.[3] A strange meeting: a
common able seaman and mutineer entertaining two of His
Majesty's captains. Adams could have had no way of knowing
that in the eighteen years since the mutiny public opinion in
Britain had swung around and that there was now a degree of

sympathy for Fletcher Christian and a feeling that Bligh's conduct had been unreasonable. Adams clearly set out to distance
himself from Christian and to paint him black in an effort to
ingratiate himself with those he assumed would hold Christian
– a fellow officer – in the greatest contempt for having betrayed
his country and his captain. Pipon gathered the impression that
Christian virtually kidnapped the others: 'he [Christian] set her
[the *Bounty*] on fire, to prevent, doubtless, the escape of his
companions, as well as to preclude the possibility of any information being given of his situation.'[4] Adams was intent on
saying whatever he thought would most please the two officers.
He told them that:

> Fletcher Christian was never happy after the rash and incon-
> siderate step he had taken; but became sullen and morose;
> and having by many acts of cruelty and inhumanity, brought
> on himself the hatred and detestation of his companions, he
> was shot by a black man whilst digging in his field, and
> almost instantly expired. This happened about eleven months
> after they were settled on the island ... the conduct of
> Fletcher Christian towards the people soon alienated them
> from him, and in consequence they divided into parties,
> which ran very high, seeking every opportunity on both sides
> to put each other to death ... Christian's wife having died,
> he forcibly seized on one belonging to the Otaheitian men,
> and took her to live with him. This exasperated them to a
> degree of madness; open war was declared, and every oppor-
> tunity sought to take away his life, and it was effected in the
> manner described.[5]

In this period the ordinary lower-deck crew were referred
to as the 'people', so the reference above is to the sailors not
to all those on the island. Unlike Adams's first story, given to
Folger, in which Christians is said to have died a natural death,
in this, his first meeting with the British navy, he lays all the
blame firmly on Christian. He is blamed for burning the *Bounty*,
for numerous acts of cruelty and for stealing a wife when his
own died. Given that Christian's original and only wife, Isabella,
was no doubt there helping the other women to prepare a meal

for the captains, and was not to die for another twenty-seven years, one has to acknowledge that John Adams's departure from the truth was not an accident of memory. He told only what he felt it was safe to admit to, and what he judged his listeners wanted to hear. He was also confident that the women would not contradict whatever lies he cared to tell. Pipon revealed some frustration when he noted: 'We could not learn, precisely, the exact number of blacks or whites who were killed while this kind of warfare continued.'[6] Exactness and consistency were not a notable feature of Adams's ability to spin a convincing yarn in his own interests.

Captain Staines, in a letter dated 18 October 1814, observed that John Adams kept a journal in which he noted the work performed by each family and who borrowed what from whom, and also kept account of the general stock from which families could borrow food when short and repay later. 'The visit of the *Topaz* is, of course, a notable circumstance, marked down in Adams's journal.'[7] So Adams was literate enough to keep a journal, but there is no reason to suppose that he, a sailor, would have done so while the well-educated officers, Christian or Young, were alive, so once again contemporary written evidence for the dramatic events is not available. John Adams made a remarkable impression on all who met him and had his word accepted and his good faith taken for granted. It was an outstanding achievement for a common sailor to so impress 'Captains' and 'Sirs' who would have barely deigned to address him directly had he been aboard their ships and would certainly have clapped him in irons for disobeying orders, let alone mutiny. Strictly speaking it was the duty of these two captains to arrest him. And yet Captain Sir Thomas Staines was concerned only with his welfare:

> In the course of time the Patriarch [Adams] must go hence; and we think it will be exceedingly desirable, that the British nation should provide for such an event, by sending out, not an ignorant and idle missionary, but some zealous and intelligent instructor, together with a few persons capable of teaching the useful trades or professions.[8]

This was an amazing response from a naval officer on finding a mutineer, some native women and the half-caste descendants of mutineers. Far from attempting to return Adams to justice, he refers to this mutinous common sailor after meeting him for a few hours as a 'Patriarch', is concerned with the possibility of his death and generally treats this few dozen people with immense concern and consideration. The place and the people seem to have had the most extraordinary impact on all who visited the island. This contributes towards the difficulty of arriving at an account which reflects the historical reality. Most visitors, upon whose accounts we rely for information, were ashore for only a few hours and were shown a community on its best behaviour; perhaps they also to some extent saw what they wanted to see – a small ideal community, uncorrupted by the wider world. For example, time and time again visitors report that the Pitcairners have destroyed their stills and are teetotallers; but just as frequently there is evidence that the stills are working and the islanders are drinking – it was not difficult for them to conceal the fact for a few hours while the captain of a ship was ashore. There is no doubt that John Adams's achievements in winning the goodwill and high regard of all the captains who visited them was germane to the respect with which the islanders were treated.

Five years later Captain Henderson, master of a trading vessel, who proved to be a good friend and supporter of the islanders, published an account of the events on Pitcairn. This time, John Adams assured him, he would tell 'nothing but the truth', which, if nothing else, gave him good grounds for deviating from his earlier versions. On this occasion he claimed that it was four years after they landed that a woman, Williams's wife, died. This was followed by the violent deaths of Christian, Brown, Martin, Mills, Williams and two Tahitians. Three years later one Tahitian refused to work and he was killed:

> before he could do much mischief except his wounding Old
> Adams in the right shoulder . . . [another also clubbed him]
> . . . Before he could repeat the blow, Quintal dispatched the
> first Otaheitian, and the other, his companion, ran off to the

woods; but coming back a few days later the women killed
him in the night, while asleep . . . Thus only four Englishmen
were left, of whom one went mad and drowned himself, and
two died natural deaths.[9]

This is an interesting and unique version, in that Adams received
his wounds fighting alongside, and was saved from death by,
Quintal. However, it accounts for the deaths of only four male
natives, though it was intended to explain the deaths of the
entire number. It also conflated the two separate occasions of
strife and disguised the murder of Quintal as a natural death. It
had the merit of being rather more complex than his previous
accounts.

Contemporaries were aware of the problem. As the story of
Pitcairn became more widely known in Britain and around the
world, the obvious discrepancies in his various accounts
impelled Captain Dillon to interview Jenny, who was then
living in Tahiti. In publishing this account the editor of the
United Services Journal commented that:

> As all accounts hitherto received respecting his Majesty's ship
> Bounty, have only been obtained from John Adams, who,
> it is more than likely, would have his own private motives
> for deviating from the facts, for perverting many facts, and
> suppressing others, the following details will no doubt be
> read with much curiosity, and we see no reason why they
> should not be entitled to some degree of credit.[10]

Apart from differences already considered, Jenny was the first
person to recount the long search through the islands before
arriving at Pitcairn and so to elucidate why it had taken the
Bounty three months to arrive at Pitcairn, less than 1000 miles
from Tahiti. For the first time she revealed a plot, instigated by
the Tahitians who sailed with them, to slaughter all the mutineers while they were trying settle at Toobouai. This is significant, because it suggests that the native men who accompanied
the mutineers were not simply friends of the white men who
then abused that friendship by treating them as inferiors and by
stealing their women. The ship had been a floating cornucopia

of arms, tools, trade goods and metal whose value in native eyes was beyond imagination. It was an object worth staying with if there was a chance, however slight, of taking control of it or of acquiring even a canoe-load of precious arms and tools.

Adams's and Jenny's versions should not just be seen in simple contradiction to each other. Deliberate falsehood aside, witnesses who have lived through the same events will tell very different stories as one remembers one thing, the other something different. Such differing accounts give a more complete picture if combined. Jenny for example, tells of the warning the women gave the men at Toobouai but does not mention their warning on Pitcairn. Adams does not mention the first, but is the source of the second where the warning was communicated by one woman to other women in a song. Jenny's silence and Adams's version actually complement each other in indicating a division in the loyalties of the women. Jenny confirmed that the women were willing to save the mutineers by betraying the plans of their Polynesian men; the woman in Adams's story did not want to warn the white men. She did not tell, but those who overheard her did, so one can perceive a division between the women at that early stage. It prefigured the growing discontent of the women with the Europeans. Putting the two sources together helps one to interpret the way events developed.

John Adams died in 1829, and it was not until after his death that it was finally admitted to outsiders that he had started the bloodshed by stealing a wife from the Tahitian men. F. D. Bennett went ashore on Pitcairn some five years later, in March 1834. He was told that Adams lost his wife and that:

> Upon her death he lived with, but did not marry, a female whom he took from her Tahitian husband; and this act (which has always been incorrectly ascribed to Fletcher Christian) led to the sanguinary dissension between the mutineers and the men of Tahiti.[11]

Bennett's visit came at a significant period. For the first time since Adams was left as the sole man the islanders were disunited and not presenting a common front to the world. Adams was no longer there to be the accepted authoritative source for the history of events on the island. Two factions developed, at least one of which had no interest in defending his reputation, or maintaining the continued prestige of his family. It was only after Adams died that his distortions of the history of the island could be drawn into the light.

John Adams and his fellow mutineers would have been less than human had they not speculated on the fate of the shipmates they left at Tahiti. Given the bloody affrays that their choice of action had led them into, they must have wondered whether it would have been wiser to stay at Tahiti with the others. They must have wondered, too, what had happened to Bligh, to the nineteen men they forced into a small boat thousands of miles from a safe haven, unarmed among hostile islands. The chances were that they had all drowned as the small craft foundered; alternatively, they may have expired slowly from thirst or been butchered by natives. If they reflected on these issues, the mutineers' consciences should at least have given them the occasional bad dream. John Adams was the only one to live long enough to learn the fate of those who stayed with Captain Bligh, as well as those who chose to remain at Tahiti.

Bligh and his men had been cast adrift on Tuesday 28 April, 1789. They were close to the island of Tofua and made there to collect water and to trade with the natives for supplies, but the natives soon realized that they had no muskets and were weak enough to be taken. Bligh showed considerable courage in leading his men back to their boat, but one, John Norton, was stoned to death in the surf as they attempted to leave. Even once clear of the shore they could all have been killed had not Bligh diverted the war canoes from which they were being stoned by throwing some clothes into the sea, booty which the canoes stopped to salvage. After that frightening encounter they agreed to avoid all islands which might be inhabited and swore to Bligh that they would endure whatever privations such a policy would bring. If they had been given even one or two muskets by the mutineers their situation would have been much more secure. As it was, their voyage across the ocean to their first landfall on the east coast of Australia, then up through the Endeavour Straits to the Dutch settlements in Indonesia entailed weeks of thirst, hunger and danger, all successfully surmounted when they arrived at Coupang in Timor on Sunday 14 June. They had travelled over 3600 miles and had been in their tiny craft for nearly seven weeks. In challenging situations Bligh had once again proved his considerable abilities as a navigator and his courage as a commander. From Coupang they moved on to Batavia, Java, where they could expect to find ships sailing for Europe. While in the Dutch East Indies, however, Bligh experienced familiar trouble because of constant friction between him and his crew. Their shared experience had not drawn them closer, and their disagreements culminated in another mutiny – if a rather drunken and half-hearted one – at Surabaya, during which Bligh arrested the master, Fryer, and Peckover, the gunner. The matter was resolved and the group reunited through an investigation into the complaints by the Dutch Governor.

In the Dutch East Indies four men – Hall, Elphinstone, Linkletter and Nelson – died of fevers. Rather than seeing to the well-being of his men, Bligh secured a passage on the first available ship for himself, leaving them to fend for themselves. Of those remaining, Lamb died on the passage home and Ledward was lost at sea while homeward bound on a Dutch ship, which foundered with all hands. Bligh's behaviour in the Dutch Indies and his treatment of his men while there eventually helped to tarnish his reputation, which rose so high when he first returned to England and gave his version of events.

News of the loss of the *Bounty* had been sent ahead from Coupang. Bligh landed at Plymouth on 14 March 1790 and became the talk of the country. He was received sympathetically by the King. The obligatory court martial following the loss of a ship was a cursory affair, as all the mutineers were on the other side of the world – Bligh was hailed as an innocent victim and acquitted of any responsibility. No mention was made of any of the disagreements or troubles during the voyage nor of his conflict with his loyal crewmen in Surabaya. In spite of the loss of his ship and the failure of a considerable commercial enterprise, Bligh was given his long desired promotion to the rank of captain. He was now firmly on the ladder of success, and national sympathy for him and confidence in him was expressed by his immediate placement in charge of a second breadfruit expedition. This time he was empowered to choose two vessels, and this time he would have a party of eighteen marines under the command of a lieutenant to assert his authority. Seldom, if ever, could a mere lieutenant who had lost his ship and failed to carry out such a costly and important expedition have been so elevated. Bligh's second breadfruit voyage was due to sail for Tahiti at the beginning of August 1791, but not before he had the pleasure of seeing, in November 1790, the dispatch of the twenty-four-gun frigate *Pandora*,[1] to find and apprehend the mutineers. Two of the midshipmen from the *Bounty*, Hayward and Hallett, who had survived with Bligh (Hayward was promoted to lieutenant) were included in the crew of the *Pandora*, partly because their knowledge of Tahitian would enable them to question natives as to the whereabouts of any white men, and partly because they knew the men and would be able to identify the mutineers wherever they were found.

Meanwhile, the sixteen men who had decided to stay at Tahiti when the *Bounty* left for an unknown destination met various fates. Most of them settled down to a peaceful life with their friendly hosts, and at least five formed stable relationships with women and became fathers. Ten of them soon set about building a schooner in which they intended to return to England by sailing her to the Dutch East Indies as Bligh had done in his small vessel. James Morrison, boatswain's mate, was the main mover in this, in spite of the fact that he could expect little less than execution, since he had been active in the mutiny and had been seen about the decks armed with a musket. Perhaps he hoped that by giving himself up he might win a pardon. While in Tahiti he emerged as a leader and was instrumental in maintaining some semblance of naval routine and discipline. He always held divine service on Sundays and, with the other ship-builders, flew the Union Flag. He made good use of his time, learning the language and leaving an extensive account of native society and customs.

Two other active mutineers, Thompson and Churchill, lived together, and did very little but drink the share of the *Bounty*'s liquor that had fallen to them and enjoy the favours of those women who were freely available. They were the leaders of a small gang consisting of Burkitt, Sumner and Musprat. They fell out with the natives when (according to Morrison) Thompson 'abused' a young girl. Sexual promiscuity was part of the Tahitians' culture, but enforced sex was not, and this incident ended with Thompson receiving a severe beating from the men of the girl's family. Later a hostile crowd gathered around his house and in defending himself he shot and killed a man and the infant he was holding in his arms. As a result of the fracas this group of sailors left the Matavai Bay area on the north of the island and moved south into another chiefdom. When the chief there died, shortly after their arrival, Churchill assumed his position. This elevation to leadership was partly due to the respect in which Europeans were held, and partly because of their possession of firearms, which were such a decisive military advantage. Shortly afterwards, Thompson, perhaps jealous of Churchill's new authority, shot him in the back. In revenge for the death of a chief, Thompson was then beaten to death by the natives.

The two parties of mutineers then lived apart until the group at Matavai Bay had finished building their schooner, which they named HMS *Resolution* in honour of Captain Cook. They tested it by sailing around the island and visiting their old ship-mates. Their timing could not have been worse, for while they were on this short expedition news came overland that a ship had arrived at Matavai Bay and armed parties were already ashore searching for them.

The *Pandora* had made a good voyage out and arrived at Tahiti on 23 March 1791, only twenty-three months after the mutiny. Ironically, she had passed within a day's sailing of

Pitcairn Island. The majority of the *Bounty* crew scrambled to give themselves up as a sign of their innocence – a number of them were not mutineers anyway and had been asked by Bligh himself to stay with the ship in order not to overload the cutter. These men welcomed the arrival of the *Pandora*, which would take them home and restore them to their anxious families. But Captain Edwards was a hard and implacable man who was not prepared to treat anyone other than as an active mutineer and, as the *Bounty* men gave themselves up, all, even those Bligh had actually named as being guiltless, were thrown into irons.

Six of the active mutineers – Burkitt, Hillbrant, McIntosh, Millward, Musprat and Sumner – who were only too well aware that they had little to look forward to but a hanging from the yardarm of one of His Majesty's ships at Spithead, decided to escape, and fled with their firearms inland, high into the mountains. Although the Tahitian chiefs were keen to retain them for their skill with firearms, they never had a chance: the chiefs were constrained by the superior power of the ship and the rewards that it could provide, and guided the shore party of marines to the fugitives. When confronted, the mutineers realized that resistance was hopeless and gave themselves up without a shot fired.

On board the *Pandora*, the fugitives were confined in unnecessarily harsh conditions. A cell was constructed on deck which was entered through a small hatch in the roof and had only two nine-inch scuttles for ventilation. All the prisoners were in leg-irons and handcuffs and no one was allowed to converse with them. In this sweatbox, made noisome by the lavatory tubs in the cell, the fourteen men, mutineers and non-mutineers together, were stifled for five weeks while the *Pandora* lay at anchor, as it prepared to search the islands for the rest of the mutineers and then make the long voyage home.

After six weeks, the *Pandora* left Tahiti on 8 May 1791, to the emotional outpouring of grief and affection which was by now customary for departing ships. On this occasion the emotions were particularly intense, as the unfortunate mutineers had lived with the Tahitians for so long – many had families, and it was said that Stewart's marriage to his Tahitian wife had been remarkably blissful. They had a child only a few months old when he was taken and his wife, inconsolable, died of grief two months later.

In looking for traces of Christian and the remaining mutineers, Captain Edwards 'touched at Huaheine and Bolabola; but when they came to Whytootackee, they made particular inquiries, as Christian had made the Otaheitians suppose that he had gone there on leaving their island'.[2] Finding no trace of the missing mutineers there:

> they made sail, and on the 22d May reached Palmerston's Islands. Here no sooner had Lieutenant Corner and a party landed, than they made the important discovery of a yard and some spars having on them the mark of the *Bounty*. The *Bounty* then had been here, and every search was to be made in case the remaining mutineers should still be found within its circuit.[3]

They knew from information already given them that the *Bounty* had lost most of her spare masts and yards during her time at Toobouai and they came to the conclusion that the items they found had been carried there by wind, wave and current. Captain Edwards appears not to have run a very effective operation as the jolly boat under the charge of a midshipman and crewed by four seamen disappeared without trace during the search of Palmerston Island. At the next encounter with land, an island the natives called Otulesulu and whose inhabitants had never seen a white man, Edwards again lost contact with one of the ship's boats. This time it was the schooner the men with Morrison had built at Tahiti, commandeered for use as a ship's tender by Edwards and crewed by two of his petty officers and seven seamen.

On the 29th the *Pandora* arrived at Nomuka in the Friendly Islands, where the search was abandoned as fruitless. They were homeward bound via the Dutch East Indies, on a course close to the one sailed by Bligh and his men in their open boat, when on 28 August Captain Edwards allowed his vessel to be wrecked on the Great Barrier Reef. When the shipwreck occurred the mutineers and unfortunate non-mutineers had been strictly confined in appalling conditions for some five months. She did not sink immediately, and for twelve hours the crew struggled to save her: cannon were pushed overboard to lighten her and the pumps kept working. As the ship went over at more of an angle and settled lower in the water, the ship's boats were prepared to take off the crew. During this frightening turmoil, the luckless prisoners were kept confined. In sheer desperation they broke out of their leg-irons, in the hope that they might escape being drowned like rats. But Captain Edwards, in spite of all the problems of a shipwreck on his hands and with his ship settling lower in the water by the minute, diverted a strong party of men to replace the leg-irons and to handcuff them, as well as keeping the small hatch, the prisoners' only exit, firmly bolted. Eventually three of the men whom Bligh had named as innocent of mutiny were released to help with the pumping. When the ship was finally abandoned (Captain Edwards not being the last to leave), the lives of some of the prisoners were saved by the master-at-arms who threw them the key to their shackles, and by the outstanding heroism of the bosun's mate who, risking his own life, made his way aft as the ship foundered, drew the bolts and opened the hatch. There was not time enough for all to scramble through and four men – Hillbrant, Skinner, Stewart and Sumner – were trapped and drowned unnecessarily because of Captain Edwards's cold-blooded callousness. If Edwards's inhumanity had not been tempered by the initiative and courage of his seamen, all the prisoners would have met the same ghastly end.

The survivors were now faced with the task of reaching the Dutch East Indies, having to cover about half the distance Bligh covered in his epic small-boat voyage. This they did with all the hardships attendant on such a trip. When they finally arrived there, they were amazed to find that the schooner which Morrison had built at Tahiti, with which they had lost contact, had also found its way to the security of the Dutch East Indies. The qualities of this schooner were a tribute to the wide range of practical skills possessed by common seamen, who were able to design and build what proved to be a superb vessel:

> She parted from the Pandora near Palmerstone islands when searching for the Bounty, and was not heard of till the arrival of the Pandora's crew at Samarang, in Java, where they found her lying at anchor . . . She was a remarkably swift sailor, and, being afterwards employed in the sea-otter trade, is stated to have made one of the quickest passages ever known from China to the Sandwich Islands.[4]

She was not some gimcrack craft knocked together in the hopes that she would last for a single voyage to freedom, but a sound and lasting vessel with sailing qualities in which a first-rate shipyard could have taken pride. There is no doubt that the mutineers at Pitcairn could have built a seaworthy craft which would have taken them back into contact with European shipping had they been so inclined. They remained concealed because they continued to fear discovery, not because they had burned the *Bounty*.

After the wreck of the *Pandora*, Captain Edwards's gratuitous cruelty to his prisoners did not abate. Although there was no possibility of escape, they were kept bound tight in the bottom of the boats for much of the time. It was not until Edwards handed them over to a British ship at the Cape of Good Hope that their treatment became humane, as it was while they were in prison awaiting court martial at Spithead.

The trial of the prisoners began on 12 September 1792, well over three years after the mutiny had taken place. Bligh, originally welcomed home as a captain who had been betrayed by officers and crew, but who had brought his loyal men to safety through supreme skill and leadership, was now away, repeating the voyage and enjoying his promotion. Before the trial had ended, public opinion and, more crucially, opinion in the navy changed, as Bligh's behaviour became more widely known through the prisoners' accounts. Christian and Heywood came from well-born families, which could not believe that their sons would have betrayed their trust and thrown away their careers unless they had been subjected to the greatest provocation. Both families rallied kinsmen and friends in an effort to lighten the stain upon their families' honour.

Edward Christian, Professor of Law at Cambridge, who fought to save the name of his brother, never attempted to excuse any act of mutiny but argued that there must have been some deep injustice to have driven their kinsmen, both desperately keen on a career in the navy, to the crime. Fletcher Christian had disappeared and, in all but his good name, was beyond justice; but Peter Heywood was only fifteen years old when he left England on the great voyage with Bligh as his captain. The Heywood family had influential connections in the navy and set about using every relation, friend and all the influence they had to save his life. The key witnesses at the trial were, and had to be, the crewmen who had been cast adrift with Bligh. For that reason alone these men had little reason to love the mutineers, but a number of them, particularly the most senior man, the ship's master John Fryer, disliked Bligh even more than he disliked the mutineers, and he and others testified to Heywood's innocence. Captain Edwards's gratuitous cruelty to all his prisoners on the *Pandora* – many of whom were totally innocent of mutiny – and the unnecessary drowning of four of their number in the shipwreck also created an atmosphere of sympathy for the surviving mutineers. An armed services publication reviewing the affair some years later stated:

> We refrain from entering into the treatment of these unfortunate prisoners, but this we must say, that if the truth has been related, it was the most unwarrantable, unofficerlike, and barbarous exercise of power, we ever recollect to have known recorded of a British officer: we willingly draw a veil over the scene.[5]

Although the feeling in the court martial was that William Bligh had been less than candid in his account of the voyage, the judgment was inescapable: the six men whom Bligh had named as active mutineers and whom witnesses had seen under arms were found guilty; but the court showed some leniency and recommended Peter Heywood and James Morrison to 'His Majesty's Royal Mercy'; they were pardoned and continued to serve the navy with distinction. Heywood, in what could only be seen as a slight to Bligh, was not only pardoned, but was promoted and chosen to serve on an admiral's flagship. One of the able seamen sentenced to death, William Musprat, won a stay of execution on a legal technicality and was eventually freed. Like midshipman Heywood, Thomas Ellison was a youth, only sixteen years old when the mutiny erupted, but he lacked rich and powerful friends, and youth alone proved no protection. He was hanged with Thomas Burkitt and John Millward from the deck of HMS *Brunswick*, witnessed by a vast crowd in Portsmouth harbour on 29 October 1792. All three showed great calm and dignity. As they stood with the rope around their necks John Millward made a speech acknowledging their fault, urging all seamen always to be true to their duty. They were then hauled to their deaths on the boom of the signal gun. The final act was embellished by their own shipmate and fellow mutineer (safely pardoned) James Morrison – he fired the gun.

Save for Fletcher Christian and his eight companions, the story of the mutiny had been completed: some had died violent deaths at Tahiti; some had died *en route*; of the rest legally tried, some were found innocent, some pardoned and some hanged. It was to be another sixteen years before the British public was to receive news of those missing with the *Bounty*.

Three years after three of their old shipmates were hanged at Plymouth the four surviving men on Pitcairn still had no urge to give themselves up. Their most frightening moment came in 1795:

> a ship was observed close in with the island; at the sight of which the mutineers were so much alarmed as to hide themselves in the bush. When they came out from their conceal-ment, they found that a party had actually landed from her, as was proved by the discovery of a jack-knife on a rock by the sea-side, and some coco-nut shells. Their habitations, however, appeared to have remained unnoticed.[6]

From the late eighteenth century the Pacific Ocean was increasingly frequented by European and American ships, particularly those exploiting the whaling and sealing grounds of the southern ocean. Remote and forbidding as Pitcairn Island was, it was inevitable that a ship would eventually call for one reason or another, even if it were only a ship desperate for fresh water or suffering severe storm damage. In all, three ships were sighted before the young Pitcairners were to have their first contact with the outside world when they took Captain Folger ashore in 1808 and he became the first outsider to learn the fate of the *Bounty*. Adams also wanted news and learned from Folger that the mutineers who stayed at Tahiti had been captured, tried and some hanged. He was much relieved to learn that Captain Bligh and those men in the launch had reached port – thus his conscience was eased; but Folger was unable to give precise details of who had lived or died. The presence of a mutineer from the British navy and the fate of the others was not the concern of an American and Captain Folger, having received water and supplies of fresh food from the islanders, asked Adams if he wished his existence to remain a secret. Adams replied 'No'.

News of Captain Folger's discovery took some fifteen months to travel from him, via South America, to become public knowledge in Britain. Contemporaries were given news of the event by the *Quarterly Review*, February 1810, with a degree of scepticism perhaps not unwarranted in view of all the previous false reports which claimed that Fletcher Christian had been seen in England, on French ships fighting against the British or in the service of Spain:

> The following relation was transmitted officially to the Admiralty from Rio de Janeiro by Sir Sydney Smith. 'Captain Folger, of the American Shop Topaz of Boston, relates that, upon landing on Pitcairn's island (Incarnation of Quiros) in lat. 25 2′ S. long. 130 0′ W. he found there an Englishman of the name of Alexander Smith, the only person remaining of nine that escaped in his Majesty's late ship Bounty, Captain Bligh. Smith relates, that after putting Captain Bligh in the

boat, Christian the leader of the mutiny, took command of the ship and went to Otaheite, where great part of the crew left her, except Christian, Smith and seven others, who each took wives, and six Otaheitian men servants, and shortly after arrived at the said island, where they ran the ship on shore, and broke her up; this event took place in the year 1790.

About four years after their arrival (a great jealousy existing) the Otaheitians secretly revolted and killed every Englishman except himself, whom they severely wounded in the neck with a pistol ball. The same night the widows of the deceased Englishmen arose and put to death the whole of the Otaheitians, leaving Smith the only man alive upon the island, with eight or nine women and several small children. On his recovery he applied himself to tilling the ground, so that it now produces plenty of yams, cocoa nuts, bananas and plantains; hogs and poultry in abundance. There are now some grown up men and women, children of the mutineers on the island, the whole population amounting to about thirty five, who acknowledge Smith as father and commander of them all: they all speak English and, have been educated by him, (Captain Folger represents) in a religious and moral way.

The second mate of the Topaz asserts that Christian the ringleader became insane shortly after their arrival on the island, and then threw himself off the rocks into the sea; another died of fever before the massacre of the remaining six took place. The island is badly supplied with water, sufficient only for the present inhabitants, and no anchorage.

Smith gave Captain Folger a chronometer made by Kendall, which was taken from him by the Governor of Juan Fernandez.

>   Extracted from the log book 29th Sept. 1808
>   (Signed) William Fitzmaurice, Lieut.'

If this interesting relation rested solely on the faith which is due to Americans, with whom, we say with regret, truth is not always considered as a moral obligation, we should hesitate in giving it this publicity.

The editor of the *Quarterly Review* gave credence to the story because a seaman named Alexander Smith was one of the crew of the *Bounty* and a 'time-piece made by Kendall' was aboard her when she sailed. His opinion of American veracity reflected the poor relations existing between the two countries which were to result in war between 1812 and 1814.

Those mutineers who went to Pitcairn were fortunate that the year of the mutiny was also the year of the French Revolution, and Britain was soon embroiled in war with France. Between 1793 and the war's end in 1815 the British Admiralty had more urgent demands on its fleet than sending a second expedition to find one ageing mutineer not captured by the first. The report of Folger's news was duly noted and filed by the Admiralty. There it was forgotten and the small community at Pitcairn was left to its own devices for many more long years.

IV

Life in Eden

The final year of the eighteenth century had seen the last murder on Pitcairn with the axing to death of Matthew Quintal. The beginning of the nineteenth century witnessed the first death of a man by natural causes, when Edward Young died. John Adams was now the sole adult male. The community was overwhelmingly female and it was the actions and values of the women that were largely to influence the children and subsequent generations. Nevertheless, a particular culture and community had grown from the unique fusion of European males and Tahitian females. Visitors were impressed by just how scrupulously Adams had instilled religious observance into this second generation. An extract from the journal of Captain Henry King of the *Elizabeth* remarks on this piety. The *Elizabeth* was a whaling ship and the captain decided to 'refresh the crew' before facing the dangers of Cape Horn and the voyage home. On 3 March 1819 he wrote, 'I stood the ship close in to what the inhabitants call Ship Landing-place.' Nine young men of the island came out to him and he gave them a meal on his ship:

> Putting their hands before them, in the position of prayer, and saying grace, they began to refresh themselves . . . After their repast, they returned thanks to God, in the same pious manner as before. They then went on deck, where they gave surprising proofs of their agility, by going aloft, jumping overboard, and swimming round the ship, while it was going through the water at the rate of two knots per hour.[1]

The surf was so heavy that, like so many other seamen faced with landing in Bounty Bay, he decided it was unsafe, but finally agreed to try when the Pitcairners promised that if the boat capsized they would save him. He was equally impressed with the way in which women came swimming out into the surf to hold and steady the boat as it came into the shore. That dangerous landing had been the islanders' protection, as Lieutenant James Lowry, there on the HMS *Sparrow-hawk* in 1839, observed, 'It is a good thing for them that there is no anchorage, as they stand less chance of being corrupted by communication with the crews of the whale ships – the only ones that ever touch there, except the yearly men-of-war.'[2] Although the number of whale ships calling there increased over the years, few went ashore, most having their supplies taken out to them by the islanders. Most whalers preferred to sail on to Tahiti and similar islands where women and drink were available, and where the tough and reckless crews made such places bywords of drunkenness and licentiousness.

Once ashore, visitors were faced with a track which climbed steeply up to the village some hundred yards above sea-level. One ship's doctor found this path up to the settlement so steep that he had to be carried. Captain Beechey surveyed the island in December 1825 and his account is the most complete source of information for life as it then was and, by implication, life as it had been. He noted that the paths and trackways further inland were so steep and slippery as to be virtually impassable in wet weather to anyone but an islander. He described the highest part of the island as a ridge only three feet wide with 'two fearful precipices' either side. It was from this highest part of the island where it ended in sheer precipices and cliffs to the sea that he was shown 'Christian's Cave' where Christian had kept his supplies and had been prepared to make his last stand should the navy ever seek to capture him. Beechey writes how, on one occasion when they were touring the island:

> borrowing help from others, and grasping at every tuft of grass and bough that offered its friendly support, we were overtaken by a bunch of chubby little children, trudging unconcernedly on, munching a water melon, and balancing on their heads calabashes of water, which they had brought from the opposite side of the island.[3]

Beechey describes how the visitors often had to clamber on all fours and how he and his party could not have safely crossed many of the slopes without the help of their guides who gave them a hand and kept them from danger. Even a large landing party would have been hard put to have apprehended the mutineers in such terrain.

Beechey was most impressed with the physique and health of the islanders. He found a population of sixty-six, already encompassing a third generation. All were well housed and well fed, living indeed in a state of well-being which was Eden-like when compared with the housing, health and diet of the average lower-class British citizen in the early nineteenth century. It was the care and health of the children which impressed him most. This was due to the women and stemmed from their Polynesian culture which accorded so much respect, love and freedom to children. In spite of all the violence that had surrounded them, and in which they had taken part, they had never allowed demoralization to affect their role as mothers. The immense care the women gave to children was not simply due to any supposed maternal instinct, but also to the fact that in their culture infants were sacred beings and 'the Head of the Family'.[4] Even though there were, before disease and accident, only twelve women, they had ample knowledge of childbirth and how to cope with it. Contemporary visitors to Tahiti recorded that girls of seven or eight years old regularly played at giving birth by realistically imitating a woman in labour and dropping a doll from between their legs, complete with umbilical cord – thus demonstrating an early knowledge of the physical aspects of birth. Midwifery was not the specialist skill of one or two particular women but was knowledge common to them all. Births seem to have been controlled to some extent as, apparently, they all took place at night and after a labour of about five hours. No birth on the island had been fatal and there had been no twins or miscarriages recorded. Between 1790 and 1825 there had been sixty-two births, all successful. Only two offspring had died natural deaths as children, and one had died in an accident. The first generation born to the original settlers ended up an even eleven of each sex, including Sarah, the babe-in-arms who arrived with them, although grand-children were imbalanced at fifteen girls and twenty-two boys.

Mr Collie, the ship's surgeon, who investigated these issues with Captain Beechey, gave a graphic tribute from an un-expected (male) quarter:

> The treatment of their children differs from that of our own country, as the infant is bathed three times a day in cold water, and is sometimes not weaned for three or four years; but as soon as that takes place it is fed on 'popoe', made with ripe plantains and boiled taro rubbed into a paste. Upon this simple nourishment children are reared to a more healthy state than in other countries, and are free from fevers and other complaints peculiar to the greater part of the world . . . nothing is more extraordinary in the history of the island than the uniform good health of the children; the teething is easily got over, they have no bowel complaints, and are exempt from those contagious diseases which affect children in large communities.[5]

Clearly the islanders' isolation gave them protection from con-tagious diseases. Even making an allowance for that, in any comparison with the health of the citizens of the towns and ports of civilized Britain (where the infant mortality rate in the poorer areas would have meant the deaths of between a quarter to a half of all births, as well as damage to the health of many mothers), the ease with which this small community handled population increase must have been a revelation. The children themselves also impressed visitors with their social confidence and good manners, exercised within their large freedom.

> Their children are stout and shrewd little urchins, familiar and confident, but at the same time well behaved. They are early inured to aquatic exercises; and it amused us not a little to see small creatures, of two or three years old, sprawling in the surf which broke on the beach . . . whilst older children, amus[e] themselves with their surf-boards.[6]

Such a free and easy childhood owed very little to European culture.

The original women settlers had suffered their casualties. The deaths of Paurai and Sarah, who fell to their deaths while engaged in the dangerous work of collecting birds' eggs from the cliffs, and of Pashotu who had died from natural causes, have already been recorded. Those three were dead by 1800, and by the time Jenny left the island in 1817 two more women had died. One was Vahineatua, who had been Mills's wife and mother of his two children, and was then Adams's wife from 1793, bearing him three children. No woman had more children than she, but tragically she 'was killed, being pierced by a goat in her bowels when she was with child'.[7] The other, Teatuahitea, Brown's wife, who had overheard Toofaiti singing about the plan to kill the whites, died of dropsy. Between 1817, when Jenny left, and 1825, when Beechey arrived, two more women had died from natural causes, so Beechey found only five of the original women settlers still alive. He barely commented on them, but his description of their daughters is detailed:

> They almost all wore the cloth of the island: their dress consisted of a petticoat, and a mantle loosely thrown over the shoulders, and reaching to the ancles. Their stature was rather above the common height; and their limbs, from being accustomed to work and climb the hills, had acquired unusual muscularity; but their features and manners were perfectly feminine. Their complexion, though fairer than that of the men, was of a dark gipsy hue, but its deep colour was less conspicuous, by being contrasted with dark glossy hair, which hung down over their shoulders in long waving tresses, nicely oiled: in front it was tastefully turned back from the forehead and temples, and was retained in that position by a chaplet of small red or white aromatic blossoms, newly gathered from the flower-tree (*morinda citrifolia*), or from the tobacco plant; their countenances were lively and good-natured, their eyes dark and animated, and each possessed an enviable row of teeth.[8]

Clearly the Polynesian contribution to the constitution of the new Pitcairners was a healthy one. The myth of the 'noble savage' may have coloured his perceptions, but the simple demographic record and observable health of the islanders shows that the myth had some basis in reality – at least, in comparison with European populations.

Of the original male contingent, only Adams survived to be described by Beechey as being 'in his sixty-fifth year, and . . . unusually strong and active for his age, notwithstanding the inconvenience of considerable corpulency'.[9] It is known however, that a number of the sailors had been noted for their strength, and Christian, an officer, had also been proud of his strength and agility. All were healthy, apart from Young who died, most probably, from asthma. During the voyage however, and before the mutiny, a number of men needed the attention of the ship's doctor, including Adams whose 'name appears on the ship's venereal disease treatment list; he was debited thirty shillings for treatment by Surgeon Huggan and assistant Ledward. The list included seventeen members of the crew debited with from fifteen to forty-five shillings.'[10] Paying the ship's doctor for medical treatment was common practice, so becoming infected was a financial blow for an able seaman earning only twenty-four shillings a month. Other Pitcairn settlers who were listed as being treated for venereal disease were William Brown, Fletcher Christian and Matthew Quintal. Given that the cure for venereal disease was beyond the medical skill available, this might have been misdiagnosis, as only the Europeans fathered children and they and subsequent generations were perfectly healthy. Of those men treated for venereal disease, only Brown had no children. Adams fathered four (two after all the other males were dead), Christian fathered three with Isabella, and Quintal five, with two women, which means that those three men alone were responsible for three-quarters of all the children born to the nine mutineers. Young fathered five children, with two women, and both McKoy and Mills fathered two, each with the same woman.

As two women died shortly after they arrived at the island, there were only ten women to bear children. Of the ten however, four remained childless, which suggests that some control was being exercised by them. We have already considered the claim that Tahitian women could induce abortion by external massage, and so control births, if not conception. Although it is doubtful that the method was successful in all cases, it seems reasonable to suppose that a willingness to bear children signified, if not pleasure or satisfaction with their partner and their lot, at least an acceptance of the situation and a readiness to create life and commence the endless cycle of generation necessary to sustain any community. Jenny, Martin's wife from 1790, who was so eager to leave the island that she destroyed her house, may have remained childless because the opportunity to escape was better if one was not pregnant or caring for infants. Teatuahitea, wife to Brown; Mareva, who was the woman of Menalee, Nehow and Timoa; and Prudence, the woman of Oha and Titahiti, all remained childless. As the white men had the power to choose, one assumes that they left the women who were least attractive in their eyes to the native men. These four might well have been the most dissatisfied of the women. Of the other six women, Toofaiti seemed very eager to have a white husband and actually helped to kill her native husband Tararo, to whom she bore no children. Although she had none by Williams with whom she lived next, she had three children in less than six years when she became part of Young's household of several women, after the massacre of the whites.

None of the women became pregnant (or they resorted to abortion) during the three months that they were wandering on the ocean and their futures were uncertain. Isabella, Christian's partner, did not become pregnant during their seven months together at Toobouai and on the voyage, yet conceived immediately on arrival at the island. The *Bounty* was burned on 23 January and she gave birth to their child named Thursday October nine months after the decision to settle. Isabella was to have three children by Christian, and two by Young after she became part of his household following the massacre. Vahineatua, wife of Mills, also had five children – two by Mills and, after the massacre, three by Adams. Mary, McKoy's wife, had one baby born in Tahiti (father unknown), two by McKoy and another one to Adams after the massacre. Rather surprisingly, as we've seen, Young's wife, Susannah, whose actions demonstrated her commitment to him, was childless during the ten years she lived with him, but gave birth to a child shortly after his death, whose father was Quintal. In general however, the timing of births and the bearing of children by one male and not another does suggest that the women were controlling fertility. Sarah is the one woman whose behaviour contradicts the assumption that it was the contented women who had children. She gave birth to four of Quintal's children, despite the fact that he was undoubtedly the most violent and cruel of the men and treated all the natives, men and women, with the most abuse. Whatever the reason, the end result was that four women remained childless, two more died too soon to have had children, two women had five children each, two had four, one had three and one had one – amounting to twenty-one births from the first generation on the island, including baby Sarah.

The second generation seem to have been exceptionally fit and healthy. Beechey states that:

> Their simple food and early habits of exercise given them a muscular power and activity not often surpassed. It is recorded among the feats of strength which these people occasionally evince, that two of the strongest on the island, George Young and Edward Quintal, have each carried, at one time, without inconvenience . . . [loads] . . . amounting to upwards of six hundredweight.[11]

On his first visit to Beechey's ship Adams was accompanied by the island's young men, who were 'ten in number . . . tall, robust, and healthy, with good-natured countenances, which would any where have produced them a friendly reception.'[12] These youths averaged 5 feet 10 inches, with a range of 5 feet 9 inches to the tallest, who just exceeded 6 feet. According to Beechey: 'Their features are regular and well-looking, without being handsome.'[13] Although none of the Polynesian men fathered a child, the Polynesian genes were predominant in the shape of nose and lips, and the fact that the eyes were mainly brown, the hair black – with only one exception – and facial hair very sparse by European standards. The Tahitian inheritance was also strong where their relationship with the ocean was concerned:

> In the water they are almost as much at home as on land, and can remain nearly a whole day in the sea. They frequently swam round their little island, the circuit of which is at the least seven miles. When the sea beat heavily on the island they have plunged into breakers, and swam to sea beyond them. This they sometimes did pushing a barrel of water before them, when it could be got off in no other way, and in this matter we procured several tons of water without a single cask being stove.[14]

At the time Beechey saw it in 1825, Pitcairn's hamlet consisted of only five dwellings, with four more at a separate location, and three or four up on higher ground. He described Adams's house as being 'situated higher up the hill than the village' as he 'has retired from the bustle of the hamlet to a more quiet and sequestered spot . . . and there are four other cottages to the eastward which belong to the Youngs and Quintals.'[15] Settlement on the island was scattered for such a small area, much of which was unsuitable for building – even that reflected the influence of the Tahitians, who did not concentrate dwellings in villages. If, however, even in so small a place the 'bustle' created by five houses could appear too hectic for a European such as Adams then the sense of individualism must have been strong. As we have seen, the houses were quite substantial and owed more to European models than native ones. Their palm thatching and sliding shutters instead of tile roofs and glass windows were dictated by the available materials.

Although the mutineers had excluded the Polynesians from a share in the cultivable land, it required collective effort and teamwork to strip the *Bounty*, to move all the material up on to the plateau and to perform some of the tasks related to house-building. It is strange that a more communal form of economic life did not emerge sooner from these origins or from their previous experience of the unity of effort needed to sail the ship. The degree of individualism among the mutineers had been their downfall. At the time of the first revolt, when Adams and Williams each took a wife from the Polynesian men, there had been evidence of a collective response from the white men. But their indifference to each other at the time of the later massacre had implied that they were living in a state of virtual alienation from each other. Those killings, however, did force the remaining four into some sense of mutual interdependence and co-operation. After the women settled down in peace again, the men seemed to take part in more group activities. Beechey wrote,

> The occupations of the men continued similar to those already related, occasionally enlivened by visits to the opposite side of the island. They appear to have been more sociable; dining frequently at each other's houses, and contributing more to the comfort of the women, who, on their part, gave no grounds for uneasiness. There was also a mutual accommodation amongst them in regard to provisions, of which a regular account was taken. If one person was successful in hunting, he lent the others as much meat as they required, to be repaid at leisure; and the same occurred with yams, taros, etc., so that they lived in a very domestic and tranquil state.[16]

It is significant that the greater sociability was something worthy of special note. It was a sociability sealed with alcohol: McKoy and Quintal made their own stills and Adams and the women also indulged in drunken sprees, at least up until the suicide of McKoy.

The island and the sea provided not only a plentiful diet, but a varied and healthy one. The sailors, enured to a diet of salt beef and hard biscuit, had become well-fed peasants:

> Immediately round the village are the small enclosures for fattening pigs, goats, and poultry; and beyond them, the

cultivated grounds producing the banana, plantain, melon, yam, taro, sweet potatoes, appai, tee, and cloth plant, with other useful roots, fruits, and shrubs, which extend far up the mountain and to the southward ... Every cottage has its out-house for making cloth, its baking-place, its sty, and its poultry-house.[17]

In general it seems that the culture of Pitcairn evolved from Polynesian or European practice along the lines of the traditional roles of male and female: the men retained a western desire for private property, and the women raised the children in the free Polynesian manner. The Europeans had brought their skills and knowledge with them, as well as the arms, tools, pots and pans, canvas and cordage, and all the varied products that were on the ship; and the Polynesians brought their skills and knowledge of the trees and plants, which enabled them to produce both food and clothing. Domestic practices, in the early years, were set mainly by the women as they controlled home life and child-rearing. The women were responsible for the preparation and cooking of all foods – though this differed from Tahitian practice. The many Tahitian taboos connected with food must have been eroded during the months on the *Bounty en route* to Pitcairn, perhaps because it was against the mutineers' perception of normal domestic roles for men to cook. On evidence from 1825, the women had re-established a collective method of working, however, with the food for everyone cooked by a small number on a rota basis. The main meal was generally eaten at noon, but meal times were not rigidly fixed, food being eaten whenever it was cooked. The women ate separately from the men according to their custom.

This communal form of working by the Polynesian women contrasts sharply with the individualism of the European men. It leaves something of a mystery as to how the two systems worked together, but there is not sufficient evidence to resolve it. It is clear, however, that once there was only one white man left alive – albeit a patriarch – the women returned to their own cultural pattern of more social forms of work. The white men's insistence on each house having its own baking place and so on would have caused some of the women discontent as it would have forced them to work in isolation rather than in the more communal system to which they were accustomed.

When Young died in 1800 the oldest girl was eleven years old, the oldest boy ten, and a dozen children were only six years old or younger. The amount of labour needed to cultivate, prepare and cook the food for this group, plus all the time required to care for and socialize a new generation fell to the remaining nine women and Adams. When Jenny left in 1817, Vahineatua and Teatuahitea were already dead and the community was left with only six women – and Adams – to sustain it. As the man who recorded Jenny's story when she returned to Tahiti in 1817 noted:

> They have hogs and fowls, and are very diligent in cultivating the ground: they dress their food like the Taheitians, having no boilers. They make cloth, and cloathe themselves like the Taheitians, the man with the maro and tibuta, the women with the paren and tibuta ... The women work hard in cultivating the ground, &c. This woman's hands are quite hard with work.[18]

That a European male should notice the callouses on a native woman's hands is some indication of how hard the labour was – or how much less women laboured in Tahiti. This need for labour also meant that the children and young people of Pitcairn could not enjoy such a carefree existence as they would have had they lived in Tahiti.

The population was set to leap ahead as the second generation reached puberty. In 1805 or 1806, Thursday October Christian, the first child born on the island, married Susannah (widow of Edward Young) when he was only fifteen, and the first grandchild of a mutineer was born the following year. There was a danger of having more mouths to feed than there were arms to do the work. Sir Thomas Staines observed the problem when he was there in 1814:

> The younger part of the females were obliged to attend, with Old Adams and their brothers, to cultivate the land, and

Captain Pipon thinks that this may be one reason why this old director of the work does not countenance too early marriages, for, as he very properly observed, when once they become mothers, they are less capable of hard labour, being obliged to attend to their children.[19]

Other visitors stated that Adams would not permit two young people to marry until they had cleared for cultivation enough land to support a family. The low ratio of adults to very young children left them less time for leisure than had been customary in Tahiti. Not only that, there were too few people to sustain a variety of recreational or cultural activities in the traditional sense. What little there was seem to have been half-ashamed remnants of Polynesian song and dance. That there was little or no trace of the European tradition is not surprising – there were no European instruments, and when first discovered the islanders knew only one European tune:

> They did not appear to have the least ear for music: one of the officers took considerable pains to teach them the hundredth psalm, that they might not chaunt all the psalms and hymns to the same air; but they did not evince the least aptitude or desire to learn it.[20]

Apart from that 'same air' (not specified) for religious purposes, all the music-making was derived from Polynesian tradition. That in itself was attenuated from their first arrival on the island because there was no longer any flute music – such as Timoa had played for Susannah. Captain King, who went ashore with some of his crew in March 1819, was given a welcome which owed much to traditional Tahitian hospitality:

> In the evening, after supper, they entertained us with an Otaheitian dance, which consisted of various writhings and distortions of the body, by no means obscene, yet in no respect pleasant. While some were dancing, the rest sat down to look on, in company with six sailors belonging to the ship, when suddenly one of the young women jumped up and ran to her brother, saying 'she would not sit any longer near that naughty man (pointing to one of my sailors), for

he wanted her to commit fornication'. I asked the man why he behaved so rude to people who had treated him so well? He told me that it was a mere accident he put his foot against hers, and that he had never spoken to her.[21]

The sailor's excuse sounds a bit thin but, had he been in Tahiti or on many of the other islands, he would have found a response very much more to his liking and relief.

By the time Beechey arrived some six years later he found that the islanders rarely danced, and he had to ask them to give a demonstration, which they gave solely to please an important guest:

> He [Arthur, son of Quintal] was seated upon the ground, as head musician, and had before him a large gourd, and a piece of music wood (porou), which he balanced nicely upon his toes, that there might be the less interruption to its vibrations. He struck the instrument alternately with two sticks, and was accompanied by Dolly [Dorothy Young], who performed very skilfully with both hands upon a gourd, which had a longitudinal hole cut in one end of it; rapidly beating the orifice with the palms of her hands, and releasing it again with uncommon dexterity, so as to produce a tattoo, but in perfect time with the other instrument. A third performed upon the Bounty's old copper fish-kettle, which formed a sort of bass. To this exhilarating music three *grown-up* females stood up to dance, but with a reluctance which showed it was done only to oblige us, as they consider such performances an inroad upon their usual innocent pastimes. The figure consisted of such parts of the Otaheitan dance as were thought most decorous, and was little more than a shuffling of the feet, sliding past each other, and snapping their fingers.[22]

Traditional Tahitian dance is noted for its rhythmic swaying and sensual body movements. His underlining of 'grown-up' implies that the dancers were from the original settlers who would have known the full range and implications of the dance and Beechey recorded that there was a lot of laughter from the 'female spectators' at what was obviously a secret joke –

'association of ridiculous ideas' is his expression – between them. Clearly all elements of overtly displayed sensuality had been suppressed, and without it there was little left of their dance. Given the role that sexual desire had played in the history of the island, its suppression is perhaps understandable.

By 1850 Brodie found that the women of Pitcairn never danced, they were too modest and shy, although they did join in games of blind man's buff and 'many other innocent games'. The islanders' musical repertoire was widening and Edward Quintal had acquired a fiddle on which he expertly played hornpipes and reels learned by ear from passing ships. Brodie and another visitor added to their attainments by teaching them new vocal skills as they still had no idea of harmony. The lessons were much appreciated, but it seems that Adams had enforced puritan attitudes which became even more deeply entrenched in the second and subsequent generations. Adams may have been the agent through whom the islanders took to the Christian faith, but perhaps its message of denial also felt appropriate on that small island with its special history.

Religion was certainly the domain where European culture became dominant, but this happened slowly. It is said that William Brown baptized Fletcher Christian's first child, but the mutineers did not hold any religious services, nor, for all that is known, did the Polynesians. The first recorded clash that may in any sense be defined as religious came over the disposal of the five skulls. It was a clash which Young instigated and won by trickery and it was the first assertion of Christian over pagan practice, although it is by no means certain that 'religion' rather than 'social custom' was the motivating force. Beechey makes two observations which imply that during the period of the killings men were buried pretty well where they fell: one confirms Christian's yam patch as the location of his death and burial. Yams were grown some distance from the village on the other side of the island, up on the higher ground: 'Here the mutineers originally built their summer-houses, for the purpose of enjoying the breeze and overlooking the yam grounds, which are more productive than those lower down. Near these plantations . . . a spot is pointed out as the place where Christian was *first* [my italics] buried.'[1] He also remarks that near the village, 'Within the enclosure of palm-trees is the cemetery where the few persons who had died on the island, together with those who met with violent deaths, are deposited',[2] implying that the bodies were not left to rot in the open but were collected for 'proper' burial after their original interment.

Only after the deaths of McKoy and Quintal did Adams and Young determine that new attitudes and values must be instilled into the younger generation if the horrors of the past were not to be repeated. They started to teach the young to read and write, and the source of their lessons and precepts was the Bible: 'They now, however, resolved to have morning and evening family prayers, to add afternoon service to the duty of the Sabbath, and to train up their own children, and those of their late unfortunate companions, in piety and virtue.'[3] After Young's death Adams suffered a deep sense of isolation and guilt, and turned increasingly to the Bible: the printed word being both the only source of his language and the path to absolution for his crimes. It was the textbook from which the children were taught English:

> He [Adams], nevertheless, had an arduous task to perform. Besides the children to be educated, the Otaheitan women were to be converted; and as the example of the parents had a powerful influence over their children, he resolved to make them his first care. Here also his labours succeeded; the Otaheitans were naturally of a tractable disposition, and gave him less trouble than he anticipated: the children also acquired such a thirst after scriptural knowledge, that Adams in a short time had little else to do than to answer their inquiries and put them in the right way.[4]

It was a move which did him no harm when he was found by the authorities. The image of this gentle patriarch converting a community of pagan women, taking the care to instruct the children in the Christian religion and insisting upon daily prayers as well as Sunday services was highly acceptable to the evangelical spirit of the age. It confirmed his repentance for his crimes as genuine, and him as worthy in turn of benevolence and mercy from the legal penalties that were his proper due. It was, however, a genuine and long-standing endeavour on Adams's part, for the teaching of children had been happening for some time before Folger arrived in 1808:

> The girls and boys were made to read and write before Captain Folger, to show him the degree of their improvement. They did themselves great credit in both, particularly the girls. The stationary of the Bounty was an important addition to the books, and was so abundant that the islanders were not yet in want of any thing in this department for the progress of their school.[5]

It was through the existence of the printed word rather than patriarchy that English became the dominant language, in spite of the fact that the women were more numerous and talked to the children in their own language. Adams taught them English and contact with the outside world through visiting ships confirmed its primacy. It is clear too that Adams gave the children some knowledge of the world beyond Pitcairn. On Folger's first contact the children of the mutineers were well aware of their own origins in Britain – even if they had not heard of the United States of America. In return for the hospitality shown to him and his crew, and in payment for the supplies they provided for his voyage home (1819), Captain King repaid them with gifts in kind:

> I gave them a whale-boat, in return for their refreshments, some books, razors, combs, and, in short, everything they stood in need of; but nothing pleased them so well as the books: as they wished much to read and write ... They got nearly two hundred books, of various descriptions, from officers and crew; – even the sailors belonging to the ship behaved with a degree of modesty in the presense of those naked females, that would have surprised a Joseph Andrews.[6]

The islanders' thirst for books confirms the value they placed on literacy and the efforts they went to in order to support a school. The fact that the whaler was able to furnish them with two hundred books is very interesting. Apart from the compara- tively high cost, it contradicts the reputation of whaling-ship crews as the toughest and most lawless men sailing the oceans. In all, on sailing, they felt that they were 'leaving a people whom we considered in a moral point of view as far superior to any of the human species we ever beheld'.[7] Such sentiments were to be repeated time and again in descriptions of the islanders' conduct and community.

There is no doubt that Adams did undergo a change in behaviour and, as this happened long before he had been dis- covered, it might be taken as genuine. This intention to educate and to instil a strict moral code into the children was reinforced when, 'about ten years after [being left the sole man], Adams had a most extraordinary dream, which was that the angel Gab- riel came down from heaven and warned him of his danger for his past wickedness'.[8] It has been suggested that these visions (he had had others) were *delirium tremens* rather than religious mania but, given his subsequent behaviour, religious mania seems to have been the long-term result, whatever the initial cause. He became even more insistent on religious observance. Not well educated himself, he confused the import of Ash Wednesday and Good Friday and came to the conclusion that every Wednesday and every Friday should be total fast days, causing the hearty-eating Polynesian women to faint in the fields. It was during this period that Dinah, Adams's eldest daughter, slipped from his high moral code and had an illegiti- mate child by Edward Quintal. Adams ordered that she be shot for the sin of fornication. All the islanders argued against such an extreme penalty for what Tahitians had never considered a sin, and no one would agree to carry out the sentence. He then prepared to do it himself, but Arthur Quintal intervened and would not permit it. Adams then forbade the couple to marry. Captain King observed that, 'Adams on this occasion, probably changed his mind through interest, for he will not suffer his daughters to marry for fear of losing their labour in cultivating his plantation'.[9] This was the first cynical, or even less than laudatory, comment applied to Adams. Adams was aware of his own lack of knowledge and frequently bowed to the opinions of those more widely informed than himself, and Captain King persuaded him that he should let the unhappy couple marry. Also on the advice of visitors, he was to allow Wednesday to be treated as a normal day again and after his death, Friday was also abandoned as a fast day. Sunday was observed as a day of complete rest and no cooking was allowed.

This image of Adams as a terrifying Old Testament figure willing to slaughter his own daughter for transgressing the moral code is very much at odds with later accounts, which present him as amiable and loving. This is not necessarily contradictory: Adams may well have mellowed with age. It is interesting that his first visitor, Captain Folger, was wholly without criticism and could hardly have praised him more highly, giving special note to the way in which he instructed the children in religion. Adams's own conversion together with the perception that he was more liable to be well received, and perhaps forgiven for his crimes, if he showed the world a blameless God-fearing community could well explain his severity in the early years. His growing trust that he would not be punished, and his final assurance on that score, because of the encomiums his community received and the respect which visiting captains, some of whom were Honourables, accorded him – a common sailor – in dining and conversing with him as an equal, must have done much to give him the confidence to relax his strictures.

Although some of the over-zealousness abated, Adams's rather dour interpretation of the Scriptures, together with the small number of people involved and the struggle for existence, turned the Pitcairners into a serious people, so that by the 1840s they were without verbal humour:

> During the whole time I was with them I never heard them indulge in a joke, or other levity; and the practise of it is apt to give offence. They are so accustomed to take what is said in its literal meaning, that irony was always considered a

falsehood in spite of explanation. They could not see the propriety of uttering what was not strictly true for any purpose whatever.[10]

It would not be surprising if the experience of deceit and trickery which had been an integral part of the killings had left the community with a distaste for anything but an honest expression of intent. What, at first glance, seems more surprising is the degree to which the community was 'European', given that Adams was the sole European for so long. There was however, good reason for it: language was the key. In spite of its remoteness Pitcairn was no longer isolated. From the time it was discovered the community had an ever-growing contact with passing ships, and English was the means of communication with their crews. This gradually reinforced the European dimension of the culture.

On the other hand, when Captain Pipon visited Pitcairn in 1814, he observed that the clothing for both sexes was still basically Tahitian:

> The first who came on board the Briton was Thursday October Christian . . . about twenty-five years of age, a tall fine young man about six feet high, with dark black hair, and a countenance extremely open and interesting; he wore no clothes except a piece of cloth round his loins, a straw hat ornamented with *black cock's feathers*, and occasionally a *peacock's* . . . a great share of good humour and a willingness to oblige . . . he was accompanied by another young man, by the name of George Young, a very fine youth of about seventeen or eighteen years of age, who also spoke English perfectly well, – indeed it was their common and general language.[11]

The clothing of the women was also made of traditional native material. Pipon's reference to 'linen' is to the native-made bark cloth:

> The women, or rather the young girls, although they have only the examples of their mothers to follow in their dress, (who are Otaheitian women,) are much more modestly clad

than any of the females we saw at the Marquesas. They have
invariably a piece of linen reaching from the waist to the
knees, and generally a mantle, or something of that nature,
thrown loosely over the shoulders, and hanging as low as the
ancles; this, however, is frequently thrown aside and often
entirely off, so that it is intended to shelter them more from
the heat of the sun, or any severity of the weather, than for
the sake of modesty, for frequently the upper part of the
body is entirely exposed, and it is not possible to behold finer
forms.[12]

His view of the young people of the island was highly flattering.
'The young men born on the island are extremely fine and
very athletic. The young women are still more to be admired,
wonderfully strong, of most pleasing countenances, and a degree
of modesty and bashfulness that would do honour to the most
virtuous nation.'[13] This combination of beauty and virtue was
universally commented on by early observers. Bennett seems
to be the only observer who was less than enthusiastic about
the looks of the islanders, mainly because, it would seem from
the tone of his comments, he did not admire non-European
features. But he is obliged to acknowledge that, 'their disposition is frank, honest, and hospitable to the extreme', and to
admit that their manner was pleasing:

> A modest demeanour, a large show of good humour, an
> artless and retiring grace, render the females peculiarly pre-
> possessing. Some of the younger women have also pleasing
> countenances; but, on the whole, little can be said in favour
> of their beauty. They bear an influencial sway both in dom-
> estic and public politics; and this they are better calculated
> to do, since they are intelligent, active, and robust, partake
> in the labours of their husbands with cheerfulness, live virtu-
> ous in all stations of life.[14]

It is as if, as he writes, he is obliged by his observations and the
treatment he received to acknowledge the good qualities of the
people. The most significant of his comments, which shows his
shrewdness, are those on the *power* of the women in domestic

and public spheres: this was later to be expressed in formal law.

When Beechey arrived some ten years later, although obviously impressed by the islanders simply as fine examples of the human race he was less impressed with the dress of the young men. Adams was 'properly' dressed in a sailor's shirt and trousers and a low-crowned hat, but the dress of the young men was the cause of some amusement to the ship's crew as it consisted of oddments of European clothing which had been given by the various ships. Friday October Christian (his name was changed from 'Thursday' when it was discovered that the settlers were a day behind, having lost a day by nearly circumnavigating the world) was drawn as he appeared on that visit: his wearing of a waistcoat without a shirt caused even more amusement than the feathers in his hat. Originally the mutineers had continued to dress in European style, with clothes made from canvas taken ashore from the *Bounty*, while the women made theirs in the traditional manner by beating out the material from tree bark. The boys and, as they grew up, the young men had dressed in native cloth and style. After increasing contact with shipping, though, the men had adopted European dress (of sorts) supplied to them by passing ships, while the girls continued to dress in the Polynesian fashion. The native dress was not to last much longer, and by the time Lieutenant James Lowry arrived in 1839 on the HMS *Sparrow-hawk*, 'the women and girls dress in a loose sort of dressing-gown, not confined at the waist, and coming close to the neck', a version of the dreadful Mother Hubbard which missionaries imposed on islanders throughout the Pacific.[15]

All visitors were most impressed with the modesty and virtue of the women, virtue that is, as understood by Christian morality; and this was in such sharp distinction to the sexual mores of most Pacific islanders that it appeared that European culture had suppressed and replaced Tahitian culture. An alternative view is that the Tahitian reputation for debauchery was much exaggerated anyway. James Morrison, one of the mutineers who stayed at Tahiti, and lived with the natives when there were no European ships and crews to disturb the even tenor of life, wrote that in normal times the lower classes were much less licentious than the Tahitian aristocracy. However, he continued, 'their whole system was overturned by the arrival of a ship, their manners were there as much altered from their Common Course, as those of our own Country are at a Fair'.[16] He goes on to state that to the islanders iron was as valuable as gold was to Europeans and he supposed that if Europeans had received strange visitors who handed gold to those that pleased them there would have been many willing to sell themselves for such riches.

In any event, morality on Pitcairn eventually conformed to what evangelical Christians would have liked in England. The conflicts over women had been at the root of bloodshed on the island, so the change to virginity before marriage and strict monogamy after it might be ascribed to this particular mutual experience rather than the domination of one culture over another. Pipon was witness to the depth and regularity of worship: 'They invariably say grace before and after meat, and frequently repeat their prayers. They know the Lord's Prayer and, I believe, the Creed.'[17] Once again, it was Bennett who found their religiosity more trying than many others, or more trying than many others were prepared to admit: 'In conducting the most trivial affairs they are guided by the Scriptures, which they have read diligently, and from which they quote with a freedom and frequency that rather impairs the effect.'[18] The status of John Adams and his possession of a Bible no doubt directly influenced which religion was followed. It is doubtful anyway whether the community on Pitcairn was large enough to sustain Tahitian religion, with its complex social rituals and its multiplicity of deities; whereas the Christian, indeed the Protestant, religion, with its emphasis on individual reform and a personal relationship to God, was more sustainable within such a small population.

The early nineteenth century was a time of great religious activity in England and the discovery of the community immediately brought forth suggestions that one of the many missionary societies should take responsibility for its moral welfare. In spite of the degree of religion already practised by the community. Captain Delano, who knew the Pacific Islands and the activities and effect of the missionaries on them as well as any man, reacted strongly against the suggestion that missionaries should be sent to Pitcairn:

> To send missionaries among them, according to the proposal of some good people, would be an unfortunate experiment upon their peace and virtue, unless the individuals selected should be much more enlightened and liberal than any of that class of persons with whom I have been fortunate enough to be acquainted . . . let it be our fervent prayer that neither canting and hypocritical emissaries from schools of artificial theology on the one hand, nor sensual and licentious crews and adventurers on the other, may ever enter the charming village of Pitcairn to give disease to the minds or the bodies of the unsuspecting inhabitants.[19]

Subsequent events confirmed this view as all too prescient.

Other characteristics which impressed outsiders were the open-handed generosity and the integrity of the community. The very first visitor, Folger, recorded that he was treated with immense hospitality, given generous supplies of fresh foods, and met with such simple courtesy that he 'left this most interesting community with the keenest regret. It reminded him of Paradise, as he said, more than any effort of poetry or the imagination'.[20] Another witness was a passenger on the barque *Noble*, which called at Pitcairn *en route* to California because it was short of water. He and four passengers landed on the island on Sunday 24 March, 1850 and were given permission by the captain to spend the night ashore. The ship was to lie off the island during darkness, and pick up the passengers and final supplies the next day. This plan was foiled by worsening weather, and after two days of beating up into the weather the ship was finally forced away, leaving the five stranded – an example of the danger all sailors feared when they left their ships to land on Pitcairn.

Brodie later published his account of his stay, which described how impressed he was by the communal spirit of the islanders. All the island men smoked, but they were almost out of tobacco – yet with only half a pound left on the entire island, he was unhesitatingly given a share. As another example of their generosity he relates how, on 14 April, after he had been there about three weeks, the New Bedford whaler *George and Susan* arrived. It could not, however, take them on their way as it was outward bound to the whaling grounds. While collecting supplies, the ship's captain happened to mention that lime juice now cost the high price of sixty dollars a barrel in America. The islanders immediately started accumulating lime juice in barrels, so that when their uninvited visitors (who were penniless) were finally rescued they could take the juice to sell at their port of arrival. As it happened, *Colonist*, a English ship *en route* to North America with 120 passengers, and also short of water, arrived and took them off a few days later, before the barrels could be filled.

Brodie spent his time on the island busily noting the life of the people and recording the history of events as it was told to him by the islanders. In his view the community was unique:

> Such a society, so free, not only from vice, but even from those petty bickerings and jealousies – those minor infirmities which we are accustomed to suppose are ingrained in human nature – can probably not be paralleled elsewhere. It is the realisation of Arcadia, or what we had been accustomed to suppose had existence only in poetic imagination, – the golden age; all living as one family, a commonwealth of brothers and sisters, which, indeed, by ties of relationship they actually are ... there is neither wealth nor want, a primitive simplicity of life and manner, perfect equality in rank and station, and perfect content.[21]

This generosity and communal goodwill owed most to the influence of the Tahitian women, rather than the European men, but the vast majority of ships which visited were American or English, as were the goods bartered from the visitors, and this eroded the Tahitian element of the culture. As we have seen, Tahitian dance and music declined with European con-

tacts, and leisure and recreational activities came to be dominated by association with the Church. From the early years
every contact reinforced European influence and the Tahitian
language and culture were swamped. It was recorded that the
Pitcairners showed a great dislike of any negroes among ships'
crews. Even in their very first contact with the external world
through Captain Folger they had insisted that they were 'Englishmen'. As the second and subsequent generations flourished
as a mixed-race group, they were faced with a choice: they
could claim to be displaced Europeans, or they could be native
Pacific Islanders; they chose to be the former. It was John
Adams's most lasting contribution to the history of Pitcairn.
Because they were English-speaking Christians the islanders
were never referred to or treated as being anything other than
of British descent. Had they been perceived as natives, such a
small group may well have been taken for enforced labour or
slavery, and thus destroyed. They laid claim to the support and
protection of the Royal Navy and the navy accepted that claim,
which led to Pitcairn's eventual incorporation into the British
Empire. Before that step was taken, however, the growing
population threatened to exhaust the island's natural resources.

V

Beyond the Horizon

When the mutineers and the Polynesians first colonized Pitcairn the vegetation was in pristine condition. The island had been uninhabited for hundreds of years, and had no grazing animals. Small rats and lizards were the only indigenous quadrupeds, and there was only one species of land bird, a small fly-catcher, so every inch of suitable soil was covered with mature trees, shrubs or grasses. This cover held the soil in place and retained enough moisture to provide permanent water sources. Within thirty years of landing, agricultural exploitation was causing soil erosion, water and fuel shortages, and a lack of timber large enough for building. Indeed, their first discoverer, Captain Folger, entered in his logbook reservations about the availability of water, and he questioned the utility of the island to mariners.

> I think them very humane and hospitable people; and whatever may have been the errors or crimes of Smith [Adams], the mutineer, in times back, he is at present a worthy man, and may be useful to navigators who traverse this immense ocean . . . Be it remembered that this island is scantily supplied with fresh water, so that it is impossible for a ship to get a supply.[1]

He may have been there during one of the island's occasional droughts, as his comments were unduly pessimistic – the islanders were to water many ships in the future.

Few though they were, within some thirty-five years the Pitcairners had felled most of the useful timber. Beechey records:

> The toonena is a large tree, from which their houses and canoes are made. It is a hard, heavy, red-coloured wood, and grows on the upper parts of the island. There was formerly

a great abundance of this wood, but it is now become so
scarce as to require considerable search and labour to find
sufficient to construct a house.[2]

The population was felling timber far faster than it could grow;
it was also clearing ever larger areas for crops. The introduction
of alien species – goats and hogs – was destroying the vegetation
in the wilder, less accessible terrain. Eventually, as increasingly
large tracts of virgin forest were cleared, even the cultivated
crops became less productive:

> the bread-fruit, from some recent causes, is beginning to give
> very scanty crops. This failure Adams attributes to some trees
> being cut down, that protected them from the cold winds,
> which is not improbable; for at Otaheite, where the trees are
> exposed to the south-west winds, the crop is very indifferent.[3]

Captain Beechey was on the island, surveying and mapping it,
from 5 December to 21 December 1825 at a time when the
population had grown to sixty-six. In his opinion the island
was very favourable to cultivation and well able to sustain such
a population, but there were already fears of the consequences
of a poor harvest:

> The temperate climate of Pitcairn Island is extremely favour-
> able to vegetation, and agriculture is attended with compara-
> tively light labour. But as the population is increasing, and
> wants are generated which were before unthought of, the
> natives find it necessary to improve their mode of culture;
> and for this purpose they make use of sea-weed as a manure.
> They grow but one crop in a year of each kind. The time
> of taking up the yams, &c. is about April. The land is not
> allowed time to recover itself, but is planted again immedi-
> ately. Experience has enabled them to estimate, with tolerable
> precision, the quantity that will be required for the annual
> consumption of the island; this they reckon at 1000 yams
> to each person. The other roots, being considered more as
> luxuries, are cultivated in irregular quantities. The failure of
> a crop, so exactly estimated, must of course prove of serious
> consequences to the colony, and much anxiety is occasionally
> felt as the season approaches for gathering it. At times cold

south-westerly winds nip the young plants, and turn such as
are exposed to them quite black: during our visit several
plantations near the sea-coast were affected in this manner.
At other times caterpillars prove a great source of annoyance.[4]

In addition to population growth, increasing trade with the
outside world also contributed to the growing exhaustion of
resources. In the six years between 1813 and 1818 only two
ships called at the island, between 1819 and 1824, thirteen, and
in the six years between 1825 and 1830, visits increased to
twenty-three. These visitors were supplied with water and all
types of fresh food in return for other products. This bartering
of supplies not only created a more intensive agriculture but
also produced new needs as the islanders became habituated to
manufactured goods. Growing commercial activity beyond the
needs of simple subsistence led to concerns about the long-term
prospects of life on the island.

The first outside economic interference with the Pitcairn
community came, with the best intentions, from Captain
Henderson, who traded from Calcutta to South America with
his ship *Hercules*. He was one of the earliest seafarers to call at
Pitcairn and was so impressed that he decided he would do all
in his power to assist them. On his return to India he placed
an advertisement in the *Calcutta Journal* of Tuesday 13 July,
1819, asking for funds with which to buy tools and agricultural
equipment for the islanders which he would deliver on his next
voyage. The following week the newspaper published further
details of Pitcairn as given by Captain Henderson. It is clear
from this that he had had earlier correspondence with England
on the subject of the Pitcairners, for on that first visit, he states:
'I delivered to Adams a box of Books from the Missionary
Society of London, and a letter from Adams's brother, who is
still living in Wapping, London.' He also records that 'I left
them a ram, two ewes, and a lamb'.[5] The introduction of animals
from outside, especially the hogs and goats of the mutineers,
was doing immense damage to the environment and new species
were always an additional risk. As there was no further mention
of sheep on the island, one assumes that they failed to adapt to

the conditions or were slaughtered by the islanders for lack of sufficient grazing land. Goats, which the mutineers themselves had turned loose in order to supply themselves with 'wild' meat, were most destructive. Captain Beechey's ship carried a bull and a cow for the islanders but, perhaps fortunately for them, the cow died, so the now useless bull was slaughtered to feed the sailors who were on short rations. John Bechervaise, one of Beechey's seamen, who was lucky enough to be in the shore party, recalled how, despite any worries about shortages, the islanders supplied the ship with all the food they could spare and with wild goats in particular: 'During my stay I saw October Christian and young Adams run down several [goats], which were sent as presents to the ship'[6] – they emulated Robinson Crusoe in running them down on foot.

Not all later introductions were unwelcome. The breed of ducks the mutineers had brought with them was improved when Captain Waldegrave left some 'Moscovy' [sic] ducks. But another bull and a cow which came to them from Tahiti after the failure of Beechey's attempt were slaughtered because they damaged the fruit trees. Such large grazing animals really required too much precious land (and we might wonder at the variety of livestock carried aboard these ships and the amount of fodder and water which was required to sustain them on these long voyages). A smaller pest which came with these visitors, the mosquito, did not harm the environment, but did make life less pleasant. There were forty-five people on Pitcairn, including Adams and five of the original women settlers when Henderson promoted their welfare. The Pitcairners won an influential group of lobbyists in Britain and its empire, and Captain Henderson was to argue that: 'I cannot refrain from offering my opinion, that it [Pitcairn] is well worthy of the attention of our laudable religious societies, particularly that for the propagating the Christian Religion.'[7]

Meanwhile the British community in Calcutta had responded to Captain Henderson's appeal with interest and generosity. On his next voyage he was able to deliver to Pitcairn, as a gift from those residents, tools of all kinds for working land, as well as

timber and iron, cooking utensils and a professionally constructed 22-foot-long cutter, to enable them to fish further out
to sea than was possible in their home-made canoes. In addition
to his planned contribution, passing ships introduced other
plants and trees, such as the orange, to add variety to those food
plants the mutineers had carried with them.

As the population grew with the birth of a second and third
generation, the ownership of the land was sub-divided through
inheritance. It was divided equally between female and male
children: on marriage both husband and wife were immediately
given a portion of land from each of their parents. Small-scale
ownership can add to the problems of planning and control for
mutual benefit, but ownership on Pitcairn had never bestowed
absolute rights. It had always been accepted that those who
cared for crops had rights to the produce, even if they did not
own the land: 'From earliest times it has been customary for
any Islander to be free to plant coco-nut, orange and mango
trees on anyone's [land], and retain their ownership; each family
possesses a registered trade mark which is chipped into the trunk
of trees.'[8]

As more of the natural tree cover was cut for building and
fuel, more land was put down to fruit trees and other cultivation.
Inevitably, as the population increased so did the area of cultivated land, which meant the steeper slopes had to be cleared
and used, increasing water run-off and soil erosion. The big
fear, in the early years, was that through an unseasonable frost
or drought or blight there could be a crop failure which would
leave them starving. But as it was now a regular calling place
for passing ships, that danger lessened. If ships' demands for
supplies increased agricultural exploitation of limited resources,
they also virtually removed the chances of the population dying
from an unreported famine. In spite of this, there was a growing
current of opinion urging the removal of the Pitcairners from
the island.

John Adams was deeply concerned with the future well-being
of his community and, aware of his increasing age, worried that
his death would leave the island leaderless and vulnerable. In

October 1823 he discussed his anxieties with Captain Hall of the London whaling-ship *Cyrus*. Adams said that he needed a younger man, better educated then himself, to take his place and to teach the young. Hall gave him permission to solicit one of his crew to live with them as a permanent settler. John Buffett, aged twenty-six, described as 'a well-educated Bristol shipwright and joiner', had the right mix of skills and abilities, and volunteered to stay. John Evans, a nineteen-year-old friend of Buffett, also volunteered to stay, but was not invited to by the islanders, nor given permission to leave by his captain; he deserted his ship anyway by the simple expedient of hiding ashore until the ship was obliged to sail.

Buffett took over the teaching in the school and the church services, and John Adams groomed him for leadership, a role he tried to fulfil after Adams's death. Both men soon married and started their own families. John Buffett had been on the island scarcely eight weeks when he married Dorothy Young. Evans, who was not a forceful character and played no significant role in the island's affairs, was the 'son of a coachmaker in the employ of Long of St Martin's Lane, who has married a daughter of John Adams, through whom he possesses and cultivates a certain portion of land'.[9] One might suspect, however, that his subsequent treatment was not unconnected with his advantageous marriage and with the struggle for resources and land ownership.

Five years later, in 1828, two uninvited adventurers arrived in a small boat from Valparaiso, Chile. One, Noah Bunker, was a sick man and died soon after his arrival; the other, George Hunn Nobbs, a well-educated Englishman, supposedly the illegitimate offspring of an aristocrat, announced that he had arrived to settle on the island. There was very little the Pitcairners could do about such unwelcome immigrants short of throwing them into the sea. Nobbs was an adventurer and soldier of fortune. He had served as a midshipman in the Royal Navy, then as a lieutenant in the Chilean navy and was better educated and more aggressive than Buffett. His actions were to split the hitherto united community.

John Adams died within a few months of Nobbs's arrival. Before he died, sensing trouble with the newcomers, he urged the islanders to elect one of the men born on the island as its chief, but not one of the few males old enough for such a position felt confident enough to assume such a role in the face of the superior education and worldliness of Buffett and Nobbs. George Nobbs married Sarah Christian and set about undermining Buffett's position of authority. When Adams died on 5 March 1829, the succession had not been decided, and leadership became a struggle for pre-eminence between Buffett, who had been with them for six years acting as pastor and teacher, and the newly arrived Nobbs. It was a power struggle during which Nobbs set up his own school and attempted to replace Buffet as *de facto* leader of the island. Nobbs gradually gained pre-eminence and managed to force payment from the islanders for the schoolmaster (himself). All children aged six to sixteen were to attend school from 7 a.m. to noon, and he was to be paid a shilling a month for each pupil, whether or not they attended. As he had less time to tend his own land he claimed the right to call on men to work for him, their labour valued at two shillings per day. It became, in effect, a system of paying the school fees of the children in agricultural produce and livestock, at a laid-down scale of value. Under Nobbs's influence and direction a fierce legal code was written, providing for all manner of offences. Flogging by the cat-o'-nine-tails was reintroduced, and fornication was punishable progressively first by a whipping, then by the forfeiture of lands and property, and finally by banishment. This code replaced the verbal authority previously exercised by Adams.

Buffett who had been a virtuous teetotaller on his arrival, fell from grace and lost support by indulging too freely in the product of the still, and he worsened matters by fathering two illegitimate children. But Nobbs remained unpopular with a substantial minority and could never command a unified community. The death of Adams and the intrusion of these outsiders was commented upon in the *United Services Journal*, a journal devoted to military and naval matters:

Here then was a picture of a peaceful and contented society, on an island where everything harmonized precisely with the wants and wishes of its occupants; the mind dwelt with delight upon such an 'Eden' being in existence. But 'ogni medaglia ha il suo rovescio', and we are pained to say that the simoom of arrogance and ignorance, engendered by itinerant fanatics, has withered the palmy days of Pitcairn. While Smith [Adams] lived, his sagacity sufficed for the protection of his flock, – but his death in March 1829, left them open to intruders. Of these, one Nobbs, a reptile of the class called 'consecrated cobblers', fastened upon them, and in return for corrupt pastoral duties, claimed exemption from labour and right of support: and this, amongst a people more righteous and just than himself, for a man is no more religious from canting perverted scriptural phrases, than a bat is a parrot because it can fly.[10]

It was a period of growing division, which reawakened memories of the blood-stained past, and made many of the older inhabitants fear for the future. They had attracted the powerful and benevolent attention of John Barrow (later Sir John), Second Secretary to the Admiralty, and his concerns over their spiritual well-being reflected the religious conflict in England. The Church of England was worried by the rise of Methodism and by the growth of any sect of religion outside of its control. Barrow was a member of the Establishment in all senses of the term, and his fretting over the allegiance of these few dozen people on a speck of land in the far Pacific, although laudable in many ways, seems out of all proportion to the other world-wide responsibilities and duties of the Admiralty:

This Nobbs is probably one of those half-witted persons who fancy that they have received a *call* to preach nonsense – some cobbler escaped from his stall; or tailor from his shop-board. Kitty Quintal's cant phrase – 'we want food for our souls' and praying at meals for 'spiritual nourishment', smacks not a little of the jargon of the inferior caste of evangelicals. Whoever this pastoral drone may be, it is but too evident that the preservation of innocence, simplicity, and happiness of amiable people, is intimately connected with his speedy removal from the island ... Captain Waldegrave says they are so strongly attached to those beautiful prayers that are found in the liturgy of the Church of England, that there is no danger of a dissenting minister being received among them. It is to be hoped that this is the case; but it may be asked, will they escape from the snares of George Hunn Nobbs?[11]

While Barrow worried about which denominational heaven might receive the prayers and souls of the Pitcairners, he also took action to preserve their bodies. Before he died Adams had communicated his concerns about overpopulation and the future safety and well-being of the Pitcairners to Captain Beechey, who in turn communicated them to John Barrow. Barrow was not only a powerful bureaucrat, but a widely travelled man and powerful advocate of scientific explorations. He was then writing his *The Eventful History of the Mutiny of the Bounty*, which was published in 1831. He admired John Adams and took an interest in the affairs of Pitcairn, and he was in a position to ensure that they received the assistance of the Royal Navy. Adams had suggested to Beechey that the population was outgrowing the resources available and that it was time that it was transported to some other British possession, such as New South Wales or Tasmania, where they could be granted sufficient land to support their growing numbers over the foreseeable future. John Barrow was not enthusiastic about the suggestion that Pitcairn be completely abandoned, because, as he put it: 'The time will come when they will emigrate of their own accord. When the hive is full, they will send out swarms.' He was, however, willing to do what he could to fulfil the wishes of the Pitcairners, and wheels were set in motion.[12]

Quite obviously the island, or any other island, could support only a given population, but in 1831, when these matters were under active consideration, numbers were not excessive, at 135. They were however, poised to explode. There were forty-eight males and eighty-seven females of various ages. As those females matured, married and produced families, the population would grow to exceed the available resources. The ratio of male to female may account for the appearance during this period of one or two births outside marriage, which were taken as indicators of a loosening of moral fibre, but may be taken as a fairly predictable result of such a marked imbalance of the sexes. If the settlers had remained undiscovered up to this point they might well have developed a polygamous society to cope with the imbalance. Overpopulation might also have led to infanticide which, in turn, would have placed their practice of the Christian faith under pressure.

Whatever the social effects, overpopulation did affect the lives of individuals, particularly girls of marriageable age, who faced only spinsterhood, which in that moral climate and closely supervised society, would not bring the compensations of freedom. Some had already found the island too constricting and had quit 'the hive'. Matthew's daughter Jane Quintal, for example, was found living on the island of Rurutu in 1829. She gave her reason for leaving Pitcairn as the lack of men for a husband. She had left with a sailor from a whaling ship who subsequently abandoned her. Jane was described as 'a tall, fine, half-caste woman, dressed in neat European clothing. Her manner was artless, and she spoke the English language with correctness'. She told her questioner that after being abandoned 'I married a native of this island [Rurutu]. I was obliged soon to get married, they are so particular; all the missionaries. I could not talk to any male creature who was single, so I got married.'[13] The power of the missionaries was considerable wherever they set up a mission. Pitcairn was under the eye of the missionaries of Tahiti, which was suggested as a suitable location should the Pitcairners be evacuated *en masse*.

One Pitcairner, Jenny, was already in Tahiti, and her feelings were generalized by a reporter who wrote: 'Jenny says that they [the Pitcairners] would all like to come to Taheiti or Eimao. We were thinking that they would be a great acquisition at Opunuhu alongside of the sugar works, as they have been accustomed to labour, for the Taheitians will not labour for any payments.'[14] Clearly her interviewer had an eye to the potential commercial value of a labour force that had European attitudes towards work rather than the Tahitians' easygoing indifference to systematic labour.

Nevertheless, the subject of abandoning Pitcairn in the supposed interest of the inhabitants had been raised. Through the influence of men like Sir John Barrow, the British government had taken unofficial responsibility for the islanders and, with the long delays imposed by the slowness of communications, the Colonial Office was persuaded to transport them back to Tahiti where Queen Pomare IV and her chiefs were willing to welcome them and to give them land. By then it was four years after Adams had first conveyed his fears to Captain Beechey, and in spite of later reports which made clear that the islanders were neither in danger of famine, nor keen to leave, two ships were dispatched:

> It was too late to halt the bureaucratic machine, however, for arrangements had been made with the Naval Officer-in-Chief in India and the Governor of New South Wales to send Captain A.A. Sandilands, with H.M.S. *Comet* and the Colonial Government barque *Lucy Ann*, to carry out the removal.
>
> Arriving at Pitcairn in February 1831, Sandilands soon found that many of the islanders did not want to leave their home at all ... [they were persuaded] ... Motives were mixed: reluctance to offend the British authorities, who had gone to so much trouble and expense, was probably the strongest; and after that a desire to see the land their Tahitian mothers and grandmothers had spoken of with so much affection. That there was any real fear of Pitcairn's water or food resources proving insufficient is doubtful.[15]

Pitcairn was left by its people, abandoned to the elements for the first time in forty years.

The Pitcairners' arrival at Tahiti and the subsequent events were witnessed by an individual who remained anonymous at the time, but who sent a report of his observations to the editor of the *United Services Journal* to use as he thought fit. The editor wrote:

> The following account, at once the most recent and circumstantial, of the state of Tahiti, and the deplorable condition

of the primitive islanders of Pitcairn, who have been transported to the licentious head quarters of the Missionaries,
has been addressed from the spot by a scientific gentleman,
who has kindly placed it at our disposal.[16]

Dated Tahiti, 15 May 1831, it records that a number of Tahitian
chiefs who were under the influence of the missionaries were
in rebellion against the Queen and some of her chiefs, because
she was in favour of ignoring laws advocating the suppression
of traditional native ceremony – laws which had been laid down
by the missionaries. One such ceremony was, for example,
the presentation of *tapa* cloth, which was traditionally done by
wrapping it around a naked woman who was then revealed
when the material was unrolled to be given to the dignitary
being honoured. Essentially, however, it was an attempt by the
Queen and some of her loyal chiefs to preserve traditional culture and customs, which were, inevitably, intertwined with
traditional gods and religion. All of which, of course, was inter-
linked with, and sustained, the Tahitians' social and economic
system. They were not used to working for gain as opposed to
producing for need. They rarely sold their produce, as hospitality was considered not only a duty, but a pleasure; and, unless
their easy way of life was completely crushed, the islanders
would not work for those enterprises designed to commercialize
and exploit the available resources. The missionaries may have
been naïve enough to think that they were simply objecting to
native religion and sexuality: their actions actually destroyed a
whole way of life. The conflict between the two forces had
developed to the point where they were confronting each other,
ready for battle:

> Things were in this state when two sails were announced in
> sight, which proved to be the Comet, a British man-of-war,
> and a transport, having on board all the inhabitants of Pit-
> cairn's Island. The first could not have entered at a better
> moment, nor the latter at a worse. They entered the bay of
> Papiete the following morning, and two days after the people
> from Pitcairn were landed . . . you have, of course, heard of
> these interesting islanders. Nothing could be worse than to

bring these good and virtuous people into this gulf of corruption. The first moral lesson they received on their arrival, was to see about fifty women of Tahiti swim off to the ships in which they were, and commit in their presence, with the sailors, such acts of debauchery, that they instantly desired to return to their own island . . . If we are to credit the assertions of these people, they did not willingly quit their island, but did so at the instigation of those who went to seek them, and on condition that they should be brought back to Pitcairn, if they were not pleased with Tahiti. Notwithstanding, this promise was not fulfilled, for although they say to the Commander that they would have preferred dying of thirst in their own island to living amongst so corrupt a people as those of Tahiti, the Comet sailed, and left them here, not, however, before its Commander had secured them a piece of land and provisions for six months.

The evacuation had tragic consequences, for he went on:

Six weeks have now elapsed since the departure of the ships; and six of the inhabitants of Pitcairn are already dead, of whom two were fathers of families, leaving each six children; and in a small vessel which I have freighted to go to the neighbourhood of Pitcairn, twelve of them have embarked, for the purpose of preserving the stock they left on their departure.[17]

The writer even offered to buy a schooner large enough to transport all the Pitcairners home, and was very scathing about one of the missionaries, Mr Darling, who had some prior claim to hire the vessel:

wishing to visit some islands in this schooner, [he] would not forgo his voyage . . . The probable consequences will be, that these unfortunate people must all die if some means of restoring them to their island are not soon found. Nothing, however, can touch the heart of the Reverend Gentleman; within three or four days he is going to sail, leaving these unhappy people to their fate, without the least apparent concern.[18]

His fears were only too well founded, for another eleven Pitcairners were to die of disease before their passage home could be secured. He goes on to say that 'The people of Pitcairn were certainly the most interesting people on the earth. Twice I have visited their island, and twice I have been enchanted with their frank and cordial hospitality, with the purity of their manners and the goodness of their hearts.'[19] The generous and wealthy friend of the Pitcairners who wrote this report turned out to be Moerenhout:

> the well-known trader and later consul for France, who with the consent of John Adams had taken a number of the young men in 1829 on a pearl-diving expedition to the Tuamotu archipelago. It was Moerenhout who arranged for an advance party, led by John Buffet, to return on one of his chartered pearling schooners to see to the maintenance of the plantations and livestock, and who made repeated attempts to get the remainder away.[20]

This enterprise was finally achieved through a subscription raised by the missionaries and supported by the European residents, added to what money the Pitcairners could raise by selling some of the possessions that had been left to help them settle into their new location, together with 'a quantity of copper bolts from the *Bounty*, which they had brought with them', and 'on 2 September 1831 they were all safely landed in their beloved home'.[21]

All, that is, save the seventeen who had died in their brief contact with the outside world. The Pitcairners were now demoralized – one-fifth of their kin and neighbours had been wiped out in some six months, and exposure to the licentious port life of Tahiti had shocked and disorientated them. Some of the islanders had acquired, or reacquired, the taste for alcohol during their brief stay in Tahiti and, once they were back on Pitcairn, the old still was again put to work. Drunkenness and licentiousness returned to the island. Contemporary reports agree that the previous moral character and engaging innocence of the islanders had been damaged if not altogether lost. Bennett observed the ill effects of their brief excursion into the wider world:

But the injurious effects of a more extensive intercourse with the world were but too evident in the restless and dissatisfied state amongst them . . . it is much to be feared that the social compact which formerly bound this people has been broken by the rude contact of the world.[22]

From the top of Pitcairn one can see nothing in the world but the curving horizon where sea and sky meet in an endless circular rim of empty ocean. It must, at times, have imposed a sense of physical restriction and – with few other people, a tiny peer group, and virtually no choice in selecting one's spouse – similarly limited social, cultural and affective horizons. This awareness would have been all the more acute as the number of contacts with the outside world increased. But in these early generations there was a sense of 'home', which drew them back. Of the eighty-six people who left Pitcairn to start a new life in Tahiti all sixty-nine survivors returned, mourning the pointless deaths of their kin and neighbours – not one choosing to remain in the outside world.

Although they could return to their beloved Pitcairn, they could not return to the previous isolation and unity. Their disastrous experience of the outside world had done nothing to heal the divisions opened up by the arrival of George Nobbs. Since the death of John Adams there had been no agreed leader and no authoritative system of settling disputes or of deciding acceptable behaviour. Friday October Christian and Edward Young, sons of mutineers and the two eldest native-born men, who might have taken command of the community, died during their brief removal to Tahiti. On their return George Nobbs retained majority support, but John Buffett kept the loyalty of a substantial minority. It was a period of anarchy in which, according to a contemporary observer, the whaling surgeon Bennett: 'Drunkenness and disease were amongst them – their morals had sunk to a low ebb – and vices of a very deep dye hinted at in their mutual recriminations'[1] – even both the competing leaders had taken to drinking the home-produced rum. Faced with this return to old ways, a section of the community petitioned the London Missionary Society to send a qualified teacher to live on the island to replace both Buffett and Nobbs as teacher and pastor, and to be leader of the community.

In October 1832 the schooner *Maria* arrived at Pitcairn Island from Tahiti. From her disembarked Joshua Hill who informed the islanders that he had been sent by the British government to take charge of their affairs. He had not been sent by the government, nor was he from the London Missionary Society: Hill was an adventurer and confidence man who had roamed South America and various Pacific islands, duping people into believing that he was well connected with the British authorities and insinuating himself into local affairs until exposed. Like so many people, he had been intrigued by the story of Pitcairn and had attempted to involve himself in the islanders' affairs before they were moved to Tahiti – but his services had been rejected by the British government. His departure from Tahiti may not have been entirely voluntary and was not unconnected with the manner in which he had duped Queen Pomare and her British missionaries. Whatever his origins, he was far better educated than anyone on the island, and boasted of his aristocratic connections and friends in England. He had conned far more sophisticated people than the islanders into accepting him for what he purported to be; they did not doubt him. Once on the island he dismissed Nobbs and Buffett and became both pastor and teacher.

Six months after Hill had taken it upon himself to be master of the island's affairs, HMS *Challenger* arrived on 30 May 1833 under the command of Captain Charles Freemantle. He wrote:

> I found on the island a Mr Joshua Hill, a gentleman of nearly seventy years of age, who appears to have come from England expressly to establish himself amongst these people as a kind of pastor or monitor . . . He landed on a Sunday, when he found Nobbs, who acted as their pastor, intoxicated . . . It appears to me so extraordinary a circumstance – a gentleman of Mr Hill's age and apparent respectability, coming from England for the express purpose of residing on Pitcairn's

Island – that I at first thought he must be some adventurer, more likely to do harm than good . . . as he had broken up all their stills, and formed them into a Temperance Society, I gave him all the assistance in my power to support him in his situation.[2]

It is a pity that Captain Freemantle did not stand by his first thought. It was his support for total abstinence that fixed this outsider on to the backs, not to say over the heads, of the unfortunate Pitcairners. They were unversed in the outside world and its affairs and relied on the British navy to protect them. They had accepted the authority and judgement of the naval captains who visited them because they were afraid that the protection of the Union Flag might be removed if they disobeyed or offended these authorities. Captain Freemantle's well-intentioned support for Hill, which appeared to solve the previous disunity under Buffett and Nobbs, was to result in a deepening of conflict and greater unhappiness.

The overwhelming importance which naval authorities and missionaries gave to banning alcoholic drink on Pitcairn distorted their judgements – anyone who was against drink must be better, in their eyes, than anyone who was not. As to whether Nobbs was drunk on the Sunday Hill arrived, we have now only Hill's assertion. Because their religious commitment and teetotalism affected opinion of them in Britain, the issue of alcohol and of who drank was a crucial one. John Adams's favourable reception had been, in large part, due to the fact that he had turned his back on the demon drink – something which, at that period, won approval from influential people in Britain who had leisure enough to take a hand in controlling the recreation and habits of working people. It is open to question whether John Adams abstained with any consistency, however, because, as we have seen, one reads that alcohol was abandoned at one period on Pitcairn, only to read of its availability at a later date – it always seems to reappear. Even when Adams was in his most rigorous phase – when he wanted his daughter executed for having an illegitimate child – it seems that he was not averse to a drink. Captain King, who was there in 1819, and persuaded Adams to relent and to let his daughter marry her lover, noted that, once Adams gave his agreement, 'I gave him some porter, wine, and spirits, to regale themselves with at the wedding'.[3]

Adams's claim to have destroyed all the stills was another of his deceptions, as there was alcohol on the island both before and after the evacuation to Tahiti and before and after his death. Although ships called at Pitcairn Island with increasing regularity, few people actually went ashore, and of those who did, even fewer stayed for more than a few hours. It would be as well to suppose that the islanders were not, as John Adams clearly was not, above telling people what they wanted to hear and showing them what they wanted to see. Bechervaise, who spent two weeks ashore in 1825 and was a seaman like Adams, often dined and yarned with him and others, and commented 'from them we got several bottles of rum, which had been made years, and which were thought of a superior quality'.[4] So, wine and spirits were an acceptable gift in 1818, bottles of home-distilled spirit were available in sufficient quantity to give to a visitor (an unimportant sailor) in 1825, and even Buffett and Nobbs were drinkers before and after the traumatic evacuation to Tahiti in 1831. Captain Freemantle, who was there in 1833, trusted:

> that they may continue to live in that state of innocence and contentment they did previously to their departure for Tahiti; which, it is to be hoped, they may, if they do not return to the use of that spirit they have so well learned the art of distilling, and which was brought about by the Englishmen, a specimen of which I obtained. It was not unlike whisky, and very good.[5]

If Adams's word was to be trusted, distilling spirits stopped years before Beechey's visit in 1825, and Freemantle appears to believe this (he hopes that they do not *return* to its use), in spite of obtaining a 'specimen' so much later. Once John Adams was no longer on the scene fostering illusions to please his audience, one is afforded a few glimpses of a different world. It is also significant that Bechervaise (whom Adams and the others did not feel obliged to impress) was not only given 'several' bottles of the stuff, but was told by Adams that: 'They soon found out the tea root and made from it rum, and to that may be attributed all the loss of life and misfortunes felt during the first nine years of their inhabiting this spot.'[6] This conversation, no doubt casually spoken and casually repeated, adds strength to Jenny's claim that alcohol was distilled *before* the massacre and lends weight to the assumption that it was Edward Young who was responsible and not McKoy – for all the apparent certitude of a precise date in Young's journal. It is apparent from the evidence that Pitcairn was actually never 'dry': even if the initial abuse of alcohol had played some part in the violent history of the island, it was also present during the period of its moral reform. Selfishness and injustice were at the root of the violence, not drink. In 1833, however, Joshua Hill's ability to present himself as an enemy of drink overcame Captain Freemantle's initial impression that he was an impostor. Once his position was accepted as legitimate by the Royal Navy the islanders were obliged to conclude that he had the authority of the British government behind him.

Joshua Hill, the impostor, replaced Nobbs, the adventurer, who had displaced Buffett, the outsider chosen by Adams. Hill was now more powerful than any previous leader had been because to all eyes he represented British authority. He created a 'Commonwealth' with himself as President over a committee of seven 'Elders', who actively preferred him to Nobbs and of whom Edward Quintal was the chief. He then dictated and imposed a fierce and inappropriate legal code. Following Tahitian custom, the women had had equal rights to land ownership and equal inheritance on the island – Hill abolished those rights for women. A prison was built, mainly with the intention of incarcerating those whom Hill called 'lousy foreigners', Nobbs, Buffett and Evans.

Bennett observed that 'the worst passions . . . had divided the island into two factions . . . the origin of this calamity was attributed to the recent arrival on the spot of an elderly Englishman, named Joshua Hill . . . the fraternal equality that had hitherto existed in their society was thus destroyed'.[7] Hill received his most active support from the Quintal family, while Buffett and Nobbs were supported by the Christians and the Adamses. This alignment mirrored the vein of opposition and division first glimpsed in the early days of the mutiny, when Christian threatened Quintal with a pistol for disobeying orders back in Toobouai. Quintal had burned the *Bounty* against Christian's wishes and, of course, Adams had killed Quintal. One might legitimately wonder whether the years when John Adams was the sole male survivor between 1800 and 1829 were as unified and idyllic as most observers were led to believe, or whether the young men had grown up so much under Adams's shadow that they had never before had the confidence to express themselves. The fact that the islanders could not agree to elect one of their own men leader and accepted outsiders into that position by invitation (Buffett), accident (Nobbs) or trickery (Hill), rather implies that existing rivalry on the island was deep enough to preclude the native-born.

Eventually, in March 1834, in his capacity as head of the 'Commonwealth', Joshua Hill ordered the banishment of Buffett, Nobbs and Evans on the grounds that they were not native-born and had no right to be on the island. They were forced to take passage on the whaling-ship *Tuscon*, which was on her way to Tahiti: their bereft families followed them some months later.

Banishing the three men who were a threat to his leadership was to be the high point of Joshua Hill's career on Pitcairn. Possibly a sense of collective guilt in allowing the wives and children of the three banished men to be forced off the island caused a revulsion against Hill and his harsh rule. They, at least, were all born Pitcairners even if their husbands and fathers were not. Hill's subsequent loss of authority illustrates how power to govern depended on either acceptance or force. His power collapsed when his most influential supporter turned against him. Hill ordered Arthur Quintal's young daughter, who was accused of stealing some yams, to be whipped; Quintal refused to permit the punishment. A furious Hill drew a sword and threatened to kill Quintal if he did not submit. Quintal, who was unarmed, leapt across the table and, in a struggle from which he emerged cut and permanently scarred, he disarmed Hill, leaving his authority in shreds. In this particular case, the exercise of superior physical force may have had a good result; but it was a return to dangerous precedents. The history of the island demonstrated only too clearly what happened when the strongest submitted to nothing but their own will and forced it on others. Following this incident, however, by general vote of the community, Nobbs was sent a letter inviting him to return from his exile and to resume his position as pastor and teacher.

Before Arthur Quintal withdrew his support from Joshua Hill, Nobbs and the other two exiles had been active on their own behalf and had written letters detailing their treatment at the hands of Hill to the Naval Commander in charge of the South Pacific. Nobbs refuted Hill's accusation of drunkenness and explained how difficult it had been to suppress drinking by the others: 'A short time after our return to Pitcairn's Island [from Tahiti] some of the natives (Edward Quintal, William Young, and Fletcher Christian), determined to re-commence distilling rum – a practice they had been accustomed to in John Adams' time.'[8] When Nobbs tried to stop them, he claimed, he was abused by them all and threatened with violence by Quintal. He then described how Hill, once he had convinced the population that he was acting with the authority of the British government, had ousted Nobbs from his position as teacher and leader of the community and then pursued a vendetta against the three Englishmen – Nobbs, Evans and Buffett:

> an act was passed (by force) to deprive our children of their mothers' inheritance, merely because their fathers were foreigners (Englishmen). In August Mr Hill sent his colleagues to seize the muskets of these persons whom, he said, were opposed to the government of the commonwealth . . . Several of the natives protested against such conduct; Mr. Hill threatened to give them a flogging, and, moreover, said,

that if they did not obey him, he would cause a military governor to be sent from England, with a party of soldiers, who would take their land from them and treat them as slaves.[9]

Nobbs complained that during a serious illness which kept him in bed for three months Hill would not allow him access to the community medicine chest of which he, Nobbs, was part-owner.

Buffett wrote a similar letter, pointing out how well he had always been accepted by the islanders since he had acceded to John Adams's request that he settle on the island. During their unhappy sojourn at Tahiti the Pitcairners so valued his services that they had asked him to stay with them, and he and his family had been chosen as the first to return to Pitcairn, three months before the others, in order to save the livestock. Yet Hill had ordered Buffett to leave the island with his wife and five children, and Buffett was in no doubt that the reason had been economic as 'there is not land sufficient'[10] for everyone. Buffett had married a Young, Nobbs a Christian, and Evans a daughter of John Adams. By passing a law forbidding female inheritance, and by expelling their husbands, Hill was effectively depriving those female branches of the Christian, Young and Adams family of their land. Buffett wrote:

> I had a mock trial, on which Mr Hill was judge, jury and executioner. After Mr Hill beating me over the head, breaking it in two places, likewise my finger, I was suspended by my hands in the church, and flogged until I was not able to walk home ... Charles Christian, the oldest man on the island, was brutally troubled, and turned out of his house, for trying to prevent me being flogged.[11]

Evans was also flogged and all three were forbidden to contact visiting ships. The prison had been built specially with them in mind. Eventually the three men had feared for their liberty, health and life, and on 8 April 1834 all left Pitcairn aboard the *Tuscon* leaving behind their wives and children.

Once in Tahiti the three men were able to convince the

missionaries, Mr H. Nott and Charles Wilson (who carried much influence), of the justice of their case, and they enlisted the help of Mr G. Pritchard, the British consul. They sent word to Pitcairn by the *Pomareu*'s Captain Henry that Mr Nobbs was to be reinstated (11 June 1834), but Joshua Hill refused to accept these instructions and so the vessel took off the three wives and their children to follow their husbands into exile.

Hill had in his time persuaded the missionaries of his value and had arrived at Pitcairn bearing a letter from them. He tried to regain his status by organizing his supporters to send a petition. This petition, dated just one week after he refused to accept Nobbs back on the island, is headed from the 'Principle Native Islanders. 19th June 1834'. It supported Hill and contrasted a supposed unity under him to the earlier divided situation when Nobbs had replaced Buffett as the teacher and leader: 'At times we have had two schools and two churches, whilst at other times we have had neither one nor the other.'[12] In attacking Nobbs's character, the petition refers back to the time when he and Bunker first arrived in a small boat: it claimed that they were alone only because they had murdered the crew who had sailed with them from South America. Such an accusation could have been investigated only in South America, but to support it they stated that after they had landed at Pitcairn 'Bunker committed suicide, and Nobbs destroyed his papers'.[13] If it was true that Bunker committed suicide it is a very interesting revelation, for in the earlier accounts it was stated that Bunker was very ill when he arrived and soon died. Given the long period of time over which more and more details of the murders on Pitcairn emerged, it is not unreasonable to take this as another example of the ability of the islanders to maintain a collective falsehood.

It was only during this period of deep social divisions that one party or the other deemed it advantageous to reveal certain facts. It was during this time, perhaps due more to these divisions than to Adams's death, that most of the damning accusations about his being the wife-stealer were made; as was that of Young's responsibility for planning the massacre of the others.

Looking at the names of those ranged on one side or the other again suggests that old conflicts lay beneath the surface. The three incomers exiled by Hill had married a Christian, a Young and an Adams – of the ten heads of families who signed the petition in support of Hill six are Quintals and one a McKoy. It may be unwise to overstress the importance of family names as underlying the split, because obviously there had been much intermarriage between families and, with equal female inheritance rights, the self-interest of one family group may well have been opposed to another whose name it shared. This could account for the other four heads of families signing the petition.

Edward Quintal had been Hill's right-hand man and the man who had flogged Buffett, but when Arthur Quintal denied Joshua Hill's authority, Edward joined other heads of families in a petition requesting that Mr George H. Nobbs should return to Pitcairn and be their leader. This marked a return to the old unity and it was signed by Edward, John and Arthur Quintal, Charles and Fletcher Christian, William Young, George Adams and William McKoy – although 'signed' is not the precise truth, for not one signed, each one made his mark. This rather revealing document calls into question just how effective Adams's teaching had been, and how misled were the succession of visitors in estimating the pupils' accomplishments. Many otherwise illiterate people learn to write their names – the fact that not one of these men could do even that suggests that demonstrations of skill witnessed by visitors owed more to rote learning than to an ability to write.

This would fit well with Tahitian culture, in which memory was developed well beyond European practice and natives could repeat their family roots and history over many generations, and even include collateral lines. This is apparent in the observations of Captain Lord Edward Russell in 1837:

> We were astonished at the intelligence and quickness of the reply to any questions we put to most of these people. They went through the Kings of England without mistake; knew perfectly well all the reigning monarchs of Europe, and leading men of our own country, which made them doubly

interesting to us. To find a race of men, inhabitants of one of the South Sea Islands, speaking our language, and following our customs, could not fail to interest us all; and, when we see they have been brought up in everything that is good and proper, that as yet no immorality has crept in among them, and every sin abhorred, and they continue to live in all simplicity and truth, we are, at once, disarmed of every ill-feeling arising from a reflection on the manner in which they came thither, and forget the crimes of their fathers.[14]

Whatever John Adams's limitations had been in teaching literacy to the first generation, one can only admire his longer term achievements. Consciously or not, by fixing English as the language and the Church of England as its religion, he ensured that this mixed race community would be treated with all the respect and support that Englishman gave to Englishman. Captain Russell (and others before and after him) were mistaken in thinking that the culture of the islanders was English. English women did not have the vote at eighteen (or younger if they were married), could not claim equal inheritance and education as did Pitcairn women – in practice their economic, social and political life was predominantly Polynesian, whatever the language in which they expressed themselves or the god they worshipped.

The correspondence received by the naval authorities demonstrated all too clearly that Joshua Hill was abusing his influence, so Captain Lord Edward Russell was instructed to sail to Pitcairn to hold an inquiry and resolve the islanders' problems. While he was in exile, Nobbs received the petition from eight heads of families and decided to return with his family, as did Evans. In this he had full backing from the missionaries for whom he had been working in the Gambier Islands. He had been officially informed that Hill had no authority stemming from, or connected with, Her Majesty's Government.

Buffett, who had been working as a mate on a trading schooner during his exile, returned to Pitcairn on the *Actaeon* with Captain Russell. Lord Russell, son of the Duke of Bedford, was, by happy coincidence, just the right man to expose as fraudulent Hill's claim that the Duke was his friend as well as his wider claims of connections with the rich and powerful. Captain Russell held a public inquiry at which the opposing factions presented their views with a deal of acrimony, but it cleared the air and exposed Hill as a charlatan. The islanders' affairs were returned to much the same state as had existed before the arrival of Joshua Hill: 'Mr Buffett was kindly received by his old friends, and found his family and children well. Mr Nobbs, another Englishman, was elected schoolmaster, by the general voice; and, although not so good a man as could be wished, still will be much service to them.'[15] Joshua Hill was ordered to leave the island, but he continued to live there, powerless and humiliated, for a year until he was finally taken into exile by HMS *Imogene* in 1838. In the judgement of H. E. Maude: 'One has only to read Hill's many literary effusions to surmise that he must have been suffering from advanced paranoia and was in all probability mentally unbalanced throughout his stay on Pitcairn.'[16]

Hill's banishment is usually presented as an end to division, but the report by the Captain of the *Imogene*, although as favourable as ever to the native Pitcairners, claims that the three recently returned exiles were no more popular than Hill:

> They are a very kindly, hospitable, and amiable race, and strikingly virtuous and correct, though among the natives it is to be regretted that two cases of deviation from the course of strict morality have not long since occurred; – and it is much to be regretted, that among the three English settlers there have been cases perpetrated of deep, base, and disgraceful profligacy. George Nobbs, John Buffet, and John Evans, the people of the island are most desirous should be removed from it. Nobbs is the teacher and tailor, Buffet is a joiner, Evans, who seems to have preserved his integrity, and as far as we could learn, to be without reproach, is a sailor by profession; and with respect to the community, a mere vegetating animal. Mr. Hill, a fourth Englishman, who had established his residence here, we brought away at his own request. He made himself obnoxious to the natives, having assumed

a power and control over them which he had neither authority to do, nor ability to execute effectually; and some being led away to side with him, the seeds of dissension among the people were thus sown. It is probable, however, that he produced more good than evil amongst them, as, with the exception of some arbitrary proceedings, his conduct was marked by the strictest moral integrity. His removal being accomplished, harmony will be restored in the community of the islanders, who, nevertheless, are most desirous to be relieved of the presence of the above-named persons, instead of whom they would gladly receive a competent religious instructor.[17]

The evidence of an eyewitness must be taken seriously, especially one whose duty it was to investigate and inquire, but, given subsequent events and the career of George Nobbs, it would seem that the good captain was not over-perceptive. To describe Hill as having the 'strictest moral integrity', when he imposed floggings on trumped-up charges, passed laws which effectively deprived women of their inheritance and exiled men with dependent wives and children, is to view the world and morality through a very limited spy-glass. He could see nothing beyond the fact that Hill did not enjoy a social drink or engage in sexual relationships: in other words, as long as 'drunkenness' and 'fornication' were avoided, moral integrity was assured. In fact, the islanders did come to unite behind the leadership of George Nobbs, who, for all his occasional human failings, provided moral and practical leadership.

The upsets and divisions had been largely, if not entirely, caused by outsiders coming to the island and disrupting the Pitcairners' customary manner of regulating their affairs. There was little they could do if people arrived in a small boat: they had to accept the newcomers on humanitarian grounds. Other outsiders were too powerful to be resisted. Most ships that called at Pitcairn treated the small community with fair dealing and peaceful trading. But there were exceptions. The crew of one whaling ship came ashore for a fortnight and threatened to violate any woman they could lay their hands upon. The island men were forced to stay together, armed, to protect the women and for two weeks they were obliged to let their crops go untended. The crew claimed that the islanders had 'no laws, no country, no authority that they were to respect – American vessels denying that they were under the protection of Great Britain, as they had neither colours nor written authority'.[18] It was a sad lesson, but one that had to be learned – no small Eden could live in tranquillity unless it was protected by forces stronger than those who wanted to violate it.

Pitcairn Island was still not a British possession. The Royal Navy stationed in the Pacific called there occasionally and kept a friendly eye on the island, but this was strictly unofficial. The navy seemed to take a perverse pride in John Adams and the offspring of the former mutineers who had, exceptionally, eluded naval justice. When Captain Elliott arrived in 1838 on a routine cruise of the HMS *Fly*, the islanders reported to him the threat to their women from the whalers and they pleaded with him to give them the official protection of Great Britain – in effect, to incorporate them into the British Empire and to give them written laws.

HMS *Fly* was a tiny sloop, and she and her Commander were among the very lowest ranks in naval importance. The request was an awesome responsibility for a low-ranking officer with no official instructions, and his confidence in responding to it was perhaps due to his being the 'Honourable George Elliott' and a person of rank and consequence. He rose to the occasion and drew up a constitution and a legal code which would give the islanders some 'written authority' to show the lawless. He did it well, as the constitution suited the circumstances and culture of the community. In its treatment of women and young people for example, it owed nothing to British precedents but re-established the Pitcairn women's right to property and equal inheritance. It included a number of other path-breaking political elements: elections were to be annual, women had equal voting rights with men, and the vote could be exercised from the age of eighteen – these were political rights not to be enjoyed by British citizens until well into the twentieth century. The legislation included compulsory school attendance, again well in advance of practice in the home country. The islanders' experience of exile, of banishment and of the leadership of outsiders had finally united them sufficiently to take their affairs back into their own hands as John Adams had urged before his death. The constitution laid down that only a *native-born* person could be elected magistrate and official head of government. The magistrate's discharge of his duty was performed in the name of the Queen of England and confirmed through the captains of visiting naval ships, the officers of which would also act as Courts of Appeal. Henceforth, Elliott promised, every effort would be made to have a naval ship call at Pitcairn at least once a year in order to hear any such appeals.

Although the British Parliament did not officially incorporate Pitcairn Island into the empire until 1887, 'the Islanders still date their formal incorporation into the Empire from 30 November 1838, the day on which the new Constitution was signed on board H.M.S. *Fly*'.[19]

There is no doubt that Commander Elliott's bold acceptance of an unlooked-for responsibility, and his shrewd and intelligent discharge of it, were unofficially accepted by all as making Pitcairn Island British and therefore under the protection of its flag and the guns of the Royal Navy.

Under Elliott's regulations, fashioned to fit the Pitcairners' normal practice, the community settled down to its placid agricultural pursuits and to lives passed in the cycle of the seasons and the inevitabilities of birth, life and death. In 1839 the population passed the hundred mark with an even fifty-two of each sex. Inevitably too, the last of the original founders of this remarkable settlement died. Mauatua, the loyal wife Fletcher Christian called 'Isabella', who was reputed for her beauty and called 'Mainmast' by the men, died in 1841. Her death left as sole survivor Teraura, who sailed with the mutineers when she was fourteen years old. Known as Susannah, she had been Edward Young's first wife; it was she who decapitated Titahiti while he slept, and desire for her had caused Quintal's death. When she was aged thirty she married fifteen-year-old Thursday October Christian, the first male born on the island, bore grandchildren to the mutineers in addition to her children by them, and was to live on with her rich memories until 1850.

By then life on Pitcairn had changed beyond the imaginings of the original settlers, who had been isolated for years and who were entirely dependent on their own resources. The island's economy ceased to be self-sufficient from the 1830s onwards. More and more ships found this tiny speck of land, so far from other inhabited landfalls, a useful place to take on board fresh supplies. Commerce with the outside world intensified in the 1840s and 1850s with the development of the whaling industry of the South Pacific. Pitcairn was located near to the whaling grounds and as whaling ships were at sea for months at a time, being able to collect even comparatively small quantities of fresh food and water was an immense attraction. Prior to the visit of

HMS *Tagus* and HMS *Briton* in 1814 the Pitcairners had sighted only four ships in twenty-four years – from which only Captain Folger had made contact. In the decade from 1813 to 1822, Pitcairn was visited on average by one ship a year, which was hardly frequent but enough to keep the wider world aware of any serious problems the islanders might encounter. But in the twenty years between 1833 and 1852, 355 ships are recorded as having called at Pitcairn – an average of one almost every three weeks. Seventy-five per cent of these were American, and the majority were whalers. The Pitcairners set about supplying their needs with a great deal of efficiency.

Trade with these ships became an important element in the islanders' agriculture. They concentrated on raising fruit and vegetables for trade rather than on growing solely for their own needs. This trade was conducted collectively and honestly. Each family had an equal right to a share in supplying a ship with whatever it needed. But if there was no competition between the islanders, neither did they take advantage of the laws of supply and demand; prices were fixed and maintained, even when articles were in short supply or when some ships were in more desperate need than others. As well as the expected fresh foods such as yams, coconuts, oranges and sweet potatoes, they also produced lime juice to be sold by the gallon, chickens to be sold by the dozen, and:

> Water melons, pumpkins and beans were obtainable in almost any quantity and water up to some 3,000 gallons a day (from the tanks on the west side of the Island) at from 30/- to 40/-, according to the quantity required; wood, which was getting scarce, cost three dollars a boat load. Clothing, tools and other articles were accepted for these products, in addition to money.[1]

The souvenir trade also grew in importance, and employed the skills of both men and women. Ships' crews and passengers bought workboxes, walking-sticks, straw hats and baskets:

> The effect of all this social and economic intercourse with outsiders can well be imagined: the Pitcairn culture was again

being steadily Europeanised, one might even say American-
ised, as the influence of the whalers was at this period paramount. Much of the Islanders' furniture, hardware, tools and
even food came from New England.[2]

The contact gradually made the islanders dependent on
imported goods, which replaced home manufactured utensils
and Tahitian clothing. All the early visitors comment on clothing made from tree bark and one in 1814 felt that:

> Whilst speaking of their dress, one must not omit mentioning
> with what taste and quickness they form a bonnet of green
> leaves . . . I was a witness to the making of one of these . . .
> it was wonderful to see with what alacrity and neatness it
> was executed. I am convinced our fashionable dress-makers
> in London would be delighted with the simplicity and yet
> elegant taste of these untaught females.[3]

The loose convenient clothing native to the Pacific was
replaced, and for special occasions women's dresses became
'long-waisted and bone-ribbed, after the patterns sent on shore
by ships' captains' wives, and also from time to time sent to
the islands by friends in England and elsewhere, [these] took
the place, for Sunday wear, of the primitive frock that had been
worn so long'.[4] Eventually, European clothing became standard
wear for every day of the week.

These economic developments were not without their set-
backs. Pitcairn was occasionally hit by cyclones. In 1845 one,
accompanied by torrential rain, caused landslides; along with
wind damage, they destroyed 4000 banana trees and 300 coconut
palms, and caused much other crop destruction. The very scale
of the disaster demonstrated the extent to which production
was now commercialized.

This increased reliance on trade and the improved – that is,
Europeanized – standard of living which resulted from it started
to put further pressure on the environment. The one-tenth of
the island observed by the early visitors under cultivation had
increased by 1850 to 'about half the island, consisting of six
hundred acres. The rest is considered too rocky for cultivation'.[5]

Inevitably, the more land that was taken under cultivation, the less there remained of the virgin forest for timber, for animals to graze in or for maintaining the water table. By mid-century soil erosion was increasingly a problem, and regulations designed to conserve the environment were put in force, the scarcity of timber being the major concern. Apart from its use as fuel for cooking (to some extent the husks of coconuts were replacing wood for this purpose), much had been used for boiling sea-water to manufacture salt.

The islanders did not follow a system of rationing scarce goods through pricing – that would have led to increasing differences in wealth and the consequent social divisions, and everyone retained the right freely to cut timber for personal use such as building, fencing and all domestic requirements; but its *use* was strictly regulated. For example, trees large enough to provide timber for house-building could be used only for that purpose. If anyone cut too much for their own building, or did not commence the proposed building within a certain time, they had to give that timber, without charge or recompense, to the next person who wanted to build. It could be neither hoarded nor squandered. Branches of a given size could not be used for fuel but had to be used for fencing enclosures or a similar constructive purpose; only the smallest brush could be burned. Some trees were absolutely protected even where they were privately owned: 'Any person who may want any trees to break off the wind from his plantations or houses, is to make it known; and no one is allowed to cut them down even if they be on his own land.'[6] Rights of ownership were subject to the collective interest. Goats were the domestic animal most destructive of woodland, so in order to preserve it the number of goats was limited according to the size of the family, with no family allowed to own more than nine.

In the early days of the settlement sea birds nesting on the cliffs had been a constant source of eggs and meat for human consumption, and they were so numerous that they were even collected as pig fodder. Now the birds did not exist in their former numbers, and there were regulations controlling their exploitation. There were regulations too, concerning all dom-estic livestock, from chickens to hogs, detailing when trespassing animals could be killed or when forfeited. There was a scale of punishments for anyone killing a cat, as rats had grown to be a serious threat to the crops. In fact, by mid-century the Pitcair-ners were reported to be eating very little meat because of the amount of fodder needed to raise animals. 'When they have no visitors, they have meat but twice a-week, plenty of vegetables at all times, and they drink only water and cocoa-nut milk.'[7] Drinks were flavoured with fruit juices and sweetened with sugar-cane.

Surprisingly, given the location, fish were not plentiful, and from the mid-1840s seemed to desert the shores – a result, some said, of soil erosion, with substantial landslides affecting inshore waters. Women caught squid from the rocks by hand, although this was a risky method as they had to be snatched in the intervals between the surf crashing over the rocks. They also fished from canoes a little off shore with spears in the Tahitian manner, using flaming torches to attract the fish at night. When larger boats were acquired, as, for example, the one presented by subscription from Calcutta, they were able to fish further off shore with long-lines. They were also able occasionally to venture further afield to other islands which were found to be part of the Pitcairn group – Oeno Island some 65 miles, and Henderson Island some 120 miles distant. Henderson Island was larger than Pitcairn – about five miles by one mile and about 80 feet above sea-level – but was totally unsuitable for human habitation. Indeed, when the islanders first ventured to Hender-son Island in 1851 they found eight human skeletons lying together, voyagers who had found the safety of land only to perish through lack of food and water. But the island was covered with scrubby bush, which could be used as fuel, and the area was sometimes tried for fishing.

Concerns over the water supply were largely resolved through the digging of water-tanks. Brodie reported that 'three . . . have been lately cut out of the solid rock, on the west side of the island for the supply of vessels. &c.'[8] These were added to until there were five or six of these tanks, each holding 3000 to 4000 gallons, which secured the islanders against drought and were a necessary part of profitably supplying the needs of visiting ships.

After the check in population caused by the temporary evacuation to Tahiti, the population was again building up. In 1837 there were 95 Pitcairners, in 1850 there were 156, in 1855 there were 187. More crucially, the population was set to increase sharply as the younger generation came to child-bearing age. This they soon did, as most girls married around the age of fourteen or fifteen, a fact that helped to account for the low levels of illegitimacy and teenage promiscuity on the islands. Fears were once more expressed about whether the island could go on supporting the needs of the population, especially now that they had become used to a new and higher standard of living based on imported goods.

In spite of the laws and practices designed to preserve a sustainable environment, it was clear that with no check on population growth the time was not long distant when the number of people would exceed the resources available for them. Fortunately, they lived in a world that still had space to spare. George Nobbs, who by this time had lived down his bad start in the island and had developed into a reasonable and popular leader of the community, wrote to the British Consul-General of the Pacific Islands in 1847, raising the question of finding a larger location for the Pitcairners. The sovereign of Hawaii, under the influence of British and American residents, offered land in his domain, but given their earlier experience of the move to Tahiti, the Pitcairners decided that if they were obliged to move then it would have to be to an uninhabited site where they could continue with their own ways, uncorrupted by others. Walter Brodie, who had been stranded on the island in 1850, raised the issue with the British authorities when he returned home. He suggested that Norfolk Island, then just being abandoned as a convict colony, might be a suitable location.

Rear-Admiral Fairfax Moresby, commander in the Pacific, was

yet another naval officer who was completely captivated by the islanders, and he exercised all his influence on their behalf. After visiting them in 1851, he was of the rather over-optimistic opinion that Pitcairn, properly cultivated, could sustain up to a thousand people. But as they would have to leave the island at that point, he considered that the sooner an evacuation was made, the easier it would be to move the whole community as a group and settle them successfully elsewhere. At the time the island was suffering one of its periodic droughts and a substantial number of the population were concerned about the future.

That future also concerned their religious well-being, and there was a desire among the islanders to have a properly ordained pastor in charge of them. In 1847 the missionaries in Tahiti received a letter requesting that Mr Nobbs be properly licensed by the Church of England. This was signed by the magistrate, Charles Christian, councillors Simon Young and John Adams, and four others as senior family men (two more Youngs, another Christian and a solitary Quintal). Once again these names, and the lack of names, show an underlying (if now dormant) division between the Christians, Adamses and Youngs against the Quintals and McKoys. In this support for Nobbs only one Quintal appears out of seven signatories, and a Christian, Young and Adams fill the official positions – a direct reversal of the earlier situation, when the ten names supporting Hill included six Quintals and one McKoy. This request made its slow way to London for official consideration.

When, in August 1852, Pitcairn Island was honoured by a second visit from Rear-Admiral Fairfax Moresby, he approved of the plan and proposed to send Mr Nobbs to London to pursue the matter. As George Nobbs had neither money nor suitable clothing, the admiral made himself personally responsible for all his expenses: his clothing, passage and stay in England. He also decided to send Nobbs's daughter to school in Valparaiso, again at his expense, in order that her education might benefit others on her return. Although the islanders very much wanted this to happen they were worried about their well-being during Nobbs's absence as, apart from his religious care, Nobbs also acted as their 'surgeon'. The admiral solved their dilemma by persuading the chaplain of his ship, HMS *Portland*, to stay behind in Nobbs's place until he returned. The Reverend W. H. Holman wrote to his father in Devon on 5 September 1852 informing him of events and writing approvingly that the school hours were from 8.15 a.m. to midday, and that on Monday, Wednesday and Friday there was a singing school after supper. More germane to the long-term future of the island, he observed that due to the increasing population there were fewer yams to trade. The admiral was not the only person on the ship to be affected by the islanders and to wish to help them: 'The crew of the *Portland* requested permission, which was granted, to present the islanders with three casks of rice, twelve bags of bread, and one cask of sugar; the value of these articles being charged against their wages.'[9] This was a generous gift from men so poorly paid and one which may have meant a cut in rations before they reached home but, if other examples are any precedent, the crew would have received many gifts of food on board and meals ashore, so this was one way for the sailors to repay the kindness they had received.

The Reverend W. H. Holman spent nine months on the island, the first outsider to stay alone on the island for more than one or two days. This, as he noted in his report to Rear-Admiral Moresby, meant that he was the first visitor able to comment on the islanders' normal daily life when they were not stimulated by the visit of a ship and its crew. One suspects that the initial tone of his report is not uninfluenced by his knowledge of how much his admiral admired the islanders. However, while positive at first, he soon becomes noticeably less so than most previous visitors.

> I have no hesitation in saying that the Pitcairn Islanders are the best, the most simple, moral and naturally kind hearted people I have ever met with or heard of. At the same time they are subject (which former visitors have ventured to deny) to all the usual infirmities of human nature, and also to those diversities of tempers and dispositions which one may always expect to find in so large a community.[10]

In truth, Holman found them to be obstinate and indolent. His report criticizes them for just living from 'hand to mouth' and taking no thought for the future, in spite of quite serious food shortages while he was there. He claimed that the climate was too unreliable to sustain the islanders at their present or future numbers for much longer. During his stay they had no rain at all in November, December and January, with a consequent crop failure. Owing to over-intensive cropping, there was so much soil washed away when it did rain that the sea was earth-coloured all around the island for up to four or five miles out to sea. He felt that Pitcairn was no longer viable:

> In concluding this report I would observe that there can be no doubt that the golden days of the Island and Inhabitants of Pitcairn are already past and gone. Everything I saw convinces me that they have been gradually retrograding since the time of John Adams . . .[11]

He recommended their immediate removal to another island. He spent his time on Pitcairn urging upon the islanders the necessity of moving and was undoubtedly influential in persuading a section of the population that it was vital, as was his report in convincing the government to follow that course.

Mr George Nobbs duly arrived in England on 16 October, via Panama and fast passage by steamship, and on Sunday morning, 24 October 1852, in the church of St Mary's Islington, he was admitted into deacons' orders. On 30 November he was ordained priest by the Bishop of London in Fulham Church and named as Chaplain of Pitcairn Island. After this the Society for the Propagation of the Gospel appointed him one of their missionaries with a salary of £50 a year (a day's wages on Pitcairn was two shillings [10p]). Shortly before sailing he was received by Prince Albert at Osborne House and presented to Queen Victoria. After such official endorsement and royal recognition, his position as shepherd of his flock would never again be assailed. His visit had raised public interest, and well-wishers formed the Pitcairn's Island Fund and provided for his return passage, along with a generous amount of supplies for the islanders. It was understood while he was in London that the government would finance and arrange for the Pitcairners to be moved to another location if they so wished. On his return to Pitcairn, Nobbs spoke in favour of the scheme and a majority voted in favour of petitioning to be moved to Norfolk Island. In 1855 London informed them that their petition was accepted and that transport would arrive the following year to move them.

Once the possibility of moving had become a fact, a group led by George Adams, son of John, opposed the move. At a council meeting they lost the vote again. The sense of unity was very strong however, and the minority feared that the British might not continue to act as their shield should they stay on the island. Thus, when the transport ship *Morayshire* sailed on 3 May 1856, from a mixture of solidarity and fear, every Pitcairner boarded her: forty men, forty-seven women, fifty-four boys and fifty-three girls.[12] Pitcairn was once more abandoned, deserted again by its people as it had been by those earlier inhabitants whose traces had been evident when the mutineers first settled. One wonders whether they had been forced to leave for similar reasons.

Norfolk Island had recently been abandoned as a penal colony and lay roughly equidistant between the northern tip of New Zealand and Brisbane, Australia; it was more than 3500 miles west of Pitcairn, and took thirty-one days to reach. Norfolk Island had a more temperate climate, and was nearly ten times the size of Pitcairn. It had many advantages as well as more land – its convict labour had built good roads and dressed stone houses – but a number of the Pitcairners could not settle happily and longed to return home. A couple of years after they had settled on Norfolk Island a trading schooner offered to take them back to Pitcairn Island. About a third of them wished to return but eventually most were persuaded by friends and relatives not to separate their families or divide the community. Sixteen, however, resisted all pleas and arguments and decided to return. Or more truthfully perhaps, four adults decided to return: two brothers – Moses and Mayhew Young – with their wives decided they would go back with their children, ten girls and two boys.

The Youngs arrived back into Bounty Bay and trod the familiar ascent to Adamstown in January 1859. The cattle that had been left behind had run wild, and vines and weeds smothered the cultivated land. The four adults faced a daunting prospect, this time with no assurance of continued support from the Royal Navy or the sympathy of the British government. Theirs was a bold, perhaps foolhardy, undertaking, which held the prospect of a strange future for their children, but the human history of Pitcairn had recommenced. It was the start of a settlement that has continued to the present.

Epilogue

When Pitcairn Island was abandoned on 3 May 1856, the thread
of continuity that had joined the mutiny of the *Bounty* to subsequent events on the island was broken and our story finishes.
The resettlement of the island by Moses and Mayhew Young
and their families starts a different tale, which, although it had
occasional moments of drama, was the beginning of a more
tranquil era in Pitcairn's history. By and large, it was the
uneventful story of daily life on a small island: seasonal labour
on the land and the familiar round of seed time and harvest;
and of birth, life and death through successive generations. If
an account of events from the mid-nineteenth century onwards
should be written, this is not the place for it: here we will
sketch in only the briefest outline of the years that followed.

The two families who landed on 17 January 1859 faced a
risky future. They could not assume that the Royal Navy would
continue to keep a friendly eye upon them as it had done in
the past. The British government had shown a surprising degree
of concern for this few dozen people, but, having gone to the
considerable expense of transferring them to a more suitable
location, it could not be expected automatically to assume responsibility for those who returned. Along with this lack of
protection, they faced the physical challenge of reconstructing
the settlement. During their two-and-a-half-year absence, the
Wildwave, an American ship outward bound from San Francisco,
had been wrecked on Oeno Island (a small, uninhabitable island
65 miles to the northwest of Pitcairn). All of the sailors reached
the shore safely, and were able to land plenty of food and water
from the wreck. The majority then stayed in Oeno, while the
captain and five men sailed in the ship's boat to Pitcairn for
help. They arrived to find it deserted. Having lost their own

boat in the process, they burned down several of the abandoned houses to obtain nails, using them to construct a vessel to take them on to Tahiti and raise the alarm. The Youngs found the ruined houses and overgrown fields; but the two brothers and their wives worked hard, as no doubt did the ten girls and two boys. For over four years the families laboured and prospered, although for the ten girls and two boys rapidly growing to marriageable age, the future was going to be one of strictly limited choices.

The navy did eventually call at the island again, and that was perhaps the factor which encouraged others on Norfolk Island to follow them. In February 1864 twenty-seven more of the original islanders again saw the distinctive silhouette of Pitcairn on the horizon and landed in Bounty Bay to the warm welcome of the Youngs. This party had returned against all advice from the British civil and religious authorities, but they had lived on Pitcairn before and had confidence in their own abilities to live there again.

Whaling ships rarely called at Pitcairn now, because the industry had moved away from the area, and during the years that it was deserted there was little point in other ships going near it – it took time for news of the resettlement to percolate through the maritime world. Without regular access to the trade goods the whalers had previously supplied them with – clothing, candles, tools, fish hooks, gun powder and so on – the Pitcairners were obliged to go back to earlier Tahitian methods and skills, such as making clothing with *tapa* cloth, and using candle-nuts for lighting. Even those few ships that did call there showed the islanders less respect and were not above cheating them in trade and threatening their women. In 1864 a Peruvian slave ship tried to entice all the islanders on board: had it succeeded, the empty island would have become a mystery of the sea far greater than the *Marie Celeste*.

Without the whaling ships calling for fresh food and water, the islanders no longer produced a surplus, and had little to offer in exchange for goods from outside. In the 1860s a few passenger ships *en route* between Panama or California and

Australasia stopped to purchase supplies, and their passengers increased the demand for curios made by the islanders. This became their main source of foreign exchange, although it was not adequate for their needs.

There was an intermittent contact between the families on Norfolk Island and those on Pitcairn, and in 1872 a strong sense of family and community led the Norfolk Islanders to try to persuade those in Pitcairn to abandon it again and reunite the community. They offered to pay the cost of chartering a ship to bring them back to Norfolk Island, and guaranteed that they would have their former lands on Norfolk Island restored to them. The only condition was that all had to come. Most, particularly the young people, were now eager to accept; they felt isolated and vulnerable to outsiders; they had suffered from drought; and contacts with the outside world were irregular. But a few refused, which meant that the condition of the offer was not fulfilled, and the opportunity was lost. Very few of the younger generation were brave enough to venture into the outside world, and up to the late 1880s only five men took passage abroad. It was not usually a happy experience. Two arrived in England in 1881 where one of them was very soon 'secured as a highly prized specimen of the human species, to be exhibited in the Westminster Aquarium'.[1] He was rescued from this indignity by the Reverend A. W. Drew and duly returned to Pitcairn.

The safe future of the Pitcairners was eventually to be secured by the misfortunes of others. The southern Pacific was becoming more frequented by European ships, and the danger of those voyages soon had an impact. In 1875 the *Cornwallis*, a Liverpool ship, was homeward bound when its unfortunate captain decided to make a detour and land on Pitcairn from sheer curiosity. His ship was wrecked on its coast in a sudden squall. Fortunately, all the crew were saved, and equally fortunately for the island's food supplies they were taken off by another ship after only a few days. Another Liverpool ship, the *Khandeish*, came to grief on Oeno, and six years later the *Acadia* was wrecked on Ducie (another islet of the Pitcairn group). In 1883

Oeno claimed another victim with the wreck of the *Oregon*. These disasters threw the spotlight back on Pitcairn, and the islanders received a great deal of favourable press for the open-hearted way in which they fed, clothed and housed the crews until the arrival of a ship enabled them to return to the wider world. The crew of the *Khandeish* lived on the islanders' supplies for fifty-one days before a ship arrived to take them away. Captain Folger's original observation that having a settlement on Pitcairn could prove a boon to sailors in this vast expanse of ocean was proving to be true once more.

The crews were deeply indebted to the Pitcairners, and when the survivors of the *Khandeish* arrived safely back in civilization they launched a public appeal aimed at supplying their saviours with all the things they lacked. Young described the bountiful goods that poured in:

> The generous citizens of San Francisco responded with such heartiness that contributions kept pouring in, and every useful and necessary article that was thought of – cooking utensils, tinware of almost every description, cups, plates, spoons, etc., etc., wooden pails and tin pans, testified to their large-hearted liberality ... Clothing made and unmade, buttons, pins, needles, almost enough to stock a haberdasher's shop ... A good supply of flour ... a beautifully toned organ ... a large supply of schoolbooks.[2]

The Pitcairners had found feeding the crews quite a drain on their own food supplies at the time, but goodwill and supplies of the kind they could not produce flowed back to them. They had proved their value to mariners and restored their earlier image as a moral and ideal community. The British government was again prepared to give them its blessing. Three years after the wrecks of the *Cornwallis* and the *Khandeish*, Rear-Admiral de Horsey visited Pitcairn in HMS *Shah* and officially informed the islanders that the British government respected their desire to live on their homeland. The Navy then recommenced its annual visits. On the first of these, in 1879, HMS *Opal* brought ashore an organ embellished with a heart-shaped silver plate, which was inscribed as the gift of Queen Victoria 'to her loyal and loving Pitcairn Island subjects, in appreciation of their domestic virtues'.[3] The aftermath of the wrecks not only brought them essential equipment, royal gifts and respectability, it also introduced much needed new blood. Some of the seamen from the wrecks married Pitcairn women (there was a surplus of women on the island) and took them away, but the Coffin family was founded at this time by the immigration of an American sailor. Another man who wanted to settle on the island incurred the opposition of the entire Young family by becoming attached to a woman who was already promised to one of the Youngs. Albert Knight would have been a permanent asset as he was a skilled carpenter; he had also built a loom and was teaching the women to weave, but he was driven from Pitcairn by the Youngs' hostility and he settled at Tahiti. At the instigation of the Youngs, one of whom was chief magistrate, a law was passed in 1882 forbidding strangers to settle on the island.

In spite of the positive publicity stemming from their generous treatment of shipwrecked sailors, it was not a good time for the island. There was a growing fear that they were no longer self-sufficient and were relying on the charity of the outside world to sustain them. Captain F. P. Doughty (who had also visited the island in earlier days) wrote a report in 1884 stating that there had been moral degeneration, that the islanders were slovenly and unkempt in their persons, that they lacked pride and were aware that they were slipping behind the times but were too apathetic to take full advantage of the island's resources. It was a time when there was no outstanding personality to lead the community, and one historian of the period, H. E. Maude, makes particular reference to the endemic bad feeling between the Youngs and Christians, which effectively prevented communal action. During this period people showed less respect to the magistrate and councillors, and ignored the laws and regulations. They were eventually to be drawn together and revived under a religious impulse resembling John Adams's sudden conversion in an earlier era.

Included among the gifts that came to the island from America was a collection of literature from the Seventh-Day Adventists. The Bible had remained the book from which Pitcairners took most of their learning. George Nobbs had been taken to England to be ordained in the Church of England, and he returned as 'Chaplain of Pitcairn Island'; but he had joined the exodus to Norfolk Island, and since the return to Pitcairn the islanders had been neglected by the Established Church. But the Seventh-Day Adventist literature, along with Bible readings and discussions, did their slow work. In 1886 the Adventists sent John Tay to Pitcairn as a missionary. The islanders gave him permission to stay and present his faith. When he left six weeks later the islanders had all joined his church. As always with island affairs, this had to be confirmed at a communal meeting, and in March 1887 it was formally agreed that they would no longer use the Church of England's forms of worship and prayer. It is difficult to know how many supported the move out of genuine conviction and how many out of a wish to preserve the unity of decision-making which seemed so important to them.

In America this conversion was followed up with a great deal of vigour and no small outlay of money. The Adventists built a 170-ton ship as a missionary vessel and named it the *Pitcairn*. It arrived off the island in 1890, bringing four Americans who baptized all the islanders into their new sect. Pork was forbidden, and it must have been quite a wrench for them to forgo their favourite meat: to prevent any backsliding all the pigs were slaughtered. The Americans energized the Pitcairners, and under the direction of a resident American Adventist they took to education and self-improvement, even starting a monthly newspaper. As is the way with new brooms, it was soon worn down on the bedrock of apathy and indifference, but some elements survived, and in 1893 the school was taken under the charge of an American woman Adventist, Hattie Andre.

Later that same year one of Pitcairn's worst disasters occurred. Oeno Island again claimed a ship, and the hapless crew, as was customary, came to Pitcairn. They brought with them a fever, probably a form of influenza, against which the islanders had no immunity. Virtually every islander became seriously ill, and twelve – about one in ten of the population – died between August and October 1893.

In spite of the religious revival in the 1890s, the years up to the outbreak of the First World War in 1914 gave rise to the most critical reports about the state of life on the island. There was a universal refusal to undertake the communal labour needed to maintain the roads, the school and other public works; and crime increased. Hamilton Hunter, a Judicial Commissioner who was sent from the Fijian Islands to arrest and deport a Pitcairn man who had murdered his wife and child because he wanted to marry another, wrote that he found the islanders 'lax in morals and weak in intellect', an opinion that was echoed in a number of reports from visiting ships' captains. Much of the disregard for the law resulted from the continued friction between the Christian and Young clans, which dominated the island by sheer numbers. In spite of the tragic decimation of 1893, by 1897 the permanent population had risen to 138, of which fifty-one were Christians, and forty-seven were Youngs. Along with six McKoys, these families were the only direct descendants of the original *Bounty* settlers. There were also twenty Warrens, eleven Coffins, two Butlers and one Buffett, descended from subsequent incomers. Women outnumbered men, and it was argued that this was one of the causes of the increase in immorality. The American mission ship helped to balance the sex ratio by taking some of Pitcairn's surplus women to work in their missions on other Pacific islands.

The man credited with saving the islanders from complete social breakdown was James McKoy, a great-grandson of the mutineer. He was active in the island's government, usually serving as its executive head or President. There was a period of constitutional change as the authorities tried to find a system of government that would lift the tone of island life. James McKoy had lived in London and Liverpool, and was one of the few native-born Pitcairners with experience of the wider world. Although not always popular with the people, he had something of the authority of a John Adams, and he reinstated an old system under which all the men were obliged to work a number of hours each week on repairing the roads and maintaining the public buildings. The regime was probably not conducive to popularity, but it undoubtedly countered lethargy and demoralization. From the turn of the century, however, McKoy became more and more absorbed in missionary activity, which took him away from the island for periods of time, and his leadership faded. He is mainly remembered for his decisive action in 1900 when a burning ship was about to be driven ashore on Pitcairn: he boarded her and persuaded the captain and crew to let him pilot them to Mangerava, the nearest inhabited island, where he successfully beached her.

The mission ship *Pitcairn* maintained regular communications with the nearby islands, and when she went out of service the islanders, helped by a government loan, bought a small vessel of their own to keep those links and to increase their trade with the outside world. They tried raising coffee, vanilla and arrowroot as cash crops for export, as well as producing copra. But all these attempts failed, simply because Pitcairn lacks a safe harbour or bay where ships could lie safely while loading cargo. Although ships called at the island with increasing frequency up until the 1900s, they were no longer whalers eager to buy water, wood and fresh foods, but large ships giving their passengers a glimpse of a remote island with a romantic past. Those passengers bought curios, but that would not have been enough to save Pitcairn, if the Panama Canal had not opened.

The Panama Canal had been planned for a long time. Its attractions were obvious, and the Spanish conquerors had thought about it in the sixteenth century; but it was not until 1879 that the French started digging, only to be defeated after eight years of effort and the deaths of over 20,000 workers from disease. It was left to the Americans to complete the work and the canal finally opened in 1914. From the post-war period onwards, ships going from Europe to New Zealand went through the canal, and Pitcairn's geographical position now became an advantage:

> From New Zealand to Panama were 7,500 miles of open sea, which made it by far the longest passenger run between ports in the world; a distinct handicap in competing with ships on the more glamorous Suez route. By calling at Pitcairn, almost exactly half-way on the route, passengers were given a much-needed break in the monotony and something exciting to talk about for days before and after the visit.[4]

Ships carrying a large number of passengers now began to call on an average of once a week, and continued to do so into and beyond the 1960s.

This new traffic had a profound social and cultural effect on the islanders. In the late nineteenth century the islanders had been returning to their Tahitian roots. The contact they had had with the outside world since the resettlement had come mainly from missionary ships or small cargo schooners going to Tahiti and similar Polynesian islands, which meant that they were becoming more influenced by Polynesian culture and less by European, but that came to an end with the new line of communication and the subsequent predominance of European influence. With the new ocean route, New Zealand became the most easily accessible place, and shipping companies often gave Pitcairners passage at reduced cost. New Zealand became the main centre for expatriate Pitcairners: they began to feel at home there as well as on Norfolk Island or their own home land, and the expatriate community in New Zealand has at times exceeded the population of Pitcairn itself.

The attractions of life in Auckland or Wellington and the greater opportunities they offered to the ambitious is self-evident, but there were also aspects of life on Pitcairn that were positively forcing people to leave. The original mutineers had divided the land into nine lots, and through the division and subdivision of it among subsequent generations of children, their descendants still dominated land ownership at Pitcairn. Thus, all those who had come to the island since then were at a disadvantage, and economic distinctions, which had not been a significant factor before, were growing. Not actually owning land had, in the past, mattered less:

> as long as, in accordance with Tahitian custom, anyone had the right to plant and thereafter use coco-nut and fruit trees, irrespective of who owned the land on which they stood, and while in any case land was freely loaned for gardens to anyone who asked. But as European ideas came to supplant Tahitian, the position of those with insufficient land of their own for the support of their families became more and more disadvantageous, and many of them were the first to leave for abroad.[5]

The island's culture now came under the influence of New Zealand, in so far as the school teacher was appointed from there, and the New Zealand curriculum was taught. Medical care was improved by the provision of a dispensary and trained nurse. Money to create and improve public facilities remained scarce, though, and in 1937 the annual income of the entire island was less than £2000. This was boosted in the 1940s when the islanders hit on the simple idea of issuing their own postage stamps, which became a must for every collector's album. However, in spite of the construction of a sea wall and a jetty, and the acquisition of power winches and motors for the public boats to facilitate the export of goods and contact between ship and shore, public incomes have remained low. In 1959, for example, the islanders' earnings from fruit sold to ships amounted to barely £600 and their biggest source of money was the sale of curios – wood carvings, baskets, fans and so on. The income from this amounted to £3700, some sixty per cent of which was through mail order to the United States – confirming the continued American interest in the islanders.

Since the Second World War, Pitcairn has benefited from modernization, starting with wireless communications, electricity and telephones. These improvements did not stop the outflow of young people: perhaps improvements in education made them more fitted for prospering in the outside world, and the more frequent contact with ships' passengers and crews made the prospect less daunting. The island now has a population fluctuating between forty and sixty people (in 1997 there were fifty-four inhabitants). It has a firm place on the itinerary of cruise ships and is in constant communication with the outside world.

The tiny community of Pitcairn Islanders was often eulogized by visitors in the past; it has also been much maligned. Perhaps a descendant of the original settlers, Amelia Young, writing in 1894, should be allowed the last word:

> Human nature is human nature the world over, and fallen at that, so it is certainly a mistake to think that, because so remote from the rest of the world, no vice or sin of any kind mars the character or degrades the reputation of those who dwell so secluded from the world.[6]

Notes

The works by the authors referred to in the notes are listed in the Bibliography.

Prologue

1. Delano, 1817: p. 139.
2. *United Services Journal*, 1831 (III): p. 313.

Chapter 1: PREPARATIONS

1. For these and similar points see Ferdon, 1981.
2. Smith, 1960: p. 26.
3. Murray (ed.), 1827: pp. 213–13.
4. Christian, 1982: p. 57.
5. Lloyd, 1968: p. 250.
6. Ibid.: pp. 254–5.
7. Bechervaise, 1836: p. 165.

Chapter 2: THE VOYAGE

1. Mackaness, 1981: pp. 298–9
2. Bligh, 1975: p. 134
3. Ibid.: p. 162.
4. Ibid.: pp. 168–9.
5. Ibid.: p. 152.
6. Ibid.: p. 355.

Chapter 3: TAHITI

1. Ferdon, 1981: p. 31.
2. Ibid.: p. 97.
3. Morrison, 1935: p. 165.
4. Barrow, 1831: p. 37.
5. Murray (ed.), 1827: pp. 230–31.
6. Ferdon, 1981: p. 50.
7. Cobbe (ed.), 1979: p. 52.
8. Ferdon, 1981: p. 145.

9. Anon., 1839: p. 74.
10. Ibid.: p. 77.
11. Morrison, 1935: p. 187.
12. Ibid.: p. 236.
13. For this and similar issues see Danielsson, 1956.
14. Hough, 1988: p. 129.
15. Ibid.: p. 112.
16. Bligh, 1975: p. 197.
17. Danielsson, 1956: p. 177.
18. Ibid.
19. Ibid.: p. 232.
20. Murray (ed.), 1827: p. 282.

Chapter 4: THE MUTINY

1. Christian, 1982: p. 107.
2. Murray (ed.), 1827: p. 233.
3. Hough, 1988: p. 127.
4. Some of the native women were more widely known by the European names given to them by the sailors. Spelling of the native names also varied considerably – for example, Mauatua is also written as Mi'mitti. The identity of the natives who settled on Pitcairn with the mutineers will be made clear in context.
5. Hough, 1988: pp. 125–6.
6. Ibid.: p. 143.
7. Bowman, 1981: pp. 98–9.
8. Bligh, 1975: p. 47.
9. Bennett, 1840: p. 49.
10. *United Services Journal*, 1831 (iii): p. 589.

Chapter 5: PITCAIRN

1. *United Services Journal*, 1829 (ii): pp. 590–91.
2. Ibid.: p. 591.
3. Ibid.
4. *Sydney Gazette*, 17 July 1819.
5. Bligh, 1975: pp. 359–62 for the following description of the mutineers.
6. Danielsson, 1962: p. 217.
7. Bennett, 1840: p. 33.
8. Beechey, 1831: p. 79.

Chapter 6: REVOLT

1. Beechey, 1831: p. 61.
2. Young, 1894: p. 29.
3. *United Services Journal*, 1829 (ii): p. 591.

Chapter 7: REVENGE

1. Beechey, 1831: pp. 62–5.
2. *United Services Journal*, 1829 (11): p. 592.
3. Beechey, 1831: pp. 62–5.
4. *United Services Journal*, 1829 (11): p. 593.
5. Beechey, 1831: pp. 62–5.
6. Ibid.: p. 63.
7. *United Services Journal*, 1829 (11): p. 592.
8. Ibid.
9. Brodie, 1851: pp. 59–60.
10. *United Services Journal*, 1829 (11): p. 593.
11. *Sydney Gazette*, 17 July 1819.
12. Beechey, 1831: pp. 64–5.
13. *Sydney Gazette*, 17 July 1819.

Chapter 8: THE WOMEN

1. Beechey, 1831: p. 65.
2. Christian, 1982: p. 200.
3. Beechey, 1831: p. 65.
4. Ferdon, 1981: p. 162.
5. Young, 1894: p. 27.
6. Beechey, 1831: pp. 65–6.
7. Ibid.: p. 66.
8. Ibid.
9. Ibid.: pp. 66–7.

Chapter 9: RUM

1. *United Services Journal*, 1829 (11): p. 593.
2. Beechey, 1831: p. 68.
3. Young, 1894: p. 31.
4. *Sydney Gazette*, 17 July 1819; *United Services Journal* 1829 (11): p. 593, republished from the *Bengal Hurkaru*, 2 October 1816.
5. *Sydney Gazette*, 17 July 1819.
6. Ibid.
7. Brodie, 1851: p. 61.

Chapter 10: EVIDENCE

1. Beechey, 1831: pp. 67–8, for this and the previous quotations.
2. Delano, 1817: p. 140.
3. *United Services Journal*, 1834 (1): p. 193. Previously unpublished manuscript of the late Captain Pipon.
4. Ibid.: p. 193.

5. Ibid.: p. 196.
6. Ibid.
7. *Naval Chronicle* (XXXV), 1816: p. 21.
8. Ibid.: p. 24.
9. *Calcutta Journal*, 13 July 1819.
10. *United Services Journal*, 1829 (11): p. 589.
11. Bennett, 1840: p. 49.

Chapter 11: DISCOVERY

1. I am reliably informed that the *Pandora* was, technically speaking, a sixth-rate twenty-four-gun ship of the line. As common usage then and later (e.g. *United Services Journal*, 1829) refers to her as a 'frigate' I have preserved common usage.
2. Murray (ed.), 1827: p. 287.
3. Ibid.
4. Barrow, 1831: p. 161.
5. *United Services Journal*, 1829 (11): p. 51–2.
6. Brodie, 1851: p. 66.

Chapter 12: A NEW GENERATION

1. *Edinburgh Philosophical Journal*, 1820: p. 383.
2. Brodie, 1851: p. 165.
3. Beechey, 1831: p. 81.
4. Morrison, 1935: p. 236.
5. Beechey, 1831: p. 94.
6. Bennett, 1840: p. 35.
7. *Sydney Gazette*, 17 July 1819.
8. Beechey, 1831: p. 73.
9. Ibid.: p. 67.
10. Silverman, 1967: 36. See also *Mariners' Mirror*, 1941, vol. 27 (p. 1), D. Bonner Smith, in 'Some Remarks about the mutiny on the Bounty', gives nineteen cases, including Christian and Heywood.
11. Beechey, 1831: p. 92.
12. Ibid.: p. 50.
13. Ibid.: p. 92.
14. Ibid.
15. Ibid.: p. 79.
16. Ibid.: p. 67.
17. Ibid.: p. 78.
18. *Sydney Gazette*, 17 July 1819.
19. Barrow, 1831: p. 297.
20. Beechey, 1831: p. 83.
21. *Edinburgh Philosophical Journal*, 1820: pp. 385–6.
22. Beechey, 1831: p. 82.

Chapter 13: VIRTUOUS LIVES

1. Beechey, 1831: p. 80.
2. Ibid.: p. 78.
3. Ibid.: p. 69.
4. Ibid.: p. 70.
5. Delano, 1817: p. 141.
6. *Edinburgh Philosophical Journal*, 1820: pp. 385–6.
7. Ibid.: p. 386.
8. Brodie, 1851: p. 62.
9. *Edinburgh Philosophical Journal*, 1820: p. 385.
10. Murray, 1853: p. 128.
11. *United Services Journal*, 1834 (I): p. 192.
12. Ibid.: p. 195.
13. Ibid.: p. 194.
14. Bennett, 1840: pp. 34–5.
15. Brodie, 1851: p. 166.
16. *United Services Journal*, 1834 (I): p. 195.
17. Morrison, 1935: p. 235.
18. Bennett, 1840: p. 34.
19. Delano, 1817: p. 151.
20. Ibid.: p. 144.
21. Brodie, 1851: p. 32.

Chapter 14: RETURN TO TAHITI

1. Young, 1894: p. 40. Citing correspondence from Captain Folger.
2. Beechey, 1831: p. 96.
3. Ibid.: p. 98.
4. Ibid.: pp. 97–8.
5. *Calcutta Journal*, 13 July 1819.
6. Bechervaise, 1836: p. 173.
7. *Calcutta Journal*, 13 July 1819.
8. Ross and Moverley, 1964: p. 27. This book, *The Pitcairnese Language*, is of much wider interest than its title might suggest. See especially H. E. Maude, 'The history of Pitcairn's Island'.
9. Barrow, 1831: p. 329. In Ross and Moverley, 1964, he is described as the son of a London watch-maker. In any case, his origins were in the artisan élite.
10. *United Services Journal*, 1831 (III): p. 313.
11. Barrow, 1831: pp. 330–32.
12. Ibid.: p. 289.
13. Bennett, 1840: pp. 30, 31.
14. *Sydney Gazette*, 17 July 1819.
15. Ross and Moverley, 1964: p. 67.
16. *United Services Journal*, 1832 (I): p. 98.

17. Ibid.: pp. 99–100.
18. Ibid.: pp. 100–111.
19. Ibid.: p. 101.
20. Ross and Moverley, 1964: pp. 68–9.
21. Ibid.: p. 69.
22. Bennett, 1840: pp. 53–5.

Chapter 15: THE ADVENTURERS

1. Ross and Moverley, 1964: p. 69.
2. Brodie, 1851: pp. 160–61.
3. *Edinburgh Philosophical Journal*, 1820: p. 386.
4. Bechervaise, 1836: p. 177.
5. Brodie, 1851: pp. 163–4.
6. Bechervaise, 1836: p. 175.
7. Bennett, 1840: pp. 53–5.
8. Brodie, 1851: p. 181.
9. Ibid.: pp. 183, 184.
10. Ibid.: p. 186.
11. Ibid.: p. 187.
12. Ibid.: p. 205.
13. Ibid.: p. 209.
14. *Nautical Magazine*, 1838: pp. 521–2.
15. Ibid.: p. 521.
16. Ross and Moverley, 1964: p. 72.
17. *Nautical Magazine*, 1838: p. 743.
18. Ross and Moverley, 1964: p. 72.
19. Ibid.: p. 73.

Chapter 16: ABANDONED AND RESETTLED

1. Ross and Moverley, 1964: p. 76.
2. Ibid.
3. *United Services Journal*, 1834 (I): p. 195.
4. Young, 1894: p. 98.
5. Murray, 1853: p. 95.
6. Brodie, 1851: p. 88.
7. Ibid.: p. 168.
8. Ibid.: p. 92.
9. Murray, 1853: p. 229.
10. Letter from W. H. Holman to Rear-Admiral Moresby dated 6 June 1953, on board HMS *Portland*.
11. Ibid.
12. Ross and Moverley, 1964, present conflicting figures for the populations. On page 78 it is claimed that the Adams faction lost the vote by 153 to 45; that makes 207 people of voting age, which is clearly an error. (A vote of 53 to 45 is more likely.) When listing the

population by families – Christians 49, Quintals 44, Youngs 24, Adamses 17 and so on – they total 187 of all ages. This is close to the figure (page 79) of 194, the entire population taken aboard the *Morayshire*. I suspect that counting them aboard the ship would give the most reliable figure (194).

Epilogue

1. Young, 1894: p. 219.
2. Ibid.: pp. 196–7.
3. Ibid.: p. 212.
4. Ross and Moverley, 1964: p. 95.
5. Ibid.
6. Young, 1894: pp. 252–3.

Bibliography

BOOKS

Anon., *Missionary Records*, London, Religious Tract Society, 1839.

Anon. [Barrow, J.], *A Description of Pitcairn's Island and its Inhabitants*, New York, Harper and Brothers, 1845.

Barrow, Sir John, *The Eventful History of the Mutiny and the Piratical Seizure of HMS Bounty: its Causes and Consequences*, London, John Murray, 1831.

Bechervaise, J., *Thirty-six Years of Seafaring Life*, London, Longman & Co., 1836.

Beechey, F. W., *Narrative of a Voyage to the Pacific*, London, Henry Colburn and Richard Bentley, 1831.

Belcher, D., *The Mutineers of the Bounty*, London, John Murray, 1870.

Bennett, F. D., *Narrative of a Whaling Voyage 1833–1836*, London, Richard Bentley, 1840.

Bligh, W., *The Log of H.M.S. Bounty 1787–1789*, Guildford, Genesis, 1975.

Bowman, R. (ed.), *An Account of the Mutiny on HMS Bounty: Lieutenant William Bligh*, Gloucester, Alan Sutton, 1981.

Brodie, W., *Pitcairn's Island*, London, Whittaker, 1851.

Christian, G., *Fragile Paradise: The Discovery of Fletcher Christian, Bounty Mutineer*, London, Hamish Hamilton, 1982.

Clarke, P., *Hell and Paradise, the Norfolk Bounty Pitcairn Saga*, Ringwood, Vic. [Harmondsworth], 1986.

Cobbe, H. (ed.), *Cook's Voyages and the Peoples of the Pacific*, London, British Museum, 1979.

Danielsson, B. E., *Love in the South Seas*, London, George Allen and Unwin, 1956.

Danielsson, B. E., *What Happened to the Bounty*, London, George Allen and Unwin, 1962.

Delano, A., *A Narrative of Voyages and Travels*, Boston, MA, printed for the author, 1817.

Ferdon, E. N., *Early Tahiti, as the Explorers Saw It, 1767–1797*, Tuscon, AZ, University of Arizona Press, 1981.

Hough, R., *Captain Bligh and Mr Christian: the Men and the Mutiny*, London, Cresset Library (first published in 1972), 1988.

Humble, R., *Captain Bligh*, London, Arthur Barker, 1976.

Kennedy, G., *Captain Bligh*, London, Gerald Duckworth, 1989.

Lloyd, C., *The British Seaman*, London, Collins, 1968.

Mackaness, G. (ed.), *The Book of the Bounty*, London, J. M. Dent (first published in 1838), 1981.

Morrison, J., *The Journal of JAMES MORRISON Boatswain's Mate of THE BOUNTY describing the Mutiny and subsequent Misfortunes of the Mutineers together with an account of the Island of Tahiti. With an Introduction by OWEN RUTTER and five engravings by ROBERT GIBBINGS*, London, Golden Cockerel Press, 1935.

Murray, H. (ed.), *Constable's Miscellany, Vol. IV, 'Adventures of British Seamen'*, Edinburgh, Constable, 1827.

Murray, T. B., *Pitcairn: the Island, the People, and the Pastor*, London, Society for the Propagation of Christian Knowledge, 1853.

Nicolson, R. D., *The Pitcairners*, London, Angus and Robertson, 1966.

Ross, A. S. C. and Moverley, A. W., *The Pitcairnese Language*, London, Andre Deutsch, 1964.

Rutter, O. (ed.), *The Trial of the Bounty Mutineers*, Edinburgh, W. Hodge & Co., 1931.

Shillibeer, J., *A Narrative of the Briton's Voyage to Pitcairn's Island*, Taunton, J. W. Marriott, 1817.

Silverman, D., *Pitcairn Island*, New York, World Publishing, 1967.

Smith, B., *European Vision and the South Pacific*, Oxford, Oxford University Press, 1960.

Young, R. A., *Mutiny of the Bounty and the Story of Pitcairn Island, 1790–1894*, Oakland, CA, Pacific Press, 1894.

JOURNALS AND ARTICLES

Annual Register, 1815.

Calcutta Journal, 13 July 1819.

Edinburgh Philosophical Journal, 1820.

Mariner's Mirror, 1932, 1936, 1941.

Nautical Magazine, 1838.

Naval Chronicle, (XXXV), 1816.

Quarterly Review, February 1810.

Sydney Gazette, 17 July 1819.

United Services Journal, 1829 (II), 1831 (III), 1832 (I), 1834 (I).

Index

Adams, Dinah, 124, 177, 206
Adams, John, 12, 13–14, 62, 63,
    66, 67, 69, 82–3, 84, 89, 90,
    91, 94–7, 99, 102–13, 116,
    117, 118, 124–30, 134–42,
    143, 153, 154, 159, 164,
    165–6, 167, 168, 170–1,
    174, 175–9, 181, 182, 185,
    190, 193–6, 197, 199, 202,
    205, 206–8, 210, 211, 212,
    214, 235, 238
Adams family, 164–6, 177–8,
    192, 207, 211, 213, 225, 228
alcohol, 29, 30, 36, 61, 70,
    124–5, 127–30, 139, 168,
    177, 195, 202, 204–8, 210,
    216

Banks, Sir Joseph, 21, 22, 23
Barrow, Sir John, 196–7, 199
Bechervaise, John, 30, 192, 207–8
Beechey, Captain F. W., 30, 97,
    108, 116, 125, 126, 128, 133,
    160–4, 166, 167, 168,
    174–5, 181, 189–90, 192,
    207
Bennett, E. D., 141, 180, 202–3,
    204–5
birth, 46–8, 50, 98, 109, 114,
    124, 125, 126–7, 130,
    161–6, 170, 177, 198, 220
birth control, 118–19, 164–5,
    165–6
Bligh, William, 12, 21, 22, 23,
    25–8, 32–7, 45, 46, 55–65,

67, 68, 143–5, 147, 150–2,
    153
Bounty, HMS
    crew, 27, 28–31, 33–4, 36, 37,
        38, 60–2
    crew list, 65–6
    deaths: drowned, 144, 149;
        executed, 152; fever, 144;
        illness, 36; killed, 143, 146
    named crew: Burkitt, T., 147,
        152; Churchill, C., 57, 63,
        146; Coleman, J., 64, 71;
        Ellison, T., 152; Fryer, J.,
        63, 144, 151; Hallett, J., 145;
        Hayward, T., 57–8, 145,
        150–2; Hillbrant, H., 147,
        149; Huggan, J., 164;
        Ledward, T., 164; McIntosh,
        T., 64, 147; Mills, J., *see*
        Mills, John; Millward, J., 57,
        147, 152; Morrison, J., *see*
        Morrison, James; Musprat,
        W., 57, 146, 147, 152;
        Norman, C., 64; Norton, J.,
        153; Peckover, W., 144;
        Skinner, R., 149; Stewart,
        G., 62, 148, 149; Sumner, J.,
        69, 146, 147, 149;
        Thompson, M., 146
breadfruit, 24–5, 26, 40, 55–6,
    59, 67, 190
Brodie, W., 174, 183–4, 223–4
Brown, William, 77, 82, 84, 88,
    101–2, 103, 112, 114, 139,
    164, 165

Buffett, John, 194–5, 202,
204–7, 208–16
Bunker, Noah, 194, 212
burials, 46, 54, 77, 115–18,
174–5

children, 43, 46–9, 50, 119, 124,
125, 130, 160, 161–6,
170–1, 175, 176, 193, 195
Christian, Fletcher, 12–13, 28,
33, 57, 59–65, 67–71,
76–81, 84, 87–8, 91, 95,
100, 102, 103, 104, 109, 110,
112, 114, 133–4, 136, 137,
138, 139, 141, 150–1. 154,
174–5, 219
Christian family, 151, 195, 209,
210, 211, 213, 225, 235, 237
Christian, Thursday [Friday], 165,
170, 179, 181, 192, 208
clothing 22, 42–3, 45, 163, 170,
179–90, 181, 221
Coleridge, Samuel Taylor, 35
Collie, Dr, 162
conservation, 41, 51, 189–93,
197–8, 199, 211, 221–5, 227
Cook, James, 21, 22, 23, 24, 25,
40, 42, 56, 67, 68

Danielsson, B. E., 48
Delano, A., 183
deserters, 29, 31, 57–8, 194
Dillon, Captain, 140

education, 21, 175–6, 194, 195,
205, 213–14, 218, 225, 236,
240
Edwards, Captain, 147–50, 151
Elliott, Captain George, 217–18,
219
emigration
to England, 227, 233, 236,
237–8

to New Zealand, 239–40
to Norfolk Island, 224–5, 228,
232, 233
to Tahiti, 198–202, 235
Evans, John, 194, 208–16
exploration and science, 19–21,
23–4, 56, 160

Ferdon, E. N., 43, 47
firearms and metal, 21, 40–1,
43–4, 57, 60, 79, 143
flogging see punishment
Folger, Captain, 11–12, 14, 134,
136, 137, 153–5, 176, 178,
183, 185, 189
food
Pitcairn, 77, 85–6, 162, 169,
190, 192, 220–1, 223,
226
shipboard, 19, 29–30, 33,
34–6, 37, 38, 60–1, 226
Tahiti, 21, 22, 24, 37, 39, 40,
41–3, 54, 68
Fort George, 69
Freemantle, Captain Charles,
205–6, 207, 208

gender conflict, 15, 115–23,
125–7
George III, King, 23–4, 152

Hall, Captain, 194
Henderson, Captain, 139, 191,
192–3
Henry, Captain, 149
Hill, Joshua, 205, 207, 208–17
historical debate, 14–15, 55–6,
61–2, 80, 90–1, 95–7,
108–13, 127–30, 133–42,
201–8, 212
Holman, Reverend W. H.,
226–7
Hough, R., 56

housing, 41, 77, 86–7, 167, 169,
174, 229
human sacrifice, 40, 53

infanticide, 47, 48, 51, 118, 198
introduced species, 21, 24, 35–6,
45, 190, 191–2, 193
Isabella, 57, 84, 85, 91, 100, 104,
110, 114, 137–8, 164, 165,
219

Jenny, 14, 69–70, 77, 78, 79–80,
84, 85, 89, 90, 95–6, 102,
104, 106–9, 112, 116, 118,
119–20, 125, 127–9, 135,
140–1, 165, 170

King, Henry, 159–60, 171–2,
176–7, 178, 206–7

leisure, 49, 50, 171–3
Lowry, Lieut. James, 160, 181

McKoy, William, 63, 66, 77, 80,
82, 84, 98, 100–8, 116, 121,
124–5, 127–30, 134, 164,
166, 168, 175, 208–9
McKoy family, 213, 225, 237
Mareva, 84, 85, 88, 93, 165
marines, 26–7, 145, 147
Martin, Isaac, 63, 64, 66, 82, 84,
98, 99–100, 101–2, 103,
108, 112, 118, 125, 139,
165
Mary, 84, 85, 165
Mauatua see Isabella
Maude, H. E., 215, 235
Menalee, 83, 88, 92–4, 98,
99–101, 105–6
Mills, John, 36–7, 63, 66, 80, 82,
84, 98, 100–1, 102, 103,
110–11, 112, 113, 164,
165

missionaries, 38, 40, 181, 183,
191, 192, 196, 200, 201, 205,
212, 225, 227
Moerenhout, Mr, 202
monetary values, 21, 25, 28–9,
43–4, 164, 220, 227, 240
Moresby, Rear-Admiral Fairfax,
224–5, 226
Morrison, James, 43, 48, 53, 62,
63, 66, 68, 116, 145–6, 148,
149, 152, 181–2

navigation, 19–21, 23, 32, 34,
55–6, 76, 78
Nehow, 83, 85, 88, 92, 99–102,
105–7
New Zealand 23, 36, 228, 238–9
Nobbs, George, 194–7, 204–7,
208–17, 224–8, 236

Obarea, Queen, 40
Oha, 83, 85, 88, 89, 91, 92,
93–4, 95, 96, 104

Pashotu, 84, 85, 88
patronage, 23, 25, 27, 28, 151,
152
Paurai, 84, 85, 89
Pipon, Captain, 136, 138,
179–80, 182
Pomare, Chief, 41
Pomare IV, Queen, 199, 200,
205
population, 13, 113, 130, 170,
193, 198, 204, 224, 235,
241
property, 85–6, 117, 193, 194,
208, 211, 214, 217, 222, 233,
240
Prudence, 84, 88, 89, 95
punishment, 32, 33, 36–7, 53,
57–8, 92, 98, 121, 152,
177–8, 208, 209–11, 213

Quintal, Matthew, 63, 64, 66, 69, 80–1, 82, 98, 102, 103, 104–8, 109, 110, 112, 121, 124–7, 128–9, 134, 139–40, 159, 164, 166, 168, 175, 209

Quintal, Arthur, 97, 111, 129, 172, 177, 209–10

Quintal, Edward, 166, 174, 210

Quintal family, 164, 167, 196, 209–10, 213, 225

religion, 46–7, 51–4, 115–17, 159, 174–6, 177–8, 181–3, 196–7, 214, 235–6, 237

Royal Navy, 23, 27–31, 32–3, 155, 185, 197, 208, 210, 217, 218, 231, 234, 236

Sandilands, Captain A. A., 199

Sarah, 84, 85, 102, 106, 109, 124, 125, 166

sexual abuse, 59–60, 126–7, 146

sexuality, 38, 49–51, 88, 173, 200–1

Ships
Acadia, 233
HMS Acteon, 214
HMS Blossom, 30
HMS Briton, 220
HMS Brunswick, 152
HMS Challenger, 205
Colonist, 184
Cornwallis, 233, 234
HMS Comet, 199, 200
Cyrus, 194
HMS Dolphin, 40
Elizabeth, 159
HMS Endeavour, 23
HMS Fly, 217, 218
George and Susan, 185
Hercules, 191

HMS Imogene, 215
Khandeish, 233, 234
La Boudeuse, 22
Lucy Ann, 199
Maria, 205
Morayshire, 228
Noble, 183
Opal, 234
Oregon, 234
HMS Pandora, 145, 146, 147, 148, 150, 151
Pitcairn, 236, 238
Pomareu, 212
HMS Portland, 226
HMS Resolution, 146
HMS Shah, 234
HMS Sparrow-hawk, 160, 181
HMS Tagus, 220
Topaz, 11, 138, 153
Tuscon, 211
Wildwave, 231
number at Pitcairn, 191, 220, 239
threat to Pitcairn, 216–17

Smith, Alexander see John Adams

Staines, Captain Sir Thomas, 136, 138–9, 170–1

superstition, 35

Susannah, 84, 85, 104–5, 107, 108, 109, 125–7, 166, 219

taboos, 41, 43, 47, 48, 54

Tahiti, 12, 19, 21–3, 24, 37–8, 39–58, 61–2, 67–8, 71, 88, 118, 120, 145–8, 181–2, 184–5, 198–202, 204, 212, 213–14

Tararo, 83, 88, 89, 91–3, 95, 96, 112

tattooing, 45, 47, 81–3

Teatuahitea, 84, 85, 114, 163, 165, 170

Timoa, 83, 88, 93–4, 99–107

Titahiti, 83, 88, 89, 91, 92–3, 94, 96, 99–107, 112
Toobouai, 67, 68–71, 84, 90, 96, 140, 141
Toofaiti, 84, 85, 89, 91–3, 96, 165

Vahineatua, 84, 85, 89, 163, 165, 170
venereal disease, 37, 164
Victoria, Queen, 218, 227, 235

Waldegrave, Captain, 192, 197
Wallis, Captain, 40
wars, 24, 27, 29, 155
West Indian planters, 24–5
whalers, 160, 177, 194, 209, 211, 216–17, 219, 220, 232
Williams, John, 63, 66, 77, 82, 84, 88–9, 90–7, 100, 103, 112, 116, 165

women
    deaths, 88–9, 95, 96–7, 109, 114, 163
    plot to kill men, 69–70, 91, 121, 122–3
    political and social rights, 48–9, 52, 217
Wyetooa, 58

Young, Edward, 28, 62, 66, 81–2, 84, 88, 103, 104–5, 107–8, 110–13, 116, 118, 120, 122, 124, 125, 126–9, 133–5, 138, 159, 164, 165, 170, 208, 219
Young family, 28, 170, 194, 204, 210, 211, 213, 225, 228–9, 231–2, 235, 237
Young, Rosalind, 119